IMAGE AND REPRESENTATION

IMAGE AND REPRESENTATION

Key Concepts in Media Studies

NICK LACEY

St. Martin's Press
New York

IMAGE AND REPRESENTATION

St. Martin's Press, Scholarly and Reference Division, 175 Fifth Avenue, New York, N.Y. 10010

First published in the United States of America in 1998

This book is printed on paper suitable for recycling and made from fully managed and sustained forest sources.

Printed in Hong Kong

ISBN 0–312–21202–X clothbound
ISBN 0–312–21203–8 paperback

Library of Congress Cataloging-in-Publication Data
Lacey, Nick, 1961–
Image & representation : key concepts in media studies / Nick Lacey.
p.   cm.
Includes bibliographical references and index.
ISBN 0–312–21202–X. — ISBN 0–312–21203–8 (pbk.)
1. Mass media.   2. Imagery (Psychology)   3. Semiotics.   4. Mental representation.   I. Title.
P91.L29 1997
302.23—dc21   97–41487
                                                      CIP

To Kirsten

CONTENTS

ACKNOWLEDGEMENTS

The author wishes to thank the following people without whom etc.: Kevin Atkins who made sure everything, more or less, made sense; Richard Duckworth who showed me that some of it didn't make sense and how it could make (some) sense; Henrik Bicat who made the computer make sense of something that shouldn't have; Carla Graham and Merle Bentley for the *Blade Runner* sketches; Alex and Kate for not turning my PC off at crucial moments; my long-suffering wife who entertained the kids on the promise of riches when this was finished; my mum for having me; my students for 'test-driving' the material and no you can't have any of the royalties; my mother-in-law for helping my wife tame my animals; Roy Stafford for letting me use the 'in the picture' spread and his enthusiasm for the subject; Len Masterman for his exceptionally useful comments; Keith Povey and Eileen Ashcroft for their editing and excellent suggestions; Everton FC for not being relegated and winning the Cup; Brian Bicat for talking Brecht; Dave Croft for being Dave Croft; Catherine Gray, Frances Arnold, Jo Digby and Nancy Williams at Macmillan.

NICK LACEY

The author and publishers would like to thank the following for permission to reproduce copyright material: Barnaby's Picture Library for 'Mother and Child Cooking' by L. Howling; Emap Elan Ltd for the front cover of *More!*, March 1995; Alison Brolls and Nicole Perez at Greycom Ltd for the Nokia 'Little Black Number' advertisement and its schedule; James Brown at IPC Magazines for the front cover of *Loaded*, November 1996; Columbia Pictures Corporation for film stills from *Gilda* and *The Wild One*, courtesy of The Kobal Collection; MGM/Pathe for the film still from *Thelma and Louise*, courtesy of The Kobal collection; the artist and Metro

Pictures for 'Untitled Film Still No. 21' by Cindy Sherman; Richard Smith/Katz Pictures for 'West End Shopper Argues with a Protester'; Roy Stafford for the centre-page spread of *In the Picture* from the Summer 1993 issue; Perry Austin-Clark of the *Telegraph & Argus* for the front page of the 2 December 1994 issue; Vestron/MGM/United Artists for the film still from *Blue Steel*, courtesy of The Kobal Collection. Every effort has been made to trace all the copyright-holders, but if any have been inadvertently overlooked the publishers will be pleased to make the necessary arrangement at the first opportunity.

INTRODUCTION

> In course planning, 'common sense' often leads to teaching about one
> medium at a time . . . placing emphasis solely on the characteristics of
> only one set of practices . . . [which] ignores the fact that all individuals
> experience media as a set of interrelated and interacting systems.
>
> (Barker, 1991, p. 5)

The British Film Institute report, 'Primary Media Education: Curriculum Statement', 'proposed six areas of knowledge and understanding as the basis for . . . curriculum development' (Barker, 1991,
p. 5):

> WHO is communicating, and why? WHAT TYPE of text is it? HOW is it
> produced? HOW do we know what it means? WHO receives it, and what
> sense do they make of it? HOW does it PRESENT its subject?
>
> (Ibid., p. 6)

These 'signpost questions' lead to the following key concepts:

1. media agencies
2. media categories
3. media technologies
4. media languages
5. media audiences
6. media representations.

These key concepts inform the structure of this book, and two
others, on introductory Media Studies. By concentrating on these
approaches to the subject I hope to give the student the basic skills
they require for post-16 education, whether in their final years at
school/college or in the first year of Media Studies degrees at
undergraduate level. It is intended that the books be used as a
back-up to teacher/lecturer input.

There is an artificiality in splitting these concepts, for without technology there would be no media; without language we would not understand representation, and so on. However, for pedagogical purposes the categories are very useful.

The adaptation I have made follows the emphasis given by current syllabuses, but as it is dealing with key concepts of the subject, this book should be relevant to any future media syllabus that I can imagine. The adaptation is as follows:

1. media agencies – institutions
2. media categories – genre
3. media technologies – remains as a category but is not dealt with separately, but in relation to each of the other categories
4. media languages – image analysis and narrative
5. media audiences – audiences
6. media representations – representations.

I have paired the adapted concepts to illustrate clearly the inter-connectedness of the categories without attempting to encompass the massive intellectual field of the subject in a single book. The three books are *Image and Representation*, *Narrative and Genre* and *Institution and Audience*.

The structure of this book

Many students in post-16 education come to Media Studies with little or no previous experience of the subject. Although there is a plethora of books available, most of them are too academic for those who are still at school and some are too complex even for those who are doing a degree course.

Many text books have an implicit model of their audience as being an intellectually static individual. This text book differentiates between the pre- and post-16 student, a difference which represents the rapid intellectual development of most 16–18-year-olds. A consequence of this is that each of the key concepts is dealt with, first, at a basic level, appropriate for students at the beginning of the course. The following chapters introduce more advanced theories, such as discourse and ideology, which are then applied to the concept. The book could form part of the structure of a two-year course, with more advanced chapters being used in the later stages. Be aware, though, that it is likely that some students might find at least some parts of this book difficult though undergraduates should have few problems with it. For example, *Image and Representation* begins with a basic introduction to image analysis. The second chapter deals with semiotics which, in the third chapter, is applied with other advanced concepts, such as discourse, to image analysis.

The subject matter of Media Studies is the artefacts that influence us every day of our lives: advertising, movies, videotapes, CDs, and so on. It investigates how the media operate, what their rules, conventions and ideological purpose are, and what the artefacts' meaning for us is at the turn of the millenium.

Unlike many subjects, Media Studies is exceptionally wide in its scope, without the narrow specialisation of which other qualifications are accused. Media Studies gives us a crucial understanding of our world. It should also be a lot of fun.

The examples I have used are a mixture of contemporary and classic (in the sense of being part of a canon) with an emphasis on film which reflects my own interests and, in my experience, those of most students. However, these are not meant to supersede teachers' own preferences. Besides, students best understand the key concepts through discussion of their own experiences of media.

One final note of caution. Although this text is obviously usable as a reference book, the later chapters do refer to material discussed earlier and this may cause confusion if sections are read in isolation.

Nick Lacey

1

INTRODUCTION TO IMAGE ANALYSIS

'Seeing comes before words. The child looks and recognizes before it can speak.'

(John Berger, *Ways of Seeing*, 1972)

1.1 'Seeing is believing'

Of our five senses, it is sight that gives us the most detailed information. It is, for most people, more important than hearing, taste, smell or touch. The majority of us rely on it to such a large extent that we neglect the other senses. 'Seeing is believing' is such a powerful idea that most people accept it as true. However, in Media Studies things aren't so simple.

As R. L. Gregory (1966, p. 9) points out in *Eye and Brain*:

We are so familiar with seeing, that it takes a leap of imagination to realise that there are problems to be solved . . . From the patterns of stimulation on the retinas we perceive the world of objects and this is nothing short of a miracle.

Gregory is concerned with the biological processes of perceiving the world around us. Media studies, when analysing images, concerns itself with the factors that influence how we look at images of our world.

Images are created in order to communicate a message. Even straightforward holiday snapshots attempt to convey what it was like to be at a particular place at a specific time.

Before we consider the factors that influence our perception of images, it is illuminating to look at how our most direct form of communication – speech – works.

1.2 Speech as communication

Roman Jakobson, a Russian linguist, created a model that is very useful for analysing speech, and in Figure 1.1 we use his model to analyse, as an example, the sentence:

'I am explaining, to you, the act of speech communication.'

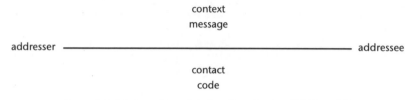

Figure 1.1 Jakobson's model of communication (1958, p. 83)

Jakobson breaks down the act of communication into six constituent factors:

- the addresser
- the addressee
- context
- message
- contact, and
- code.

In our example these factors, considered in a relatively simple fashion, are as follows:

addresser = me (Nick Lacey)
addressee = you (the reader)
message = 'I am explaining to you the act of speech
communication.'

These are straightforward, but what are the context, contact and code?

The *context* is the social situation of the communication; in the case of this book the context is Media Studies or, more broadly, education. The addressee and addresser usually have a common context.

The *contact* is the channel of communication or how you are receiving the information. In this instance the contact is visual. If you were listening to a recording of my voice then the contact would be aural, and if you were reading it in braille the contact would be tactile.

Finally the *code* is the language used. This example is, of course, written in English – it is a linguistic code. Obviously the sentence could be written in any language, for example:

'Je vous explique comment on communique des ideés.'

It should be emphasized that codes are not necessary linguistic. They could be any sign which is recognized by society to have a particular meaning. Most people recognize that a red traffic light means 'stop!'. Indeed it is a part of the formal Highway Code.

Codes can also be less formal: for example, the clothes we wear form part of a social code. We expect people who are wearing skirts to be female and are surprised if they are not. We are surprised because these people are not acting normally, they are breaking a social code. Some codes are almost universal – for example in most societies a nod of the head means a 'yes'. But beware, there are some places were it means 'no'!

To return to Jakobson's model and the sentence 'I am explaining to you the act of speech communication', see Figure 1.2.

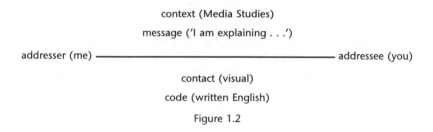

context (Media Studies)

message ('I am explaining . . .')

addresser (me) ———————————————————— addressee (you)

contact (visual)

code (written English)

Figure 1.2

We can clearly see from this model that the act of speech communication is not simply a matter of hearing a spoken message. In order to understand a communication fully it is essential that all the other constituent factors be analysed. But how does this help us with image analysis?

Before we consider this, we must understand that we spend every day of our lives analysing, not just any communication we receive or send, but everything that happens around us. As the quotation from R.L. Gregory at the beginning of the chapter implied, everything we perceive through our senses is interpreted in some way:

'What's this taste or smell (and so on)?' Even recognizing objects requires some interpretation, because by naming something we are putting a specific linguistic label on the object, a label someone from a different country wouldn't necessarily use.

It should be noted that the model, as it stands, ignores the possibility of interference which may obscure any or all of Jakobson's dimensions. This can range from interference on a telephone line to a person speaking with a bad cold.

To understand, therefore, how we interpret and analyse images, we must first consider how we interpret the world around us.

◀ Exercise 1.1 ▶

Choose from a magazine an advertisement which has at least one person in it. Decide what the advertisement is trying to tell you and, using Jakobson's model, try to break it down into its component communicative parts. Save your analysis for later use.

1.3 Interpreting the world around us

It is obvious that you – the reader – have a greater understanding of the world than a young child. The reason for this is you have more experience of the world and have had a formal education. This demonstrates that we have learned to understand the world, that understanding does not come naturally. The fact that this understanding is learned means that the particular society we are born into has a great affect on us. People born into different societies have a different understanding of the world because they will learn about it in different ways.

In the initial stages of image analysis it is helpful simply to describe what we see using terms that are as neutral as possible. At this stage of analysis we are simply engaging in the process of identification; this is analysis at the level of *denotation*. For example, if we describe a particular colour as 'red' this is denotation; we may associate this colour, however, with passion or danger (this association happens at the level of *connotation* which will be dealt with later in the chapter). Theoretically, at the level of denotation almost everyone will describe an image in exactly the same way; that this is not the case suggests that even denotation is affected by an individual's understanding of the world.

◀ EXERCISE 1.2 ▶

In order to demonstrate how we interpret our world, I am going to ask you to do something that appears contradictory. Imagine the image in Figure 1.3 is real. You (the addressee) are facing this group of six men (the addressers) in Newcastle at about six o' clock on a Saturday evening in July, when the photograph was actually taken (the context). None of these men are talking to you, so there is no message (however, this does not mean that we are not interpreting the situation). You are waiting for a bus at a bus stop (contact). Don't forget that what they are wearing constitutes a social code.

Figure 1.3

- What information are you receiving in this situation? Make a note now of what your feelings would be as you look at this group, before you read my interpretation below.
- If you have done this in a classroom situation, compare your interpretation with those of other students. The fact that everyone doesn't have the same feelings demonstrates that each person has interpreted the image for themselves.

This is how I would have interpreted what was happening in Figure 1.3 if I were in that position:

The group of six men are young, but not very young (late 20s/early 30s), so they may have a degree of social responsibility; they're waiting for a bus (possibly can't afford the taxis that are available); their appearance is casual (all are wearing jeans), neither scruffy nor smart; they're unlikely to have spent the day shopping as they aren't carrying any bags (an unlikely activity for a group of men anyway); they may have been to a sporting event (not football in July) and are now on their way home; four of them are facing me, a fact which I find threatening.

In order to reach this interpretation of the situation, I have used a whole series of assumptions, such as the fact that it is a norm of our society that older people tend to be more responsible. I have used the context and my understanding of clothing codes (if they were all wearing dinner jackets or tramp's clothing my understanding of the situation would be very different) to guess their reasons for being there. My knowledge of the potential for inner city violence, gained through news reports, warns me that the situation is potentially dangerous to myself. If I had suffered violence in the past in a similar situation, I would probably be scared. If they were six women, or men I knew, then I wouldn't be afraid at all. If I were a woman, then I imagine the situation would be even more threatening.

This may, or may not, be similar to your interpretation. Any interpretation depends on who you are and your experiences in life. What should be clear is that we interpret what our eyes are seeing all the time.

If we consider the situation further and look at each individual's body language, we find we have more (coded) information which we can interpret. From left to right:

1. looks slightly disbelieving ('how did we miss that bus?'?) or, maybe, surprised;
2. has a cheerful expression on his face but, while undoubtedly male, wears a pony-tail, which is not conventional;
3. partially obscured, difficult to draw any conclusions;
4. again very calm, if anything, a cheerful expression;
5. looks angry and mean and is staring straight at me! His arms are at his side as if he's ready for anything!
6. thoughtful ('what shall we do now we've missed the bus?') or possibly has an itchy chin.

If everyone had the same expression as number 5, I'd have been very worried, but overall they seem a harmless group.

Because there is no verbal communication between me and the group I have used their body language to interpret what they may be thinking. These codes are part of non-verbal communication (NVC).

1.4 Non-verbal communication (NVC)

In assessing the men individually I have been reading their body language, which is one aspect of non-verbal communication (NVC). NVC is a particularly important channel of communication which all human beings – with the exception of those who are severely mentally ill – use, often unconsciously.

Michael Argyle, in his excellent book *The Psychology of Interpersonal Behaviour*, describes eight aspects of NVC:

- facial expression
- gaze
- gestures and other bodily movements
- bodily posture
- bodily contacts
- spatial behaviour
- clothes and appearance
- non-verbal aspects of speech (for example, tone of voice or grunting agreement).

Each of these aspects has its own code with which, as fully socialized members of Western (that is, northern European, North American, Australasian) society, we are all familiar.

◀ EXERCISE 1.3 ▶

Using any photographs of people, such as those in a family album, describe the meaning of as many codes of NVC as you can.

Because we all understand the codes of NVC, to a greater or lesser extent, there is little point in explaining them in detail here. However, it is worth pointing out that while most people assume such codes to be based on common sense, psychological experiments have shown most of them are, in reality, culture-specific. This means that they too, like language, are learned. Just as we learn language as a child we also learn how to communicate non-verbally; then we spend our lives using NVC without even thinking about it, just as we can usually speak without having to consider consciously what we want to say.

A few examples of NVC:

- *Facial expression* Eyebrows are important features in facial expression – indeed, I used them in assessing the mood of characters 1 & 5 in Figure 1.3. Argyle (1983, p. 33) describes the following meanings of eyebrows: fully raised = disbelief; half-raised = surprise; normal = no comment; half-lowered = puzzled; fully lowered = angry.

- *Gaze* This term is used to describe the focus of a person's look and is a particularly powerful form of NVC. When two people's gaze meets, this is *eye contact* and this is particularly meaningful. We are used to the cliché of lovers gazing into each other's eyes and the manic stare of a psychopath. When analysing images we should be particularly interested in gaze: are people in the image looking directly at the audience, at each other, or off the edge of the frame?
  To test the power of gaze, the next time you're engaged in conversation with someone, just look into their eyes and wait for their, and your own, reaction (don't choose someone with a violent disposition).

- *Gestures* Another experiment you might like to try is engaging in conversation without moving your hands. It is exceptionally rare for someone who is explaining not to make gestures with his or her hands. Once you are conscious of gestures you are making, as you talk, the effect can be quite comic. In a classroom situation, watch your teacher's hand movements and if they ask 'are there any questions?', say: 'Why do you move your hands like that?'

- *Posture* This also communicates much information, from the slovenly pose of the lazy student to the erect stance of an officious person.

- *Body contact* This is highly restricted in western culture, as it conveys a high degree of intimacy unless it either happens in a professional context – at the doctor's, for example – or forms part of etiquette, like shaking hands. Both the professional context and etiquette possess their own set of codes which define what is permitted.

- *Clothes and appearance* Whether we like it or not, the clothes we wear make a statement about us. We may, at one extreme, be very fashionable or, at the opposite pole, the person who has no sense of how colour combines. Uniforms are formal declarations, often of authority; types of clothing may be associated with a sub-culture (for example, leather jackets and bikers). Even our hair cut makes a statement – from the long-haired hippies (man!) to the shaved head of the facist.

Because these non-verbal rules are learned, they change as society changes. This is also true of language; one of the reasons pre-twentieth-century literature can be difficult to read, at least at first, is because the meaning of some words has changed. In *Keywords*, Raymond Williams describes how certain terms' meanings have developed. This is a particularly interesting text for Media Studies students.

Similarly, different cultures have different norms. A Venezuelan friend found the rules of *spatial behaviour* in Britain difficult to come to terms with at first; the British require more body space than is conventional in South America. When he returned home, however, he found he was holding conversations walking backwards. In terms of his non-verbal behaviour, he had become a fully fledged, insular Brit.

We spend every second of our waking lives unconsciously interpreting the information our senses receive from our environment. This interpretation is possible because we automatically follow the codes we have learned in order to give meaning to the world, whether they are linguistic or non-verbal. If we had to do all this decoding consciously then we'd probably go mad from information overload.

Incidentally, the men in Figure 1.3 were half way through a stag day (the thoughtful one is, appropriately, the 'stag'). Despite this, they weren't threatening. At the time they were waiting for the eighth member of their party, having spent the day losing money at the racetrack. I was, in fact, standing in the imagined position, taking the photograph.

We must next consider what is the difference between interpreting the world around us and analysing images.

◀ EXERCISE 1.4 ▶

Using the above information, interpret any non-verbal behaviour in an advertisement and use your own experience to decode anything else that is being communicated.

1.5 Image analysis

Photography is, literally, 'writing with light'. While we would not question the need to read writing, we often do not realize that we also have to read images. We assume that because photographs represent the 'real world' they are in some way natural; all we need do is look at them. The first objective in Media Studies should be, I think, to move from this passive consumption of images to an active reading of them. This is image analysis.

The object of analysis in media studies is to understand the meaning of a text (whether it be a novel, a film, TV programme, image, and so on). 'Text' in media studies means any object (artefact) that contains information, and not just – as text is traditionally understood – written material. *Coronation Street* is considered just as much a text as Charles Dickens' *Oliver Twist*; *Terminator 2: Judgment Day* is as much a text as *The Times*.

When analysing images from advertisements, films, television and so on, it is common to distinguish between their form and their content. This distinction can be applied to any text, whether it is an image-based text, a written one (such as a novel) or a combination of words and images (for example, newspapers).

- Form refers to how an image was created, including the position of the camera, or the position an artist takes in relation to the subject of the image.
- The content is simply what is in the image.

For the purposes of convenience it is assumed in the following that the images are created using a camera. However, all the points made can be applied just as easily to images that are drawn or computer-generated. Initially, for the same reason, we shall concentrate on aspects of images to be analysed without specific reference to their meaning; but it must be borne in mind that in actual analysis these aspects are only interesting because of the meaning they generate.

1.6 Form

Although information about how an image was created, or how a photograph was taken, can be very useful, that information is often not available. In most analyses it is sufficient to assume (often we have no choice but to assume) that all the information we require is available in the image.

Framing

When analysing images, the formal aspects are almost wholly to do with the image's frame.

We are accustomed to seeing frames on paintings, even if we pay them no attention, but we often consider that snapshots – such as Figure 1.3 – do not have a frame. This is not the case. All images have frames – the frame is the boundary between the image and what surrounds it; it is the image's edge.

The frame defines the position from which the image was created. It's the border between the space we are allowed to see, and that which is out of our sight. The relationship between on-screen and off-screen space is particularly important in film and television, and will be discussed later.

The formal aspects that the frame does not determine are: the depth of field (what is in focus) and the quality of film (or related technology, such as video) used to create the image.

- *Frame dimensions and shape*   All frames have a shape: an A4 piece of paper measures 211mm × 298mm or 298mm × 211mm, depending on whether it is portrait or landscape. As the names suggest, you are likely to have the paper upright for a portrait and horizontal for a landscape drawing.

Frame dimensions and shape are usually only significant if they are unconventional. For instance, if a picture of a man and woman together is long and thin this will emphasize their closeness more than a frame which allows more detail of what surrounds them.

The standard cinema film dimension is called the *Academy ratio*, after the Hollywood Academy which standardized it in the 1930s (see Figure 1.4). Image dimensions are usually given in ratios, rather than in height and width, because the same image can vary enormously in size. When you get your photographs developed, it is common to get larger prints of those you particularly like: it will have changed in size but the ratio between the top or bottom and sides will remain the same.

Similarly, we are all used to seeing different-sized televisions, but just because we are watching a portable TV, it doesn't mean that we don't get the same picture as on a 63cm television; it's just a smaller version of the same image. If you project a film on a screen close to you, it will give you a smaller image than on a screen further away. What doesn't vary, however, is the relationship between the image's height and width; this is called the *aspect ratio* (Figure 1.5).

The Academy ratio is 1:1.33: that means the image is one-third longer than it is high, so 1m in height = 1.33m in width and 5m height = 6.65m width. This ratio has historical precedents in painting.

Cinemascope, one of the wide-screen systems, has an aspect ratio of 1:2.35.

Figure 1.4 The Academy ratio

The aspect ratio of television is described confusingly as 4:3. This is because it describes the width before height and is in fact the same as 1:1.33. When films that were originally made in a wide-screen format are shown on television, part of the original image is cut off. If they are shown in their original dimensions then there has to be a black band along the top and bottom of the screen, to get the correct ratio. The term 'letter-box' is sometimes used to describe this. The ratio of most films released in the cinema today is around 1:1.65.

Figure 1.5 The aspect ratio, 1:2.35

- *Angle*   The angle of vision refers to the camera's angle in relation to the vertical; the most common is the 'straight on' position. There are two other common angles: high (clearly above the object) and low (below). (See Figure 1.6.)

- *A low angle* is often used to indicate a position of power – the audience is forced to look up at a character, so low angles are conventionally used to represent heroes.
- Similarly, *a high-angle shot* necessitates the audience looking down at a character (or object) and suggests the character (or object) is in a subservient position. It should be stressed that just because a high-angle shot is used, it doesn't necessarily mean that the person is in a subservient position; this is merely a convention and the actual meaning is determined by the context.

- *Height*   Height is obviously the height at which the shot is taken. The most common height is at eye-level, just under 2 metres (see Figure 1.7).

Figure 1.6 Cameras in position above and below an object which they are both filming

Figure 1.7 Height

- *Level* The level refers to the camera's horizontal angle. As with the vertical angle, the norm is 'straight on' or 0 degrees. However, the camera can also be tilted on its side to the left or right so the figure could appear as in Figure 1.8.

(a)   (b)

Figure 1.8 The same figure with camera tilted to (a) right and (b) left

● *Distance* Finally, distance simply refers to the distance of the object from the camera. There are seven categories (the descriptions in parentheses are given as examples):

1. extreme long shot (a landscape)
2. long shot (a group of people)
3. medium shot (one or two people)
4. medium close-up (part of body)
5. close-up (face)
6. extreme close-up (part of face).

For example, look at Figure 1.9, which shows the same figure shot in long shot and close-up.

It isn't necessary to define these distances precisely: one person's medium close-up might be another's medium shot; it's their function, which I will consider later, that matters.

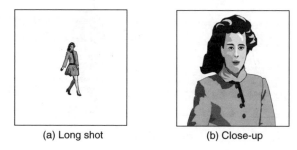

(a) Long shot   (b) Close-up

Figure 1.9 Long shot and close-up

◀ EXERCISE 1.5 ▶

Once again using your advertisement, add all the formal aspects present to your analysis.

● *The depth of field* This refers to the distance between the nearest and furthest area from the camera which is in focus. Deep focus photography will have the whole scene in focus, whereas a more conventional style will highlight objects within the frame by having the background out of focus.

A soft focus effect can also be created by using special lenses or filters and prevents the appearance of hard edges in the image.

- *Lens type* The standard single-lens reflex (SLR) for still cameras is 50–55mm for 35mm film and is commonly held to approximate human sight.

- Wide-angle lenses, which can be used for deep focus photography, make the scene appear deeper than it actually is, so objects in the frame appear to be further away than they actually are.
- An extreme wide-angle lens gives a 'fish-eye' effect in which everything is distorted.
- Telephoto lens create the opposite effect, pulling objects closer together; for example, athletes running toward a camera can seem to be running is a very tight pack until the cut to a side shot shows the true distance they are apart.

- *The stock, or type, of film* This refers to the speed at which it responds to light.

- A fast stock will tend to produce grainy images and is used in low light or to shoot fast moving objects.
- A slow stock will give a fine-grained image but will require plenty of light.

Slow stock is the norm in cinema. Most of the time, television companies use videotape, which is cheaper and gives a bright image.

- *The mobile frame* All we have considered so far are still images. Many images we see are moving, whether in the cinema or on television. Indeed, the word 'cinematography' means 'writing with movement'.

The mobile frame could encompass in one shot all the elements described so far, although this would be highly unlikely.

There are six types of moving images:

1. *pan* (short for panorama) in which the camera moves horizontally from a static position. A pan could move through the 360 degrees of a circle;
2. *tracking* (or *dolly*), in which the camera moves on tracks, giving a particularly smooth movement;
3. *tilt*, as referred to above, to the left or right;
4. *crane*, in which the camera is moved on a device that can move up, down and laterally (the ultimate crane shot is the helicopter shot);

5. *handheld*, which gives the frame a shaky look, particularly when it moves; often used to indicate a point-of-view shot (that is, we are seeing what the character is seeing);

6. *zoom* (*telephoto*), is technically not movement at all. The camera stays still and the focal length is altered during the shot bringing us closer (the zoom), or further away (wide angle), from the object; what doesn't change, though, is the aspect – we are still looking at the object from exactly the same position.

These are the main formal features that should be investigated in any analysis of the mobile frame.

To state whether an image is, say, a high-angle shot, from floor level, tilted to the right, tracking left is, however, only the first part of the analysis. We use appropriate terminology to describe the image, but description is not analysis. Analysis describes the features of an image and shows what these features mean. But before we consider the meaning of the formal aspects of the image, we must investigate the second component of analysis: content.

1.7 Content (*mise-en-scène*)

The term *mise-en-scène* means literally 'put on stage' and is used in film studies to demonstrate the film director's control of everything that appears in the film frame. In image analysis we must assume that everything in the picture has been 'put there for a reason'. The premise we must operate from is that everything in the image has meaning; it is a series of codes waiting to be interpreted.

There are three main components of *mise en scène* analysis:

- the subject
- the lighting
- the setting of the image.

The subject

The subject of an image may be a person, or a number of people, in fact anything that can be seen. It may represent reality or be something completely abstract. It may be the only thing within the picture or there may be many subjects, making it difficult to work out what is, in fact, the subject of the picture.

When trying to make sense of the subject we will bring our cultural knowledge, our understanding of social rules, to bear on it. For example, we know that a vehicle with four wheels on a road is most likely to be a motor car; however, someone who has never heard of such a subject would be unable to name it. If the subject is a person, then we would consider all the aspects of non-verbal communication (NVC) as we did when analysing Figure 1.3.

The positions in which subjects are placed form the image's composition. The main subject of an image is usually placed one third of the way across the image from either edge; this convention arises because the 'natural' position of the subject, the middle, would divide the image in half, which can be aesthetically displeasing. In conjunction with this, the horizon, if present, should be placed either one-third or two-thirds up an image. This convention is called the 'rule of thirds'. (Applying the rules to your own photography will give it a more professional look if that's what you desire.)

The lighting

This refers to how the image is lit. The lighting may be daylight or the flashlight we commonly use when we take snapshot photographs indoors. However, particularly in cinema, light can be used in numerous expressive (coded) ways. For example, with the use of filters, daylight can be made to look like moonlight. Alternatively, lack of light, shadows, might be used to conceal someone or something about a person (particularly used in *film noir* detective stories).

The lighting in many of the images you will study will not be natural, it will be controlled in some way. This is particularly true of advertising and cinematic images. Even if it is 'natural' lighting (that is, the light used is what is there) for the purposes of analysis it is still assumed to be making an expressive point. After all, in most cases, the photographer chose not to use artificial light, or chose that particular position in relation to the sun.

There are three main aspects to the study of lighting:

1. where the lighting is coming from: front, side, back, above or below?
2. is this lighting of equal intensity? (unlikely)
3. where is this light coming (or supposed to be coming) from?

(If you look carefully at films you will notice many examples of bizarre changes in lighting between shots of what is meant to be the same scene!)

The most common form of lighting is 'three-point lighting' made up of the key, fill and back light.

- *The key light* is the main source of illumination and is directed on the subject, usually from 45 degrees above and to one side of the camera. It is a hard, direct light which produces sharply defined shadows. It can be bright (high intensity) or dim (low).
- *The fill light* is a soft or indirect light that 'fills in' the shadows formed by the key light.
- Unsurprisingly, *the back light* shines from behind the subject, usually to differentiate it from the background.

We will examine later the expressive possibilities of this lighting system.

The setting

The setting is self-explanatory; we would have different expectations, for example, of a tropical setting from one in the Arctic. Imagine people wearing swimsuits in the latter. (The 1993 movie *Cool Runnings* advertised itself with the incongruous image of Jamaicans in the snow.)

It is useful to split the image into *foreground* and *background*, or *figure* and *ground*. Usually the subject, being the most important part of the image, occupies the former and the setting forms the background.

◄ EXERCISE **1.6** ►

Again, using your advertisement, add an analysis of the *mise-en-scène*.

1.8 What does it all mean?

The production of meaning is the crucial issue of analysis. What does the image mean and how does it communicate this meaning? If we refer back to Jakobson's model of speech communication earlier in the chapter, we can see that the dimension we have been investigating, when looking at form and content, is code.

Code is probably the most important of Jakobson's dimensions. As stated earlier, codes are any subjects or symbols (like words) which have a generally agreed meaning. So far we have considered only what the codes are – angle, distance and so on; this is called the level of *denotation*. What codes actually mean depends upon a consensus which we will consider below and in section 1.12; this is the level of *connotation*.

FORMAL ASPECT	CONVENTIONAL MEANING
• Angle	
High	Subservient position
Normal	Neutral
Low	Position of power
• Distance	
Long shot	Sets a scene and/or places subjects into context
Medium shot	Places audience at a 'safe' distance, near enough to observe but not intrude
Close-up	Places audience in an intimate position and signifies an emotional moment
• Composition	
Conventional (symmetrical/rule of thirds)	Posed, calm composition
Unconventional (asymmetrical)	Documentary style, real life as it happens
Dynamic	Disturbance, conflict
Static	Calm
• Depth of field	
Deep focus	Expressive, *mise-en-scène* very important
Selective focus	Indicates what is important in scene
Soft focus	Nostalgia and/or romance
• Lens type	
Telephoto	Voyeuristic
Standard	Normal
Wide angle	Drama
• Film stock	
Fast (grainy look)	Documentary style, looks 'real'
Slow (high resolution)	Normal
• Mobile frame	
Pan	To survey an areas or follow a subject at a distance
Tracking	To follow a movement from a close proximity
Tilt	To follow a movement up or down
Crane	To move dramatically toward or away from a subject
Handheld	Point-of-view shot
Zoom in	Allows us to see more detail from a distance (telephoto)
Zoom out	Places subject into context
• Lighting	
High key	Optimistic
Low key	Sombre
Fill	Natural; a lack of fill creates extreme contrast between light and dark often seen in *film noir*
Back	Glamour, creates a halo effect around the head

Figure 1.10 Examples of codes and their connotations

It is, to an extent, a false exercise to analyse codes on their own, because their meaning is usually determined by the other factors, such as context and message. We can, however, give some examples of what codes conventionally mean – their connotations – before considering the other parts of the communication (see Figure 1.10). This will also serve as revision of points made so far; however, it must be emphasized that the presence of a high-angle shot will not *guarantee* that a subservient position is being represented.

◀ EXERCISE 1.7 ▶

Analyse and compare Figures 1.11 and 1.12, using what you have learned in the chapter.

Figure 1.11 Rita Hayworth (*Gilda*)

Figure 1.12 A documentary image of a housewife

There follows a brief analysis of the two images in Figures 1.11 and 1.12. This is not the 'right answer' (there isn't one) but it does demonstrate how to read the codes of the images.

Neither of these images has a clear message although, like the 'lads' in Figure 1.3, they are both communicating with the addressee. The context in which we are viewing them is Media Studies; a discussion about these images in a different social situation (for example, at home or in an art class) could yield very different results. The contact is visual (there is more to this dimension, which we shall consider in Chapter 3).

If you have seen the film *Gilda* (1946), from which Figure 1.11 is taken, then your reading is likely to be different from an analysis which considers the image in isolation. Your knowledge of Gilda, played by Rita Hayworth, would influence the way you decode the image. For the purposes of this exercise, I shall ignore the image's filmic context.

The most striking formal aspect of Figure 1.11 is the lighting. Hayworth is shot for glamour with a heavy use of backlight, which creates a halo effect in her hair and emphasizes her 'hour-glass' figure by clearly delineating the shape of her waist and hips.

The low-angle of the shot puts her in a position of dominance, as does her gaze, which is directly at us. The half-closed eyes are calculating, as is her pose, with head to one side: it is as if she is deciding what to do with us. Hayworth's glamorous image is also reinforced by make-up, particularly on her lips, which are half-parted in a seductive fashion. The lips are ready for the cigarette, which is held in an assertive position, the smoke from it caught by the key light, helping to create a 'smouldering' atmosphere.

The key light also creates the only clear shadow in the image, that of her hand holding the cigarette. Her long fingernails cast a rather vicious shadow onto her chest, suggesting that her assertiveness borders on aggression. The cat-like claws link with the fur she is holding in her other hand. The fur is a sign of luxury and decadence (particularly as she is trailing it along the floor), and she appears to have taken it from around her shoulders. Clearly this is the image of a 'sexy' woman. However, the fur draws our attention to the elaborate ring (showing wealth) on her left hand, and thus to the fact she is married. While the image suggests that this woman is sexually available to men, the ring hints at transgression: any relationship with her would be adulterous.

Hayworth is given no context, and the background is black. She appears to be an abstraction of feminine sexuality, at once alluring and dangerous.

By contrast, Figure 1.12 shows a housewife and mother. The lighting is naturalistic, signifying it is 'documentary' style; this could be a photograph taken by the husband. The work of the housewife, and mother, is shown to be fun; she is smiling and can prepare an elaborate-looking meal and look after 'junior' at the same time. The open door, showing a back garden, suggests the weather is warm, which adds to the positive atmosphere engendered.

The deep focus of the image allows us to see the scene in detail. The counter draws our eye toward the back wall and we see the paraphernalia of cooking. The woman's dress is plain and practical, as is her hair style. The proximity of mother and child suggests they are operating as a team, and although the woman is leaning across the child, her smile negates any possibility that this is causing irritation.

Could the woman in the kitchen appear like Rita Hayworth? Probably, but the worlds of home and eroticism are usually represented as being very different and often inhabited by different people. This raises questions about the representation of women in particular, and gender in general, some of which will be considered in later chapters.

Having considered the formal aspects of image analysis we will now, before returning to code, investigate Jakobson's other dimensions.

1.9 Context, contact, and the message

Context

The context is the social situation in which the message in embedded. As if often the case in analysis, it is easiest to understand the effect a variable is having by imagining what would change if the variable changed. In this case, imagine the difference in a communication if the context is changed.

For example, you have analysed an image of Rita Hayworth in a Media Studies context. Put that same image in a different situation, say on a bedroom wall, and it would communicate differently. One is less likely to respond to it as a poster on a wall by analysing its formal codes; desire is a more likely response.

Similarly, your reading of the housewife would be very different if it were in your family album, which you were looking at in the home. Looking at a family album in class, however, would return it to an educational context.

Particular media are associated with specific social settings. For example, the institutional setting of cinema creates in the audience certain expectations: the dimming of the lights is a cue that the performance is about to begin; it is common for sweets to be eaten during the performance; the back row is reserved for snogging couples.

Much of our media experience takes place in the home, which may be a family setting (with competing voices) or a one-person household. In many households it is normal to 'talk over' the radio or even the television, but this would be frowned upon in a cinema or theatre.

The people present when a text is being experienced can also influence the addressee's reception of the message: watching a sexually explicit film can be embarrassing for adolescents and parents in each other's company, whereas enjoyment would be the more likely emotion if each generation were watching the scene on their own.

Think of the different experiences you have when watching texts in an academic context compared to the home where the emphasis is usually on entertainment. How do you feel when your academic knowledge of, say, the codes at work in images, starts to impinge upon your 'normal' viewing habits (many students have 'complained' to me about not being able to watch films any more without thinking about them!)?

In other words, the context is information from outside the communication or text, which influences how it is read.

Contact

The contact is, in simple terms, the channel of communication. It is the manner in which the addressee receives information. This has possibly the least influence on the meaning generated by the communication but, nevertheless, needs consideration in any analysis. The contact is the medium used to convey the message.

When Marshall McLuhan coined the phrase 'the medium is the message' he was over-simplifying the act of communication. However, McLuhan's words do illustrate how a medium can transform the meaning of the message that the addressee is receiving. The medium is the physical means by which communication is facilitated. It determines in what form information travels from addressee to addresser.

- *Cinema* This projects the film image onto a screen and the addressee usually experiences it as a member of an audience. Theatre uses a similar auditorium but is a 'live' experience (no two performances can ever be alike; cinema 'performance' can).

- *Television* This is an electronic medium which sends both sound and visual information. This information can be transmitted as a broadcast, or narrow-cast (via cable or satellite), signal.

- *Radio* This is also electronically transmitted, obviously sound only, usually in a broadcast form although it is also available on cable. Radio can also be transmitted locally through induction.

• *Print*   Print media are purely visual; they are usually distributed physically but can be electronically transmitted using facsimile machines and the telephone network. The print media include newspapers, magazines and books: these are usually experienced privately because we read them silently (this was not always the case; early newspapers were often read to an illiterate audience, leading to discussion of current issues among a community).

The text most often affected by contact is film. Film is seen at its best in the cinema but most films are watched on television, whether they're broadcast or on video. The quality of image on standard television is very poor when compared with that in cinema: the audiences are literally seeing different things. Spectacular films lose most on the small screen, and some films become almost meaningless (director Peter Greenaway's films can be virtually unwatchable on TV).

Video is also an important point of contact for it gives the audience power to stop, pause, rewind, review, or fast forward a text. This makes it an excellent resource for Media Studies students who are studying sequences but has also contributed to 'moral panics' about 'video nasties': it is imagined that 'innocent' children use it to analyse particularly gory or pornographic bits of film.

Contact is the medium through which the addressee is receiving the text. Its influence in the reading of the text depends upon how many channels the medium uses (for example, television's sound and vision or radio's sound only) and the quality of the medium (compare radio's VHF, or FM, with its short wave).

It is obviously better to experience a text in the medium for which it was intended; for example, films in the cinema and not on television. It can, however, occasionally be enlightening to read a text in a different medium. For example, if you record the soundtrack of a favourite film and listen to it, you will probably hear things that you have never previously noticed.

An important part of contact is how it creates a relationship between the addresser and addressee. This is explained in the next chapter.

Message

The message is the information that the addresser is sending to the addressee. However, there can be no certainty that the addressee will read the message as it is intended; for example, an advertisement's message is usually about the effectiveness of the product or service being promoted, but an addressee may disagree with, or misunderstand, the message.

Messages are, in most instances, very easy to decode; after all, most addressers want to communicate with the addressee. The exceptions to this are texts which want to make the addressee work at creating meaning; Art cinema occasionally seems to relish being obscure, sometimes to the point of suggesting that there may in fact be no message or meaning.

On other occasions the message is not understood because the addressee has no knowledge of a text's codes, possibly because he or she is not the intended audience. These codes, of course, can be learned; anybody can learn to appreciate, say, cubist art or opera.

In most cases images are used to illustrate and reinforce the message and, as we shall see in the next section, words are often used to anchor the image' meaning. An exception to this, in Britain, is cigarette advertising which is heavily reliant upon the image because it is illegal to use words to state anything positive about the product. Clearly, in silent cinema the image must carry alone virtually all the information about the narrative. The only other channels available are intertitles, which give written information to the audience, and the accompanying music.

Though images are clearly the most important bearer of the message in photography and painting, the artefact's title is bound to influence an addressee's reading of the text. Leonardo da Vinci's Mona Lisa could have been entitled 'Virtue' or 'Whore', creating, possibly, completely opposite messages.

In cinema also, the image is often the prime provider of information, even over-riding that of the dialogue. In *Citizen Kane* (1940), directed by Orson Welles, the scene where the young Kane is adopted takes place in his parents' hut and we hear the conversation concerning the boy. Kane is playing outside in the snow with his sledge and Welles' use of deep focus places the boy at the centre of the *mise-en-scène* and the audience can see him, through a window, playing in the distance with his sledge. The significance of this is revealed only at the end. In *Gilda* (1946), a classic *film noir*, Glenn Ford's voice-over narration is demonstrated as patently false by what we see; his messages are clearly unreliable.

Television relies more heavily on words to convey information, as the image it beams into our homes is not, currently, as rich or as detailed as that of the cinema (although 'home entertainment' technology promises to change this): video also suffers the same limitations and films on video lose much of their visual impact.

In radio, most information is transmitted by words. Any image used is, obviously, wholly created by sound. Different acoustics, for example, are used to create an outdoor or indoor setting. A reverberant acoustic could be used to signify a large hall, or swimming pool.

In popular music image and sound invariably come together. The music and lyrics carry most of the message but it is important that the artist 'look the part'. An artist looking like REM's Michael Stipe but singing a bland, romantic 'Europop' song, would be incongruous; whereas, say, Ice-T's looks suit his music.

While it must be remembered that all of Jakobson's variables are important, the function of communication is to convey a message. The message is usually unambiguous and easily understood. Images have a vital role in conveying a message, but words, because of the smaller possibility of ambiguity, are usually more important.

◀ EXERCISE 1.8 ▶

Preferably in groups, analyse a series of messages which use images to accompany them. On a scale of one to ten, rate how important you think the image is to the message: '1' would indicate it was redundant (that is, it did not belong there); '10' signifies it is the bearer of the message on its own. What conclusions can you draw from your collection?

1.10 Codes

In our earlier consideration of form and content we have already described the formal codes of image analysis. Codes are objects or symbols which have a consensual meaning; in addition, less tangible things, such as light and camera angles, qualify as codes because they too have a generally agreed meaning. Images do not, however, merely use formal codes to communicate, they also employ codes with which we are all familiar.

Earlier in the chapter it was stated, that 'before we (analyse images) we must understand that we spend every day of our lives not just analysing any communication we receive, or send, but everything that happens around us.' It is no surprise that the media uses the same codes we use in everyday life to send and interpret messages. For example, someone who fully lowers his or her eyebrows is usually angry: the position of the eyebrows is understood as a code for anger. It makes little difference, in terms of your reading of the code, whether this person is with us or is being represented by an image (if the individual is really angry then it's probably better that he or she is an image!). Although Exercise 1.2, where you had to imagine your response to a group of men, was described as a contradiction in terms (because you were asked to imagine the image as real), as far as coding is concerned 'lack of reality' makes little difference.

However, as we have seen in our consideration of formal codes, the media does not only draw upon codes from 'real life'. In fact the relationship between 'real life' and the media is not one-way; how could it be, as the media forms part of the 'real world'? Indeed, the influence of the media upon the 'real world' is a source of much contentious debate: our moral guardians seem to believe that by watching 'sex 'n' violence', particularly on television, the nation's youth will become corrupt (these issues are dealt with in *Institution and Audience*). Clearly the media does have an influence on us – who would advertise if it did not? – but the relationship is complex and hard to quantify.

To consider coding specific to the media, in addition to the formal codes already considered, we must investigate the use of:

- anchorage
- image choice and cropping
- juxtaposition
- genre and
- colour.

Anchorage

We are more than capable of interpreting images which stand on their own. However, it is unusual, in the media, to see images that are unsupported by any words. In newspapers the words are an image's caption and the accompanying report; in advertising the words range from the pithy slogan to a detailed description of products or services; in cinema and television the only images we do not expect to 'speak' to us are those of silent cinema.

The function of these words is to reinforce the addresser's intended meaning. Roland Barthes (1977) described this function as 'anchorage': the meaning of the image is anchored by the caption. For example, an image of a person sipping from a cup appears very different with the captions: 'The tea was delightful' and 'The tea was poisoned' – same image, different context, different meaning.

Figure 1.13

(Photograph: Richard Smith, Katz)

An image's meaning can often be ambiguous. For example, Figure 1.13, taken during riots in London about the introduction of the so-called 'poll tax', shows a policeman restraining a young man; a female onlooker appears to be getting involved.

◄ EXERCISE 1.9 ►

Analyse the image in Figure 1.3 and write a caption which summarizes – anchors – your meaning.

The codes of dress are very important in this image. Clearly the policeman represents authority, the young man's dress suggests he is a non-conformist, while the woman appears to be 'respectable'. The most obvious reading of this image is, I think, that the woman is giving the young man 'a piece of her mind'. Indeed, this is how the photograph was used in the press. However, the woman actually wrote to a publication which used the image and explained that, in fact, she was more concerned about police brutality and was urging the young man to stay calm (he was upset because the police had manhandled his girlfriend).

Our socially-learned expectations suggested that the young man was a trouble-maker, but the truth was very different. The only way the erroneous impression gained by our expectations could be eradicated is through anchorage, a caption explaining what was actually happening. The fact that the original caption did not do this may mean the image was being used to distort the truth, or the picture editor did not know the true circumstances.

It is a useful, and fun, exercise to write your own captions to newspaper photographs: can you make the image have the opposite meaning to that intended?

Image choice and cropping

Anchorage is not only provided by words: the actual choice of image is a factor in determining meaning. Picture editors of newspapers will often have numerous photographs of the same event, or dramatic moment, to choose from. Their choice will be determined by what appears, to them, to convey the desired meaning most effectively.

Photographs are often cropped, particularly in news publications. This consists of cutting an image both to fit the space available and also to emphasize the image's subject. For example, a long shot of a 'world leader' at a conference has a very different meaning from a cropped version which features only a 'close-up' of the leader. In the original version we see the leader situated among many other people and clearly in a public setting. Close-ups, however, imply that we are receiving a privileged insight into an individual's thoughts because it appears, to the audience, that he or she is alone.

Juxtaposition

Juxtaposition means 'being placed side-by-side'. It is obvious that any other information, written or otherwise, near an image is likely to influence the reading of that image. For example, an image of a craggy, handsome man juxtaposed with a mansion on the cover of a novel would suggest it was a romantic story. The same man, however, juxtaposed with a gun and the mansion would probably suggest a murder mystery.

The juxtaposition of images can create very different meanings from the images placed on their own. 'Before and after' advertisements, such as those for slimming or muscle-building products, create a narrative simply by placing images together: 'use this product and you will be transformed from this to this'. Clearly if the 'before and after' images were analysed on their own, the narrative would not be present. In newspapers, similar juxtaposed images – such as photographs of a building before and after it is demolished – also imply a narrative.

Collage takes juxtaposition to extremes by placing numerous, usually unrelated, images together within a frame. These same images could be placed together to form a different patterns and this would then yield a different meaning.

◀ EXERCISE 1.10 ▶

Cut out, or create, an image, and write as many different captions as you can for it; try to create opposite meanings using the same image.

In cinema, the power of juxtaposition is demonstrated by the 'Kuleshov effect'. During the 1920s, a Soviet film-maker, Lev Kuleshov, is reputed to have filmed an actor with a neutral expression on his face and followed this shot with various other images, such as a baby and a bowl of soup. The audience was asked to determine the actor's emotion and, despite the fact that his expression was always the same, the audience assumed he was reacting to the objects inter-cut with himself; in the first instance they interpreted the actor's expression as affection, and in the second as hunger. In other words, they assumed that the actor and the objects occupied the same space.

We are moving here toward a consideration of images in sequence, which will be covered later in the chapter.

Genre

Genre provides addressees, or audiences, with a clear set of expectations which are used to interpret the text. For example, we expect to be frightened by a horror text and will be surprised if it lacks at least some of the following elements: a large, old, decrepit house with a squeaky door (brilliantly spoofed in *Edward Scissorhands* (1990) when Diane Wiest's character opens such a door and shouts 'Avon calling'); thundery weather; a cellar; blood and gore; blood-curdling screams; horrible deaths; monsters; supernatural powers and so on. In a romance an image of, say, a young woman approaching an old house gives very different meanings from the same act in a horror text.

Genres are obviously not restricted by a medium; a horror text can appear on television, radio, in the cinema, or print, and audiences will use the same generic framework for each medium. (Genre will be dealt with fully in *Narrative and Genre*.)

The genre of a magazine, for example, can determine how an image is read; numerous different types of magazines could, hypothetically, use the same image on their front covers, and generate different meanings. An image of a woman on the cover of *Cosmopolitan* is intended to attract women; on the cover of *Esquire*, a men's magazine, the same image could be obviously used to attract men. (In practice *Esquire* tends to use known faces, female and male, while *Cosmopolitan* usually sticks with anonymous models.) The image in the context of *Cosmopolitan* sends the message: 'buy this magazine and you could look something like this.' *Esquire*'s message reads: 'buy this magazine and you could get a woman who looks something like this.' This is not to say that anyone actual believes a physical transformation will take place; it is probably more in the hope that something of the glamour associated with the publications will rub off on the purchaser.

Similarly, it is possible to imagine the same image being used on the cover of different types of books; the meaning generated would then depend upon the book's genre. For example, the image – and it could be the same one that hypothetically appeared on the magazines above – could be suitable for: novels (for example, romance, pornography, crime, science fiction); text books (for example, psychology, biology, business); or general interest (for example, cooking, dieting, Media Studies). Each of these genres would lead us to read the same image in a different way.

In practice, of course, the images used are different, because each genre has its own iconography (see below).

Part of our understanding or what genre a text is comes from the anchoring provided by the title. The appearance of our woman on the front of the *Angling Times* would suggest she had caught a very large fish. It is not only titles that anchor meaning, the kind of lettering, or font, can do the same: for example *Romantic*, or **Science fiction**, and blood dripping off the title will invariably indicate a crime or horror novel.

Iconography is also an important code used by genres. It refers to objects we recognize as having specific meanings when associated a the text's genre. For example, a crucifix usually represents Christianity; in a horror film it is also a totem, or weapon, against evil. A ten-gallon hat and six-shooters are indelibly linked with the Western genre; indeed it is probably impossible to make a Western without them. While the root of iconography is real life (in this instance the 'wild west' of nineteenth-century North America) for most people the understanding of these codes is derived from the media – mostly films (media representation of the original 'wild west' is usually more mythical than historical, as we shall see in Chapter 4).

◀ EXERCISE 1.11 ▶

Choose a genre (for example, horror, war, science fiction, romance) and list as many objects that you associate with it, as you can.

Iconography operates in stereotyping in a very similar fashion and is most powerfully seen in advertising. What does a middle-aged, white man, wearing a pin-stripe suit and bowler hat, carrying an umbrella, do for a living? Answer: something to do with finance or, more specifically, the City of London. The fact that this form of dress was the norm decades ago, and is virtually obsolete now, is irrelevant to the stereotype as long as audiences understand the code. (Some stereotypes, however, have little, if any, relationship to reality. The colour of a woman's hair cannot possibly have an influence upon her intelligence and yet the 'dumb blonde' is a common stereotype.)

Before we conclude this section on codes, there are a few more we need to consider that are specific to the media and not drawn from 'real life'.

'Silent' cinema developed a whole series of non-verbal codes to overcome the lack of sound (usually limited to musical accompaniment). As a result, the gestures of silent film actors today often seem 'over the top': the heroine, flung on the floor by the villain (who twiddles his moustache), raises her arms in a mixture of pleading and prayer; cut to close-up of villain, eyes wide open, with obvious make-up, relishing his power. This exaggeration of gesture overcame the lack of dialogue.

Since the arrival of sound this melodramatic style of acting has become redundant. Modern audiences, while understanding the codes of silent cinema, find them too obvious, preferring the subtler coding of contemporary texts. It could be argued, however, that this exaggerated form of gesture still exists, albeit in a different form, in the 'action' movie.

Opera and musicals also use codes generated by the medium – it is rare, for example, for people to burst into song (unless they're in the bath). To the uninitiated, the sound of Mimi faultlessly singing her final aria in Puccini's *La Bohème* – complete with the odd cough –

before she dies of consumption is laughable; those who understand the code cry nevertheless.

Just as we learn 'real life', or social, codes through the process of socialization, codes specific to media representations are learned through exposure to the media. Codes can only exist if there is a consensus between addressers and addressees about their meaning.

The object of image analysis is to find out what all these codes mean in combination. However, we must consider one other variable that may be present in the still image: colour. It is arguable that colour is a formal property of an image but its codification derives from everyday life rather than specifically from photography.

1.11 Colour

Clearly colour could not be used as a photographic code until colour film was technologically possible. As a code, colour takes its cue from social codes: red is associated with passion and violence; blue with coolness and melancholy.

Even if, say, film directors do not consciously wish to make an expressive point with colour, they need to be careful that colours do not clash within the frame; a *mélange* of green and orange, for example, may make an audience feel sick (this could, of course, be an expressive point).

One way in which colour is used is to focus the audience's attention within the *mise-en-scène*. This is done with bright colours, which draw the eye more than pastel shades.

Colour is obviously linked with lighting. Film directors may suffuse their film with a particular coloured light: red in *Taxi Driver* (1976), directed by Martin Scorsese, and blue in *Blue Steel* (1989, Kathryn Bigelow). The effect of this is to link various themes in the film.

Director Vincente Minnelli (1910–86) has a reputation as a stylist (which means, basically, his style is very noticeable) and a number of his films, for example *Lust for Life* (1956), use painters' styles as the basis for the use of colour. Another good example of the expressive use of colour occurs in Minnelli's film *Home From the Hill* (1959) which:

> revolves around a conflict between a man and his wife. The husband's den . . . is painted a deep, blood red all over and is furnished in a 'masculine' way, with leather armchairs, rifles and hunting trophies. The

rest of the house is the woman's domain – it is decorated in off-white, with chintzy patterns and in upper-class good taste; she wears pastel colours that blend in with the setting. The house is thus divided dramatically between the male and female parts, as is the family itself.

(Dyer, 1981, pp. 1154–5)

◀ EXERCISE 1.12 ▶

List as many associations with different colours as you can.

In Western society there is a tradition of associating the colours, or shades, white and black with good and evil respectively, and this feeds into many stereotypes. It is arguable that this expressive use is racist, as the word black now has negative associations and vice versa. In China, for instance, the colour of mourning is white.

While colour basically adds to the verisimilitude of an image, it must be also considered as a code because it is, potentially, being used expressively. Ironically, given everyday life for most of us is in colour, it is usually the lack of colour, black and white photography, that is used to signify a certain type of realism. It could be that the lack of glamour, or the apparent cheapness, of black and white images suggests to the audience that what is shown is real, 'warts and all'.

1.12 Analysis of advertisement: Nokia 232

Before moving on to 'Images in Sequence' it will be useful to revise once again and apply the tools of analysis described so far. For this I am going to use an advertisement for a mobile phone, Figure 1.14.

'An Unforgettable Little Black Number' – image analysis

Despite the fact that this advertisement, for Nokia 232 mobile phones, appears to be relatively simple in construction, it yields a massive amount of information when subjected to analysis. I have used all of Jakobson's dimensions as the starting point and have followed the order in which the dimensions have been described. But it is probably easier to make notes first on the points most obvious to you, without following a particular order. Do make sure, however, that you consider all the dimensions.

- *Frame* The frame is standard magazine shape, which immediately suggests it is a magazine advertisement (although it could appear in a broadsheet newspaper as a 30 × 5; that is, 30cm high by

Figure 1.14

5 columns across); it could also appear at certain poster sites, such as those at bus stops. This particular advertisement ran in 13 magazines, listed later, during the summer of 1995.

• *Angle and height*   The shot was taken from a low angle; we are looking up at the woman. The height is about at her knee-level, putting her in a dominant position.

• *Distance*   The frame encloses a medium shot of the subject, a woman, and the background of a bust on a pillar. The medium shot allows us to see most of the woman, with only her shins and feet 'cut off', so her face, dress and legs are all visible.

• *Tilt*   Unusually, the angle of this image in the advertisement is tilted slightly to the right. This appears to suggest (I do not think we believe that the setting is actually sloping) that the woman is walking uphill.
The tilt also creates three diagonal lines (formed by the bust and pillar, the woman and the darker wall behind the woman). These lines give a dynamism to the image and open a space, in the bottom right hand corner, for product details.

Mise-en-scène

• *The subject*   The most important subject of the image is clearly the woman (the subject of the advertisement, however, is the mobile phone). She is wearing a black dress and tights, long silver earrings, has an immaculate coiffure and is holding a mobile phone. Her gaze is directed at us and she is smiling. She has one hand on a pillar.

• *Lighting*   The key lighting, from about 45-degrees above her on the left, emphasizes her face, which stands out further because of the lack of fill lighting on the shadow cast by the key light. No backlighting appears to have been used, as her black dress makes her stand out from the setting. Fill light has been used on the shadow cast by the bust; if it had not been used, the woman would have been undifferentiated from the background, as the shadow cast would have merged with her dress.

• *Setting*   While clearly a studio shot, the use of a classical bust and pillars suggests a museum setting. In this case, however, because there is no clear sign that the location is actually a museum; the setting is abstract.

The wall behind the woman is shaded – the effect of this is to make the woman's face, which is brightly lit, stand out more than it would on a pale background.

- *Context, contact, and the message*   The social situation in which you are reading this image is, once again because of the nature of this book, educational and the contact, clearly, is visual. Normally, however, magazine advertisements are read in an informal context.

The message is usually explicit within advertisements because their function is to sell either a product, service or brand/company name. In decoding this advertisement we shall find that the message of this text when targeted at men, is 'Buy Nokia 232 and the female in your life will appear to be as attractive as this woman' and, when aimed at females, 'Buy Nokia 232 and you will appear to be as attractive as this woman'.

- *Anchorage*   The anchorage is provided, linguistically, by the copy ('An unforgettable little black number' and 'It's not what you say, it's how you say it.') and by the image of the product. The 'unforgettable . . .' copy is a pun because it is referring to both the woman's dress and the product. First let us consider how it is applied to the image's subject.

The 'black number' is clearly referring to the woman's dress; it is a phrase that has connotations of being sexually attractive, the 'little' means a lot of leg is being shown. 'Unforgettable' refers to the 'turn on' of the image: because the woman is (conventionally) beautiful and is wearing a '(sexy) little black number' ('sexy' is implied in the phrase), she is sexually attractive (to heterosexual males) and a model of sexual attractiveness (to heterosexual females). In other words, the woman is an object of desire and a model for appearance. The rhetoric of the anchorage is that, once seen, this woman is never forgotten (untrue, of course).

The meaning of the Nokia 232 is anchored in exactly the same way: it is a sexy, unforgettable, little, black number. The qualities of the image's subject are transferred to the product which she is holding in her hand.

Nokia's slogan ('It's not what you say, it's how you say it') emphasizes that lifestyle is a main selling point of the product and harks back to Marshall McLuhan's (a noted media commentator of the 1960s) 'the medium is the message'. The implication is that it is the product itself that is important: you can say exactly the same thing on numerous makes of mobile phones – or indeed on the conventional telephonic system – but only with a Nokia 232 will you become 'unforgettable'. As in many advertisements, what is here offered is more the lifestyle which purchasing the product will allow you to experience than the product itself. This 'explains' the low angle of the shot, which signifies the woman is powerful: buy this product and you too will be powerful.

The final piece of linguistic anchorage is the Nokia logo, which emphasizes the social nature of their product ('connecting people') and the dynamism associated with it – the three arrows pointing forcibly upwards.

• *Image choice and cropping* Because this is a 'custom-made' photograph, it is not only the particular choice of image that is important (one of many which would have been taken with different poses and/or settings) but also the choice of content: the look of this particular model, the certain type of sculpture. We have already described the model as beautiful; however, it is also likely that the choice of this woman was influenced by the presence of the classical sculpture because there is a similarity of facial shape; this is emphasized by the shortness of her hair (long flowing locks would not have had the same effect). (Of course it is possible that the model's face suggested the use of the bust; all we can state with certainty is the similarity.)

For 'custom-made' images, cropping is often not important because the photographer would know what frame size was required, so the lower part of the woman's legs have not been cut off to facilitate the image fitting an the standard magazine-sized frame. It is possible that this image was cropped along the diagonal line created by the shaded wall behind the woman, although care was obviously taken not to cut off her leg.

• *Juxtaposition* There are three items placed side-by-side within the advertisement – the Nokia 232, the woman, and the classical bust and pillars. We also need to consider the position of the copy.

When analysing juxtaposition it can be fruitful to follow the direction that your eyes, when looking at the image, appear to take naturally. In this case the key lighting and the beauty of the woman's face draws our gaze to the top left of the image where the copy 'unforgettable little black number' immediately anchors the advertisement's meaning. It also creates a slight puzzle, as it does not look like a 'fashion ad': what is the product? This is answered quickly by the observation of the mobile phone held to her ear directly between her face and the copy.

The three diagonal lines drag our gaze downwards, taking in the classical bust and pillars, toward the bottom of the page where the product name and contact (freephone number) for further information is situated.

The juxtaposition in this images creates the order in which the addressee (Nokia 232) wishes the addressee to read the advertisement.

• *Genre*   Advertisements tend to be, in themselves, without specific generic connotations. The content of the advertisement, however, can refer to a genre as a short cut to meaning (by using, for instance, a 'wild west' setting). Certain types of product have created their own advertising genres, such as motor cars and cleaning fluids; these advertisements are often self-referential and audiences can only fully understand them with knowledge of the advertisement's genre. As I have already mentioned, this advertisement could be classified, generically, as a 'lifestyle' advertisement, which enables us understand the equation that buying a Nokia 232 will give us access to a better existence.

The way an advertisement is read is also influenced by the genre of the text (or institution in the case of cinema and television) in which it is placed, and its position within that text. I originally saw this advertisement in the June 1995 edition of *Esquire* magazine. *Esquire* advertises itself as 'the award-winning magazine for men'. It is a lifestyle magazine, which means that it is aimed at a middle-class, adult audience who are probably 'thirtysomething'. In the context of *Esquire* the advertisement appears to be targeted at men and the lifestyle equation becomes: 'buy this product and you will become attractive to women like this'. This association occurs because this desirable woman is using the product. Clearly no one expects any current female companion to be transformed into this beauty, but associations of power and attractiveness are transferable.

The magazine is printed on glossy, high quality paper, emphasizing the desirability of the product. Newspapers, even with colour printing, cannot hope to reproduce this effect an newsprint. Many have weekly, glossy magazines in order to pick up advertising such as this.

The advertisement's position was on page 32, a left-hand page facing editorial; the influence of the editorial (entitled 'In Search of Yamashita's Gold') in reading this particular advertisement is probably insignificant. However, if the editorial covered, for example, the high cost of mobile phones or, alternatively, their benefits, then it is likely that it would have had some bearing on the reading.

This particular advertisement had a 2–3 months length of activity, in 1995, with a frequency of one or two insertions in consecutive months in women's and men's monthlies. The actual schedule is reproduced below (courtesy of Nokia and its agency Greycom):

You magazine, 7th May
Company, June and July
Elle, June and July
She, June
New Woman, June and July
Vogue, June
Harpers & Queen, June and July
Vanity Fair, June
OK, June and July
Esquire, June and July / August
FHM, June and July
GQ, June
Spectator, 3rd June and 17th June.

It is usually very difficult to get hold of this information and it is unlikely that you will ever need to know the schedule. I have included it simply as an example of an actual schedule.

◀ EXERCISE 1.13 ▶

Using copies of some of the above magazines, try to isolate any variations in your reading of the advertisement created by the different publications (it is unnecessary to get the actual issues in which the advertisement appeared).

This appears to have been a very full analysis but is, in fact, far from exhaustive. In Chapter 2 we shall return to the advertisement and consider it from a semiotic perspective and in Chapter 3 from a psychoanalytic view.

1.13 Images in sequence

The images we have considered so far have been still. While the principles of still image analysis can also be used on moving images – they must usually be stilled in order to analyse them accurately – there are additional codes which are unique to images in sequence.

The relationship between still and moving images can be understood at an early age: the ubiquitous 'stick person' animated by flicking quickly through the pages of a book, is a common trick learned by young children. The rapid juxtaposition of images, each slightly different from the previous one, gives an illusion of movement. The same principle is used in cinema; a still image, or frame, is projected momentarily on to a screen, to be immediately followed by another, and so on. In silent cinema the speed of projection is approximately 16 frames per second (fps); sound cinema requires 24 fps. (The figure for silent cinema is approximate because early cameras were hand-cranked and the speed depended upon the camera operator. The difference between the fps rate of silent and sound explains why, sometimes, in silent film, people appear to walk too quickly: this is because 16 fps film is being projected at 24 fps.)

The first films exhibited in cinemas were short and straightforward portrayals of events from everyday life. However, once film is used for narrative purposes then it is necessary to structure images into a sequence. A narrative is a sequence of events that are linked, usually by a cause–effect chain, in a given setting – or space – and within a specific time frame. Unless these elements are carefully constructed the audience may become disorientated: on an obvious level, we do not expect a novel's characters to change their names without reason; similarly, if the novel opens in a particular place, any change in setting must be described, or motivated, by the narrative. If the narrative is occurring on a Monday, we do not expect the next day to be a Friday.

Linking together different shots in film is similar to linking together sentences in a novel. Unless the addressee understands the codes used he or she will not get the full message. Linking images in sequence, whether film or television, is primarily the product of editing – the juxtaposition of one shot with another.

Editing

The word 'edit' often means 'to cut out': in audio-visual texts it refers to the join between shots. The purpose of conventional editing is to make this join as smooth as possible; indeed, the objective is to make the join seem invisible. This can only happen if the audience is not confused by the edit; if they understand the link between the shots, narrative cause and effect is maintained.

The potential for audiences to be disorientated by the editing process was first exploited by a French pioneer of cinema, Georges Méliès. The story runs that while he was filming (horse-drawn) traffic the film stuck inside the camera. Having fixed the problem, he continued shooting. When the film was seen later, one vehicle 'miraculously' turned into another. Méliès used the 'trick' to create illusions in his fantasy films.

Méliès' use of editing was intentionally disorientating; in narrative film, however, disorientation is usually the last thing a film-maker wants the audience to experience. The need for a narrative flow, to tell the story, led to the development of the *continuity system of editing*. This was perfected by film-makers in Hollywood and is one reason why this particular part of the USA has dominated film production in the Western world ever since.

Continuity editing

One objective of continuity editing is to create a coherent cinematic space in which the action can take place. Early cinema placed the camera as if it were in a theatre's stalls, and the players acted in front of it. This was clearly very limiting, with no different camera positions or camera movement. Once the camera moves, whether the movement is seen on screen or if it's done between cuts, it is essential that the audience know where it has moved to, or they would become disorientated. To prevent confusion the following rules are used; these rules, in fact, form the codes of continuity editing. If the audience did not understand them, they would become disorientated. The fact that audiences understand these rules unconsciously, and cannot describe them (unless they've studied film or media), is a testimony to their effectiveness.

● *180-degree rule*   The 180-degree rule (Figure 1.15) was established as the best way of facilitating continuity of cinematic space within one scene. By staying on one side of the imaginary axis, the 'axis of action', which is formed through the subject(s) in the scene, the audience will always have a clear idea of where the characters are in relation to one another and where they are within the scene.

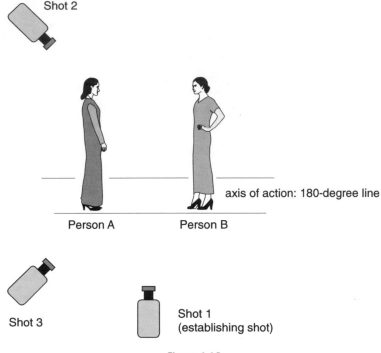

Figure 1.15

If, however, the 180-degree line is crossed (for example, shot 2), and the camera remains facing the characters, then everything would appear the other way around. For example, someone who was walking from left to right would suddenly appear to be going in the opposite direction; two characters talking to one another would suddenly appear to change position. Shot 3 would be a 'legitimate' position, as it remains on the same side of the 'axis of action' as the first, establishing shot (see Figure 1.16).

● *Establishing shot*   The position of the 180-degree line is usually established by the first shot of a scene, the 'establishing shot'. This creates the 'axis of action' and it is necessary that the characters and space are clearly seen within this shot.

● *Re-establishing shot*   Once a scene's space has been established, a number of medium or close-up shots may follow, which would fragment the space. In this case a 're-establishing shot' might be required to re-anchor the audience's perception of the scene's space.

Shot 1

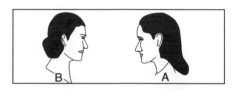

Shot 2   Confusing, because it appears that person A has turned to face the other way

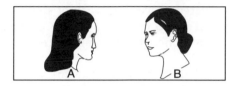

Shot 3   Person A facing the same direction as in shot 1

Figure 1.16

● *Shot/reverse-shot*   Once the scene has been established, medium shots can show each end of the 180-degree axis, although they must always stay on the same side. The angle of these two shots from the axis of action must be same. This technique is usually used in filming conversations between characters; for example, an over-the-shoulder shot could show one person talking, cut to over-the-shoulder of this person would show the other listening. This is a shot/reverse-shot pattern (see Figure 1.17).

● *30-degree rule*   Whenever a camera position is changed it must move at least 30-degrees, in relation to the shot's subject(s), from its previous position in order to make the movement obvious. Anything less tends to have a jarring effect.

● *Eyeline match*   When a character looks off-screen followed by another shot, the second shot shows what the character is looking at.

● *Match on action*   If a character starts to move in a particular direction, it is possible to cut to a shot where the character is still

Figure 1.17

moving but has covered space that was not shown. Because of the 180-degree rule, and the consistency of the character's direction, audiences tend not to notice the missing space (and time).

● *The Cut*   As stated at the beginning of this section, edit normally means 'to cut'. Unless the editing is done 'in camera' (which is what we normally do with our home videos – the cut is where we switched the camcorder off) then editing requires film to be cut and then spliced to the next shot. (Video tape is not edited in this fashion, the sequences required are usually recorded from a master on to another tape in the desired order.)

If one sequence of film or tape is immediately followed by another, then this edit is described as a 'cut'. There are, however, four other ways of splicing images together:

1. *Fade-out*: where the scene simply fades to black, which means it has ended;
2. *Fade-in*: the scenes appears from a black frame and obviously signifies a beginning;
3. *Dissolve*: the second shot fades-in and is superimposed over the first shot, which fades-out (usually taking less than a second), this usually suggests the passage of time or is expressively linking the two scenes (for example, a dissolve from a shot of an evil character to a shot of a fire may suggest that the character will burn in hell);
4. *Wipe*: the second shot flows horizontally across the first, as if it were a curtain being pulled across the frame giving the effect of an abrupt conclusion to the scene.

As has been suggested in the above description, each of these edits has a meaning; these may vary, though, depending upon the scene in which they are placed. The fades and dissolves usually indicate the passage of time (although a cut can also do this). A wipe can often imply that the second scene is happening at the same time as the first. These edits usually happen so quickly in continuity editing, that the audience rarely notices them. Indeed some dissolves are so quick that it is unlikely that anyone other than a Media Studies student analysing a sequence will perceive them.

Of course, in actual film-making, characters filmed in the same scene may in reality have been miles apart. This is particularly true when location shooting is mixed with studio work (which will probably be responsible for producing close-ups). Unless told otherwise – by an establishing shot – audiences assume that there is a spatial relationship between one shot and the next, the Kuleshov effect discussed earlier. The overall effect of continuity editing is that it is not noticed; it appears, in fact, to be invisible.

◀ EXERCISE 1.14 ▶

Using a minute of any movie (the odds are it will use continuity editing), count how many different shots there are. Show the sequence to friends, without telling them what they are looking for, and ask them how many shots there were. You are likely to get wildly differing responses.

The creation of coherent space for the narrative to be enacted is not the only function of editing. When analysing images in sequence, we must consider the effect that the juxtaposition of different images (which is what a cut produces) has upon the creation of meaning. Four relationships between images at the edit should be considered:

- graphic
- rhythmic
- spatial and
- temporal.

● *Graphical relationships* Graphics refers to a shot's brightness, and the patterns of line, shape, volume, depth, movement and stillness. The focus of analysis is on whether the graphic properties of shots are edited to create either continuity or contrast. The 'rule of thirds' is a graphical relationship within one shot.

● *Rhythmic relationships* These are created by the length of shot, how long a shot runs before the edit. If a sequence consists of shots of the same length, then a rather monotonous rhythm will be created; conversely, a series of long shots followed by rapid editing is likely to create an exciting effect (often used for set pieces in action movies). Some documentaries use the 'long take' – that is, very little editing – in order to create a sense of reality.

● *Spatial relationships* As already discussed, continuity editing uses various rules – such as the 180-degree rule – to create coherent space.

● *Temporal relationships* These are about how on-screen time is constructed. It is unusual for onscreen time to match 'real time' (that is, 30 minutes onscreen takes 30 minutes of time to show). A text can take place across any length of time; from a few hours to the aeons of *2001: A Space Odyssey*. Editing is often used to cut out redundant actions: for example, a character may stand up to leave the room; an immediate cut shows the character exiting by a door – the movement to the door is taken out. This is an *ellipsis*.

Continuity editing is the conventional system used in audio-visual texts in the Western world. There are other systems, such as montage, which will be discussed in Chapter 5.

1.14 Sound

As noted at the beginning of this chapter, the sense from which we get the most detailed information is sight. This may be the reason that sound is often given little emphasis in analysis of audio-visual media texts. However, sound carries vitally important codes for the creation of these texts' meanings (it goes without saying that it is the carrier of meaning in radio).

There are four dimensions of sound that need to be analysed:

1. *dialogue (or monologue):* the most obvious dimension – what characters are saying onscreen;
2. *sound effects*: non-verbal sounds, created within the onscreen space, the source of which is clear to the audience;
3. *ambient sounds*: background sounds which add to the atmosphere of the scene;
4. *non-diegetic sounds*: not originating from onscreen space; for example, a voice-over or sound-track music.

◀ Exercise 1.15 ▶

Record on to audio tape a movie sequence with which you are familiar. Make notes on sounds you hear for the first time. (This exercise is best done using a movie sequence, because movies tend to be much more carefully constructed than television texts.)

Dialogue

Dialogue on the soundtrack is usually carefully mixed to make it very clear. It is either recorded at the same time as the scene is filmed or may be added later (*post-dubbed*). A more experimental use of speech in audio-visual texts is overlapping dialogue, where characters 'talk over' each other: Woody Allen uses this to give a heightened realism to scenes; for example, in the opening scene of *Husbands and Wives* (1992), the announcement that a married couple are splitting up leads to frantic questioning by the Woody Allen and Mia Farrow characters. Although more than one character is often talking at the same time, the mix ensures the audience hears clearly the voice the director wants it to hear.

Sound effects

Sound effects are anything that is not spoken, has a clear source within the world represented and are usually, but not always, observable within the frame. This includes the opening and shutting of doors, characters moving around the scene and so on; an off-screen knock at a door would also be considered as a sound effect.

These sounds can be post-dubbed. For example, the sound of fist fights is usually added later, often with particularly unconvincing results.

Ambient sounds

Ambient sounds form a background to a scene and, while they do originate in the narrative space, need not necessarily be specifically identified. For example, a country scene would probably include the ambient sounds of insects and birds. These are called *spot effects*.

A scene on a city street will probably be accompanied by the spot effects of traffic, although you will not necessarily see the traffic. If this scene is followed by one inside a building on this city street, then the ambient sounds will probably continue, but at a lower volume; this helps to indicate the setting of the scene.

Non-diegetic sounds

The most potent non-diegetic sound is music. There are few films which wholly dispense with the expressive qualities of music. Even the gritty, realist BBC television drama *Cathy Come Home*, directed by Ken Loach and produced by Tony Garnett in 1968, used the song 'Stand By Me' early in the film.

Music is often used to cue drama and evoke emotion. The approach of danger in a thriller is usually signalled by 'sinister' music; a romantic moment will often be accompanied by a lush orchestration of strings. So music not only adds to meanings generated by the image, it also creates meanings. The composer John Williams' use of percussion in *JFK* (directed by Oliver Stone, 1991) created a very physical effect with its insistent, militaristic rhythms; this enabled Stone to create tension, even though the audience knows Kennedy is about to be shot in the Dallas motorcade.

Music is often used to evoke a period, so a medieval setting may be accompanied by medieval-sounding music (it does not have to be genuinely medieval, it simply needs to connote the era). Since the 1950s, when 'youth culture' was 'invented', the use of rock 'n' roll music, in particular, not only evokes an era but also produces nostalgia in an audience of the relevant generation.

Music is not always non-diegetic: in films like *Bird* (1988) – Clint Eastwood's film about jazz saxophonist Charlie Parker – the performance of music is onscreen and therefore must be considered a 'sound effect'.

An institutional dimension of music is its use in generating publicity for movies when the theme song is performed by a popular artist; each time the song is performed, or the accompanying pop video broadcast, the movie is also being promoted.

1.15 Storyboarding

Storyboarding is the visual representation of an image with additional details such as the action, dialogue and sound, any camera movement, and length of shot. Storyboards are normally used to create images in sequence.

Storyboarding is one of the basic skills of Media Studies, which is unfortunate for those of us who lack graphical skills. However, the technical quality of the drawing is not assessed by exam boards; the quality of the use of the conventions of image construction is. An example of storyboarding is given in Appendix 1. Storyboards are commonly used to plan a video but are acceptable, for examination assessment, as a media artefact in their own right. The effectiveness of storyboards can easily be demonstrated by the following exercise.

◀ Exercise 1.16 ▶

Choose a reasonably detailed video still image and write down, using Media Studies terminology, a description of that image. Then storyboard the same image. It should be clear that a storyboard can more economically convey information about an image.

Storyboards are a crucial part of planning a video. The starting point, however, should be a brief description of the video's objectives. Your objective may be a narrative or a montage of shots to illustrate the intended voice-over. This description will then act as a guide to storyboarding which, in turn, will form the basis of your videoing. It should be remembered, of course, assuming you have video editing facilities, that you needn't video your storyboard in chronological order. Be certain, however, to keep a strict log of sequences that have been videoed as it will make editing a lot easier.

The storyboard should be used as a guide and not a rigid prescription: certain set-ups may not work in practice or you may be inspired to shoot a scene differently. While it is important to be flexible, if you find you are completely ignoring your storyboard, then you should go back to the 'drawing board'.

As stated above, storyboarding is commonly used to plan videos or films. However they can also be used to illustrate sequences. In Appendix 1 you will find a storyboard of a sequence from *Blade Runner* (1982). It is intended that the accompanying analysis of the sequence should illustrate how to analyse images in sequence, using what we have learned in this chapter. The analysis is not intended, however, to be exhaustive; also, many of the terms we have discussed are not applicable to this sequence. The whole sequence is not storyboarded, but the fifteen frames included should give a clear idea of what is required in storyboarding.

2

SEMIOTICS

Chapter 1 has given a basic introduction to how to analyse images. This chapter considers the science of signs, or semiotics, which has proved a fruitful way of looking at texts of all kinds. One of the great strengths of a semiotic approach is that the reader is encouraged to look at familiar objects and ideas in a fashion that makes them appear strange; nothing is taken for granted. Because of this, it is conceptually difficult; however the effort is repaid in the resulting analyses.

2.1 Introduction to semiotics

The 'study of signs' was founded, simultaneously and without knowledge of each other's work, by Ferdinand de Saussure in Switzerland and Charles Peirce in the USA; they termed their creation *semiology* and *semiotics* respectively (the root of the term is the Greek *semeion*, sign). Semiology and semiotics mean the same, although the latter term appears to have gained greater currency.

At the heart of semiotics is the study of language and how it is the dominant influence shaping human beings' perception of and thoughts about the world.

Semiotics is also a wonderful tool for analysing images. Although the terminology (signifier, signified, paradigm, syntagm, synchronic, diachronic, and so on) may at first make the science appear obscure, semiotics is an important discipline in the study of media language.

2.2 Saussure

Ferdinand de Saussure's theories were collected, posthumously, in *Course in General Linguistics* (1916) from lecture notes compiled by his students. When Saussure described how signs are created he was referring not only to formal signs, such as those in the highway code, but any system of communication. Language is, of course, the most fundamental system we use.

Signifier and signified

Saussure's revolutionary approach defined signs structurally. He stated that the sign is the sum of the *signifier* and *signified*: the signifier is the perception of the sign's physical form which may be material, acoustic, visual, olfactory or a taste; the signified is the mental concept we learn to associate with that object (Figure 2.1). The relationship between the sign and its *referent* (the actual object the sign is representing) is the *signification*.

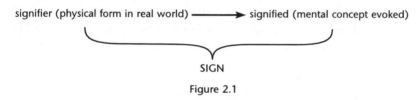

signifier (physical form in real world) ⟶ signified (mental concept evoked)

SIGN

Figure 2.1

If we perceive a furry animal with four legs that barks (the signifier), this evokes the mental concept of a dog (the signified); the combination of 'sound-image' and concept creates the sign 'dog'. Similarly, when we see the letters d,o,g, placed together, the word is a signifier, and once again the mental concept of a dog is signified, and the combination of these elements results in the sign 'dog'. Although the signifier and signified are separated for the purposes of analysis, in our perception of the sign they are inseparable. The basic act of signification operates at the level of *denotation* (as described in section 1.3).

● *The level of denotation* Denotation is simply about identifying a sign; when we perceive something, through any of our senses, the word or words (signs) we attach to the perception is the denotation. Denotations operate at the first-order level of signification.

The relationship between the signifier and signified is usually arbitrary. The fact that a furry animal with four legs that barks is called dog in English was selected from a multitude of other words (ignoring for a moment the ancestry of the English language); dogs could have been called cats or fardels. This explains why we have different languages throughout the world; if the signifier determined the signified, the word for the animal called a dog in English would be very similar, if not the same, in all languages (in fact there would probably be only one language).

Similarly, the word 'dog' can also signify 'to follow tenaciously', 'a mechanical device for gripping' and 'a worthless person'; a signifier can have many signifieds It also follows that a signified can have many signifiers – for example, some synonyms for 'dog' are bitch, canine, cur, man's best friend.

Clearly the arbitrary nature of signs means that they can have many meanings, or are *polysemic* (defined in Chapter 3). This does not mean there is anarchy in the search for meaning: all languages have rules which structure meaning in a conventional fashion and these will be described later in the chapter.

Not all signs are entirely arbitrary in nature. Some signs have a resemblance to what they represent; for example, a photograph is a sign which usually looks like its referent. The word 'buzz' sounds like what it describes, and, in English, pigs 'oink'. However, these signs are *not* what they represent – that would be impossible; they act as similes. For example, onomatopoeic words sound like what they represent, which, of course, does not mean they sound the same; in Japanese, for instance, pigs apparently make a 'bong-bong' sound. Signs which possess a resemblance to their referent are iconic, as defined by C. S. Peirce (see section 2.4).

Saussure's description of signs is important in Media Studies because it emphasizes that they are constructed. Once this is understood, the task of analysis is to deconstruct not individual signs, but sign systems, or codes, to show how meaning is created.

◀ EXERCISE 2.1 ▶

Write down a description of your environment at the level of denotation.

● *The level of connotation* Our understanding of signs rarely stops at the level of denotation. Once we perceive a sign, we often have particular associations with that sign which colour our understanding; for example, a person who dislikes dogs would have negative feelings about the sign 'dog' whereas a cat lover would feel positive about the sign 'cat'. These associations are a second-order system of signification, or *connotations* (as described in section 1.8). (It can be argued that even the first-order system of signification, denotation, is itself a connotation because we learn to *associate* a particular signified with a signifier.)

In the second-order system of signification the individual has perceived, at the level of denotation, the original sign 'dog', which has then become another signifier which evokes an associated mental concept to create another sign which consists of 'dog' + 'associations' (see Figure 2.2).

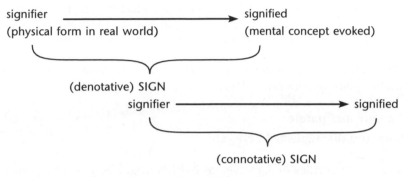

Figure 2.2

Many connotations have reached the status of a social consensus. For example, if the dog is a border collie (sheepdog), sitting down, tongue hanging out, with its head to one side (a denotative description), it is difficult to avoid the connotation that the beast is friendly. Some signs carry particularly powerful connotations, these are (Barthesian) myths, which will be discussed later in the chapter and should not be confused with Greek myths or 'untrues'.

◄ EXERCISE 2.2 ►

Add connotations to your denotative description in Exercise 2.1.

• *Meaning and context* Meaning cannot exist in individual signs, because of their arbitrary nature, but is derived from their context. For example, we can only understand the two different meanings of 'dog' in the following sentences because of the other signs (words):

1. 'The dog barked loudly at the postman.'

2. 'The man said he'd dog Noam forever.'

If we read sentence (1) to say 'the follow tenaciously loudly at the postman' then it is obviously nonsense. So a sign's value, the particular meaning 'dog' represents in this case, is created by the difference between it and other signs in the same context.

This isn't, however, just a result of the sign 'dog' having more than one meaning; all signs only have value because they are different from other signs. As Thwaites *et al.* (1994) ably sum up:

> If a sign gets its meaning from other signs, it works through a system of differences (from what it isn't), rather than identity (with itself). It means something not because it has some fixed identity, but because it is different from other signs. We could put that in a succinct but paradoxical form by saying that what is sign is due to what it isn't.

One of the fundamental structures which help to anchor meaning is the *relationship* between *la langue* and *parole*.

Langue *and* parole

Saussure distinguished between:

- *langue*, the rules of sign system (which might be grammar) and
- *parole*, the articulation of signs (for example, speech or writing),

the sum of which is language:

$$language = langue + parole$$

While *langue* could be the rules of, say, English grammar, it does not mean *parole* always has to conform to the rules of standard English (what some people erroneously call 'proper' English). *Langue* is less rigid than the phrase 'set of rules' implies, it is more a guideline and is inferred from the *parole*. Language systems are often likened to an iceberg: the *parole* is visible, but the rules, the supporting structure, are hidden (Figure 2.3).

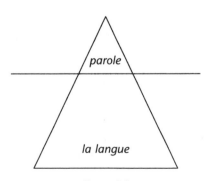

Figure 2.3

As Figure 2.3 suggests, the rules of any communication are hidden. However, these rules are necessary for the performance (the perceived element of the communication) to be intelligible. It should also be noted that the *langue* itself does not guarantee meaning. Chomsky's famous phrase 'Colorless green ideas sleep furiously' is grammatically correct but meaningless.

An example of how this would apply specifically to Media Studies is the codes of Hollywood cinema, discussed in the previous chapter, which are the equivalent of *la langue*, while the actual use of those rules in a particular film (whether conventional or unconventional) is the *parole*. Unless a person has studied the media language of Hollywood films then it is unlikely that he or she would know about, say, the rules of continuity editing; however, because most people can make sense of the editing when watching films (the *parole*) then they implicitly understand *la langue*.

◀ Exercise 2.3

Separate *la langue* and *parole* of the following texts: tabloid newspaper; broadsheet newspapers; teenage magazines.

Synchrony and diachrony

As was stated above, *la langue* and *parole* are structures which help to give arbitrary signs meaning. Saussure demonstrated another way, of structuring meaning: considering the vertical and horizontal dimensions of sign systems; *synchrony* and *diachrony*. Synchrony is the vertical dimension of meaning and diachrony is the horizontal dimension (Figure 2.4). These dimensions are, obviously, useful in the study of language. For example, if we were analysing the line from Shakespeare's *Hamlet*:

'O that this too too sullied flesh would melt,'

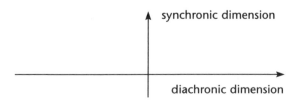

Figure 2.4

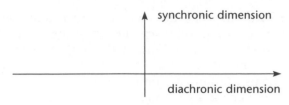

'O that this too too (sullied) flesh would melt,'

Figure 2.5

The synchronic dimension could be a particular word, say 'sullied'; while the diachronic dimension could be the whole sentence (Figure 2.5).

Analysis would usually focus on both dimensions: 'what is the meaning of "sullied" in the context of the sentence?'.

When we study a still from a film, or a freeze-frame of a video, we are, in effect, looking at the synchronic dimension; the sequence from which the still is taken is the diachronic dimension.

The relationship between the synchronic and diachronic dimensions is relative: we could argue that the letter 'u' is a synchronic dimension, while the whole word 'sullied' is the diachronic; or that *Hamlet* is synchronic and the *oeuvre* of Shakespeare is diachronic. As noted earlier, the meaning of a sign is determined by its context, it has no meaning on its own. Similarly, the synchronic and diachronic dimensions demonstrate that our analysis of individual signs or texts is determined by the perspective we bring to them. For example, if we focus on the letter 'u' in Shakespeare's line, we would probably be looking at it from a linguist's perspective. If we were considering the play *Hamlet* in comparison with Shakespeare's *oeuvre*, then we are likely to be engaged in theatrical or literary criticism.

Paradigm and syntagm

Langue is organized along two axes, those of selection and combination. Saussure called these the *paradigmatic* and *syntagmatic* axes:

- the paradigm is the *vertical* set of associations;
- the syntagm is the horizontal, or sequential, arrangement (beware, this can be confusing because the *syn*chronic dimension is vertical).

The paradigmatic dimension is not fixed but determined, in the main, by the syntagmatic arrangement, which, in turn, is determined by *la langue*. Take the sentence:

'The cat sat on the mat.'

In this context the most obvious paradigm associated with the subject of the sentence, 'cat', is that it belongs to the category 'domestic animal', so we are most likely to use this paradigm to determine the meaning of 'cat' . Other paradigms to which the sign 'cat' can belong are 'the cat family', 'lazy animals' and 'mammals'. There is always more than one sign in paradigms. For example, in the domestic animal paradigm:

'The cat   sat on the mat.'
    dog
    tortoise
    hamster
    parrot
and so on.

The only reason we understand what referent the sign 'cat' refers to is because it is *not* a dog, tortoise, hamster or any other domestic animal; as was stated above, it is the qualities that distinguish one sign from another that give the sign meaning.

To form a syntagm, the paradigmatic dimension must combine with other paradigms, which it does according to the rules of *langue*. The syntagm then anchors the meaning of individual signs (from the paradigms) by creating a context; in other words, it helps us to choose the appropriate paradigm of a sign. For example, it is unlikely that we would assume 'cat' belonged to the paradigm 'mammal', in the example above, because it could result in such absurdities as 'the whale sat on the mat'. Other paradigms in this sentence include 'floor covering' (mat, carpet, rug and so on).

Paradigms, by their very nature, expand the possible meanings of a sign; the syntagm prevents confusion by limiting the number of meanings. This is the way signs have conventional meanings despite their arbitrary nature. A classic example from everyday life of these dimensions is a three-course menu which offers a choice of starters, main dish and dessert. Diners are asked to choose from three paradigms, which have a conventional order (the *langue*), and their syntagmatic choice gives them a three-course meal.

These dimensions are particularly useful in image analysis. For example, the use of a cat in an advertisement for double-glazing relies, for its meaning, upon the paradigm 'domestic animal' combined with the syntagm, which places the cat next to the double-glazed window. This communicates that the product is effective in eliminating draughts.

The cat, of course, also belongs to other paradigms. The syntagm 'cat and window' could suggest the cat belongs to the 'lazy animal' paradigm: it is looking outside but not doing anything. However, in the advertisement the product, double-glazing, serves to anchor the meaning of the sign 'cat' within the 'domestic animal' paradigm because its function is to eliminate draughts. Placing a dog in the same position would not have the same effect, even though it too can belong to the 'domestic animal' paradigm. The syntagm 'dog and window' has different associations, such as waiting for its master to return home or wanting to go for a walk.

This replacement of one sign by another is called a *commutation test* and illustrates how powerful paradigms and syntagms can be in image analysis or, indeed, other types of analysis (for example, replace the gender of a character in a novel). By substituting objects for other signs in the same paradigm, and decoding the new meaning, we can isolate what contribution the original sign is making to the meaning of the image.

Look again at Figure 1.12 and let us consider what insight we might gain by using the commutation test. We can simply describe the image, at the level of denotation, as showing:

A woman preparing a lot of food in a kitchen with the help of a boy.

In preparing for a commutation test it is useful to suggest different signs of paradigms that are present in the image. For example:

A | woman | preparing a lot of food in a kitchen with the help of a | boy.
 | man | | girl.

By simply replacing two signs, we have three additional possible combinations:

1. A man preparing a lot of food in a kitchen with the help of a boy.
2. A woman preparing a lot of food in a kitchen with the help of a girl.
3. A man preparing a lot of food in a kitchen with the help of a girl.

If we exchanged 'woman' for 'man', as part of the human paradigm, what interpretation do we make of the image? I would then read the image to suggest that the adult was an expert, possibly a chef. The woman, according to my analysis in the first chapter, was a housewife. Why the difference? Clearly it is more unusual to see a man cooking than a woman and so, in my interpretation, I had to consider why he should be engaged in preparing food, whereas it seems a natural activity for women. These assumptions, of course, reflect the norms of our society, but it is interesting that the commutation test reveals that there is more likely to be a connotation of expertise associated with a man.

Often when the gender of a person is changed, the effect is ridiculous – imagine a man taking Rita Hayworth's pose in Figure 1.11. However, because all we have done is change one sign of one paradigm, we can be sure that any alterations to the meaning of the image is caused by gender and our assumptions about gender.

◀ EXERCISE 2.4 ▶
Analyse Figure 1.12 using combinations (b) and (c).

◀ EXERCISE 2.5 ▶
Do a commutation test on an advertisement (don't restrict yourself to switching gender).

The contribution of semiotics to Media Studies is sometimes derided because of its obscure jargon; the commutation test, however, demonstrates semiotics at its most powerful. It is a particularly effective way of unmasking myths which, as we shall see in section 2.5, sign themselves to be natural.

In addition to Saussure, two other people have made seminal contributions to the science of signs: C. S. Peirce and Roland Barthes.

2.3 C. S. Peirce

The other great pioneer of semiotics was C. S. Peirce, who created a tripartite categorization of signs:

- iconic
- index and
- symbol.

Iconic

An iconic sign bears a resemblance to that which it represents and can be an image, images or graphical. A photograph is iconic: we may recognize a photograph of a particular pet but we know that the photograph is not the actual pet. Similarly a recording of a dog barking is aurally iconic.

An iconic sign does not necessarily have to resemble *physically* what it refers to: maps are graphical iconic signs. However, in order to read, say, ordnance survey maps, we need to understand the codes used (such as contour lines).

Index

An index sign has a direct relationship, or causal link, to that which it represents. For example, a thermometer is an index of temperature. A picture of someone sweating lying on a beach is an index of heat.

Shots of the Houses of Parliament are often used in films to establish the setting of London. Obviously the image of the Houses is iconic, but it is simultaneously an index in that it represents more than itself. The relationship, of course, is that the Houses are situated in London. Similarly, the Eiffel Tower is an index of Paris; the Opera House, Sydney; the Kremlin, Moscow; and the Statue of Liberty, the USA. Indexes, or indices, can be specific to individuals; for example, the presence of a car is an index of the car's owner.

Symbolic

Language is the most obvious symbolic sign because, as Saussure described, its relationship with what it represents is arbitrary. Indeed, any arbitrary sign must be symbolic since it can only be a sign because there is a consensus about what it means. Formal signs are usually symbols, for instance those used in the Highway Code.

◄ EXERCISE 2.6 ►

Using any advertisement which includes images, preferably one used in Chapter 1, find 10 examples of Peirce's categories.

2.4 Barthes

Roland Barthes' crucial contribution to semiotics was his definition and exploration of myths. Barthes was not concerned with archetypes, untruths or Greek myths and legends, but how signs take on the values of the dominant value system – or ideology – of a particular society and make these values seem natural.

For example, a flower with red petals, green leaves and a thorny stem signifies the mental concept *rose*; this is at the first level of signification or denotative level. The level of denotation gives the basic meaning of the sign.

However, the sign 'rose' can, in turn, signify the mental concept of romance, particularly if it is red and placed in the context of St Valentine's Day. Romance is a myth that defines heterosexual love as tender and caring; the female is passive and the male active in the relationship. How does this 'flower with red petals, green leaves and a thorny stem' take on the meaning of romance?

We have already seen how the original denotative sign can become the signifier of a second-order system of signification, creating a connotation. Barthes showed that Saussure's sign can become a signifier to create, not only a connotation, but a myth (Figure 2.6).

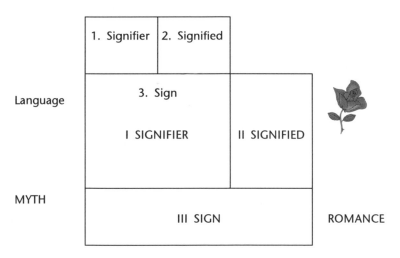

Figure 2.6

Source: adapted from Roland Barthes, *Mythologies* (St Albans: Granada, 1973) p. 115.

Because it is virtually impossible to understand 'a red rose on Valentine's day' as anything other than meaning romance, it appears that a signifying system, which is a connotation, is acting as a denotation. Myths are connotations that appear to be denotations. This 'trick' allows myths, in texts, to structure the meaning of the communication without appearing to do so, they efface their own existence. Like continuity editing, myths position the audience in a specific relationship with a sign and simultaneously disguise themselves. As we did with image analysis, it is necessary that we deconstruct the meaning of myths in order to understand how they work.

For example, consider an after-shave advertisement that includes an image of a fast car: in this text the fast car connotes masculine power and is part of a system of signs which create the myth of masculinity. Masculinity is a social creation, gender, rather than a biological definition. To be defined as masculine in Western society the male needs to be strong (musculinity), physically skilful, rugged and adept in the use of technology. The use of cars in advertising (they are almost always fast – when did you last see a three-wheeler advertized?) often symbolizes these aspects of masculinity: they are powerful (speed), corner beautifully and, obviously, are (advanced) technological creations.

In order to deconstruct this particular use of the myth we could use a commutation test (substitute a bicycle for the car?). Alternatively it is possible to use an oppositional way of reading the text; for example a feminist reading of the car in the after-shave advertisement could emphasize that the car's speed signifies men's lack of sexual staying power. This sort of reading helps in the deconstruction of myths because it emphasizes that the association, in this instance, of speed and masculinity is not natural but a social construct. In order to make such a radical reading it is necessary to use ideas, or discourses, which are alternative to the consensus; this will be considered further in the next chapter.

The identification of myths, because they appear natural, can be difficult. As we shall investigate below, even Nature is a myth: while clearly nature in its unmediated form is natural, society's idea of what makes up nature is clearly a social construct. This is particularly evident in any documentary text which talks about 'Mother Nature': this can lead to many deterministic assumptions about nature.

Myths are a potent way of making meanings in society. Other areas that Barthes investigates in *Mythologies* include: wrestling;

holiday writing; soap-powders and detergents; margarine; Einstein; striptease.

◀ EXERCISE 2.7 ▶

Using the same images as in the previous two exercises, try to decide what objects are myths and then attempt to make an alternative reading of them.

2.5 Binary oppositions

We have established that signs do not possess intrinsic meaning but are defined by relationship to other signs: signs are defined by what they are not. One of the most powerful creators of a sign's meaning are binary oppositions. Here signs are contrasted with signs which have meanings which operate in opposition. For example: town and country; man and woman; child and adult; public and private; civilization and savagery. Binary oppositions, like all signs systems, are not natural descriptions but cultural creations.

Binary oppositions are often structurally related to each other and function to order meanings. For example, the town and countryside are characterized by the following oppositions:

town	*country*
artificial	natural
polluted	clean
over-crowded	deserted
exciting	boring
commercial	non-commercial
dangerous	safe

These lists consist of connotations of both town and country. Taken together they form myths of urban and country life.

◀ EXERCISE 2.8 ▶

Try to find examples which contradict the town and country dichotomy. For example, in towns there are usually parks which can be characterized as natural.

It is possible to find contradictions, or antinomies, for all the oppositions. For instance, the countryside is polluted by artificial fertilizers, has exciting areas for activities such as rock climbing, is commercially exploited by farming, and so on.

The media often use binary oppositions to structure their representations. So a portrayal of a town, for instance, may use pollution as its starting point; the other ideas can then follow on from this: the environment is dangerous, over-crowded, artificial, and so on.

People or objects which fall in between opposites form an ambiguous category. Representations of this 'in-between' category often classify its inhabitants as abnormal. Transsexuals, in terms of the signification of gender, are neither men nor women, and so are deviant. While it is true to say that transsexuals, statistically, are deviant, the connotations of 'deviance' suggest moral corruption and sickness. The representation of adolescents is similarly contentious: they are, obviously, neither adult or child and as a result are often represented as being a 'problem'.

A text which uses binary oppositions usually assigns a positive value to one side against the other; by stating that one side is good, it follows that the other is bad. For example, 'them' and 'us' categories are often used in a nationalistic context to affirm a nation's identity.

The final part of this chapter is an analysis of an advertisement for the Nokia 232 mobile phone. This analysis is an attempt to apply both our semiotic knowledge and the tools of analysis described in Chapter 1. It is not meant to be an example of how to present analysis of images, it is far too exhaustive for that. In the Appendix there is a far shorter version of the essay, one that could, for instance, be written under exam conditions. What follows is meant to be an example of how to approach analysis of an image. In practice this would be done in note form before being turned into an essay.

2.6 Semiotic analysis: Nokia 232 advertisement

Peirce's tripartite categorization sheds some new light on the analysis in Chapter 1. Clearly the images are iconic, the words and logo are symbolic; these we have already analysed. However, the index category yields the information that the classical bust (sculpture) and pillars might represent either ancient Rome or Greece, while the reading in Chapter 1 only suggested that the setting is a museum.

The word Nokia is an interesting symbol because it is meaningless in the English language; what is signified, however, does mean 'a Japanese company'. The connotations of 'a Japanese company' are that its products will be reliable and good value for money. (A few years ago a British-based manufacturer of electronic goods, Dixons, launched a product range with a Japanese-sounding name in order to benefit from this connotation and Nokia is, in fact, a Finnish company.)

Of most semiotic use are Saussure's paradigmatic and syntagmatic dimensions and Barthes' myths.

Paradigm

The paradigm 'humanoid object' for the white woman in the image could include:

black woman
man
child
old woman
gorilla
robot
and so on.

Other potential paradigms are: fashion models; clothing as signs. There follows a commutation test using the 'humanoid object' paradigm.

Imagine a black woman anchored by the copy 'an unforgettable little black number'! Clearly the advertisement would have, at the very least, racial overtones. The colour of the woman would make her appear to be the subject of the copy and not the dress or phone.

What meaning would we get from the advertisement which featured a man wearing 'an unforgettable little black number'? It would probably be laughable – whether intentionally as in parody, or unintentionally as in incompetence. Because of this, the construction of the advertisement is gender-specific: it only works with a female as object. Whether this is sexist or not depends upon your viewpoint.

It is likely that if the advertisement was solely aimed at the men then the word 'little' would be substituted because men's relationship to size would suggest that they would not find 'little' a turn on. If it were aimed only at men then a word like 'compact' would be more appropriate as it would have connotations of 'executive portability': that is, the modern executive is very busy and has to carry a lot of equipment; a compact mobile phone would allow him to keep in touch with important business contacts without being over-burdened. If it were aimed only at women then 'slimline' might be the appropriate word because it would carry the executive connotations with the added benefit that being slim is usually thought of as a socially desirable trait in women.

The use of a child would suggest the product was a toy; it would also mean, however, that the sexual element of the image would become disturbing. (Children are occasionally used in this way – for example, in the films of the young Shirley Temple.)

An old woman would again fail the 'sexy' test, not because old women cannot be sexy (see the 70+ year-old Lauren Bacall and Helen Mirren who is in her fifties) but because the convention is that old people are not sexually attractive. In any case, youth is important for this particular product, as it aims to be trendy.

The gorilla, again, would be laughable. The incongruity of the image would be enough to draw an audience's attention but it is unlikely that they would find the gorilla more attractive than the woman.

The robot would also attract attention and a robot connotes high technology and the future, both of these connotations would be appropriate for a product which is high-tech and trendy. The lifestyle theme of the advertisement, however, would be lost. Selling the product on its technological advancement is usually a specifically male address.

The value of this paradigmatic analysis is that it shows the meanings created by the image's specific elements: the use of a young, beautiful woman is crucial to the preferred reading of this advertisement. By noting how different parts of the paradigm change the advertisement's meaning, we can isolate the actual contribution of, in this case, the beautiful woman.

◀ Exercise 2.9 ▶

Using different paradigms, analyse the different meaning the advertisement would generate.

Syntagm

The syntagmatic dimension takes us back to the juxtaposition analysed above. There we considered how the positioning of the image's elements lead the eye through the advertisement's preferred meaning. We should also consider the combination of elements, for example how the black dress contrasts with the white bust and pillars. The opposite 'colours', and the way the bust's head is tilted away from the woman, links her with the bust; the similarity of their features has already been noted.

The syntagm of the woman and the classical sculpture generates the meaning that the image, as a whole, is 'classy'. This, of course, includes the product and the dress: the 'chic' little black number.

In an analysis that is not going to explicitly consider, in any detail, ideology (covered in the next chapter), the final consideration is Roland Barthes' myths.

Myths

Barthes' myth are part of the second-order system of signification, that is, we are analysing the connotations of images. We have already described the woman as conventionally beautiful, and the 'unforgettable little black number' as having sexual associations; clearly these are connotations because notions of beauty and sexiness are socially constructed (for example, today's supermodels would not be suitable material for Botticelli nudes, and Marilyn Monroe – the sex symbol of the 1950s – was probably too ample in build for today's scrawny standards). What, then, is the myth 'female sexuality'?

The woman is not only sexy because she is beautiful, the clothes she is wearing have connotations of being fashionable; they are stylish and show off her (sexy) legs. What is sexy depends upon the person's gender; in our culture sexy suggests a woman is displaying herself for the male gaze and is therefore available. A sexy man is less likely to be on display in the same way, although this convention appears to be changing.

The immaculate coiffure not only links her with the bust, it also emphasizes her attractiveness, as does her make-up on hands and face.

Although being defined sexually can often oppress women – that is, if it is defined that their only function in society is being sex objects for males – a woman's status as a sex object can occasionally work to her advantage. An object of desire can be admired and can exploit the situation. Sharon Stone's notorious 'no knickers' scene in *Basic Instinct* (1992), despite being a male fantasy, uses this empowerment when her character, Catherine Tramell, exploits her sexuality to control men. Problems arise with this empowerment when (usually) males take the view that women who appear sexually available are sexually available for them.

The gaze of the woman in the image – directly at the audience – is also powerful. It is not a hostile gaze, as direct eye contact can sometimes can be, but (her smile signifies) an inviting one: 'look at me, aren't I powerful?' Her power is emphasized by the dynamism of the image; she is moving (the position of her legs signify a step) 'uphill' and her earrings are swaying with the movement: this woman is going places and talking (to the lover who bought the phone?) at the same time. Alternatively, this dynamic, young woman has bought herself the phone as it is a requirement for her particular lifestyle.

Considering the myth of the bust and pillars is, fortunately, more straightforward. These are classical figures and have connotations of:

purity
beauty
wealth
intellect
tradition
long-lastingness
technology.

These connotations are inevitably a product of my knowledge of what is 'classical' and do not necessarily have to be accurate. As in genre, associations only have to have a social consensus, they do not have to be rooted in reality.

As already stated, the syntagmatic structure of the image links the classical elements with the woman (and the dress). Thus the connotation of 'classical purity' is that the woman is pure. This, in turn, relates to a (hopefully old-fashioned) myth of femininity that women should be pure (that is, virgins) and set on a (classical?) pedestal. This purity is constructed as an object of desire and therefore the Nokia 232 is also desirable.

The relationship between the beauty of the woman and the sexual power this may create has already been discussed.

The connotation of someone's owning such a classical sculpture is they are wealthy and have good taste. The association of wealth, aesthetic judgement and intellect (only 'brainy' people are interested in such ancient artefacts') adds to the power of the woman. Mobile phones are still, just, associated with wealth (although as the mass market grows this will become marginalized) and the fact that this product is not being sold on price (it is not mentioned) suggests it is expensive to use. Expensive, yes, but tasteful too: hence the aesthetic importance of the association.

Tradition is a great favourite of advertisers; its use exploits the nostalgic feeling that things were better in 'the good old days'. The association with the product, with which, as we have already stated, the woman is closely identified, is twofold: the product is well-made (as things used to be) and it is long-lasting.

Of course, cutting-edge technology (which Nokia 232 implies it is with its emphasis on size) contradicts the idea of tradition. This apparent contradiction does not make the myth incoherent; it is the power of myths that such contradictions can be glossed over: products can be at the cutting edge of technology and traditional. The bust and pillar represent a stunning technological achievement of an ancient time: Nokia 232 is also stunning (and will also be superseded by another product as technology is developed).

JAKOBSON'S MODEL REVISITED

3.1 Introduction

As stated in the introduction to this book, the chapters are differentiated; that is, they each have a different level of difficulty. Chapter 1 dealt with, in some detail, a basic introduction to textual analysis; Chapter 2 introduced some of the complicated concepts of semiotics. This chapter attempts to take the ideas presented earlier in the book even further. How far you wish to wrestle with these concepts is dependent upon your predilection for hard work and/or the level of qualification you are studying for. One thing is guaranteed, the ideas presented in this chapter are difficult.

3.2 Jakobson's model revisited

You may recall that at the beginning of Chapter 1 Jakobson's model of speech communication was used to demonstrate the variables in all forms of communication. What follows is a more sophisticated version of that model proposed by Thwaites *et al.* (1994) in their excellent *Tools for Cultural Studies*. They follow Dell Hymes' revision of Jakobson. What this revised model should, at least, demonstrate is that even though Jakobson showed how an apparently simple act like speaking is complicated event, even his model is a simplification.

As we saw in Chapter 2, the sign is the building block of communication. A sign is anything that produces meaning; it must have a physical existence, refer to something other than itself, and have socially agreed meaning(s). For example, assuming we understand the language, individual words are signs: we can see or hear them, we usually know what they refer to, and there will be an agreement about what they mean. When words are combined they form language, and language is a code.

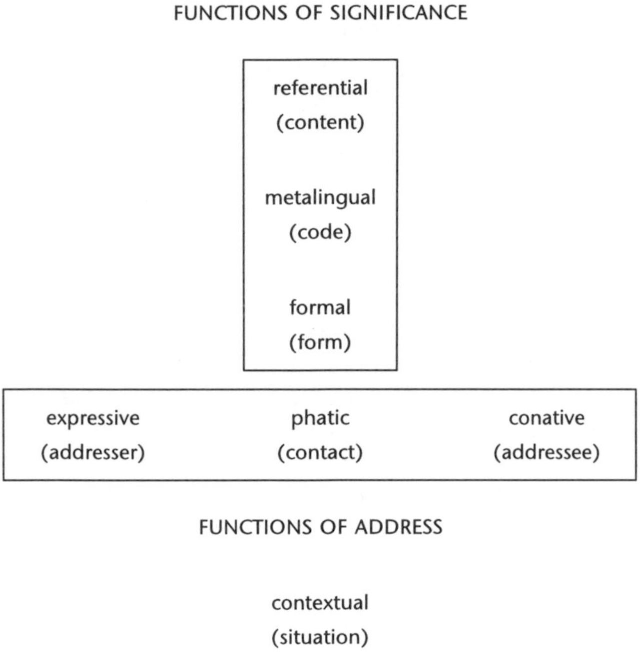

FUNCTIONS OF SIGNIFICANCE

referential (content)
metalingual (code)
formal (form)

expressive (addresser)	phatic (contact)	conative (addressee)

FUNCTIONS OF ADDRESS

contextual
(situation)

Figure 3.1

Code, which we dealt with in some detail in the last chapter, is, then, a combination of signs. This chapter is concerned with how signs are structured and how codes are created. First, though, we need to consider the functions of a sign, called the functions of significance. The revised model is shown in Figure 3.1.

It should be noted that most models of communication contain a feedback loop; in the media the possibility of an individual addressee feeding back response is very limited – most media are one-way systems. Media institutions are, of course, interested in what audiences think, but they are only interested in a certain type of response. For example, television companies are mostly interested in numbers of viewers rather than what sorts of programme an audience would like to see.

Referential function

A sign's referential function refers to 'the real world'. Signs, by definition, must stand for something other than themselves and the referent is the actual object that the sign stands for. The referential function dominates many communications. You may, for example, be explaining how to get to a particular destination.The referential function, however, is not necessarily concerned with the truth, it simply implies that the statement is accurate. For example, the directions you give to a destination might be incorrect.

Metalingual function

The metalingual function indicates which codes should be used to read the communication. If a friend tells you, with a smile on her or his face, that your work is 'rubbish', then you would probably use the codes of sarcasm to read the message; if the expression was a frown, then the metalingual function suggest the message was serious. Genre is an example of a metalanguage; once you know a text is, say, an action movie, then you have a range of expectations to be fulfilled (or disappointed).

People can possess metalanguages, for example the clothes they wear. If a policeman or policewoman speaks to you, he or she has an authority, signed by the police uniform, which the general public do not possess.

Formal function

Often, simply the way a text looks suggests how it should be read. The layout of a list, for example, suggests it contains information to be remembered or checked. Similarly, the layout of a letter can indicate whether it is, say, a business communication or informal in nature. This formal function can complement the metalingual function: in magazines, advertising and editorial usually look different, which suggests you read the former using codes of advertising – the intention is to sell something – while the latter's intention is to inform and/or entertain.

Because of their form, advertorials offer a confusing meta-language; they appear to be selling something, but look like editorial. For example, many periodicals, particularly 'lifestyle' magazines, have a fashion section consisting of modelled clothing, sometimes thematically structured (like beachwear); however, the images are anchored by information about the price and shops where the clothes can be bought and so the section is, in fact, an advertisement.

Expressive and conative functions

The addresser and addressee are the sender and receiver of the *message as structured by the communication*. Texts have implicit addressees: this book, for example, clearly has Media Studies students as its target audience, and you assume that the addresser – me – is a person qualified to write such a text.

The actual *receiver* and *sender* of the text, however, may be completely different. There is nothing to stop a one-year-old picking up this book and dribbling all over it, and it is possible I don't know what I'm writing about. In addition, while there is one addressee of this book (a person interested in and/or studying Media Studies) it has, hopefully, many thousands of receivers who have bought or been given the book. Of course there is only, basically, one sender (Nick Lacey).

Clearly, the number of readers of this text whom I know personally is extremely small. In order, then, to address my target audience I must construct in my mind an individual who is the addressee. The signs which I – the addresser – use in the text must create a relationship between the addresser and the addressee. This is done by using signs' phatic functions.

The phatic function

The sign's expressive function is how it constructs the addresser and the conative function is its construction of the addressee. These functions create a relationship between addresser and addressee by defining a group to which we both belong – in this case that of Media Studies enthusiasts(?!) – and thus create a context in which signs can be exchanged. (Although books are by their nature one-way channels of communication, please feel free to feedback your response to this text by writing to the publishers; your opinions would be much appreciated.)

In this text, I have attempted to create the relationship between addresser and addressee through the occasional use of jokey asides and reassurance. The jokes, for example, may not add any information (referential function) but I hope they serve to render the reading of this book slightly less painful (joke!?).

So the sign's phatic function is not to communicate information – that is the referential function – but to establish this relationship between the addresser and addressee. The use of this function is not, of course, restricted to text books, we use it in our everyday life. For example, on greeting a person you may ask how he or she is. Unless you know he or she has been seriously ill (the social context) this will be a polite question which does not require details of the addressee's medical history. However, the receiver of this greeting will occasionally not understand its phatic function and will describe their aches and pains anyway. Another example is the use of the weather to establish a relationship: how many of us have experienced the absurdity of standing in the pouring rain and remarking to a neighbour that 'it's not a nice day'?!

For sub-cultural groups the norms of dress may act as phatic communication, defining sympathy with the group's values. For example, male members of fascist groups commonly shave their hair; hippies grow their's long. Of course, by affirming one sense of identity, the signs are simultaneously excluding those who do not belong, in which case these signs operate in a non-phatic fashion.

As an experienced Media Studies teacher I have a clear idea of my addressee, but this is not the same as my target audience. While the book is aimed at anyone interested in advanced Media Studies, my addressee is a 16–18-year-old Media Studies student. Whether this is clear from the coding of the book is determined by your reading of it: if you fall into my addressee category and you find the text addresses you in a convincing fashion, then I have been successful. If, however, you are much older, or indeed much younger, than the addressee you may find the text occasionally 'jarring', which, while it indicates the success of my coding, does suggest I have excluded part of my target audience.

What addresser the expressive function has created in this book is difficult for me to be certain about. It is probably impossible for anyone to judge how he or she – as an addresser – appears to you who are reading this book (the receiver). Clearly I am a Media Studies teacher but I am probably oblivious to many aspects of my personality that 'leak' into the text.

Contextual function

Finally, a sign's contextual function is the social situation in which the sign exists; for example a classroom suggests that the communication is educational. A red light situated on a traffic light means we must stop; a red light situated upon a HiFi system indicates the system is switched on. In both cases the sign is a red light but the context tells us which code to use.

If you are reading this book merely because you feel it will help you get a better grade, it is likely you are using this text in an instrumental fashion. However, if you are reading it 'out of interest' then the book may be fulfilling an intellectual need.

◀ Exercise 3.1 ▶

Using any advertisement, preferably the same one used for the similar exercise in Chapter 1 (Exercise 1.1) break down the sign system using Thwaites' *et al.* model.

The use of Jakobson's revised model demonstrates how complex communication is and while it is useful in analysing images it does not tell 'the whole story'. What we have been doing, up to this point, is isolating the structural elements of the signs of communication. Before we proceed we must consider the structures of signs themselves, and in order to do this we must investigate semiotics.

4

ADVANCED IMAGE ANALYSIS

4.1 Introduction

We learned in Chapter 1 how we used our socially-learned understanding of non-verbal communication (NVC) to decode images. In this chapter we will see how we can use media texts in order to understand society.

Media Studies is often compared to English Literature because it analyses texts. The apparent lack of discrimination in the selection of these texts (soap operas are as likely to be studied as classic films or television programmes) has often been used to criticize the academic validity of the subject. However, it is because Media Studies does not have a preordained canon of what texts are worthy of study that it is so effective in enabling us better to understand society. In addition, Media Studies does not only deal in the present, it can also teach us, like Literature, about the past.

By analysing the conventions used to represent reality in the past we can better understand our predecessors' world view and often, because the past is a precursor to the present, better understand modern media conventions. Part of this understanding is derived from authorial intent or, more usefully, a text's preferred reading (they may not be the same thing).

We often find that texts are *polysemic* – that is, they have a number of meanings – and how we, as individuals, read these 'open' texts is determined by our subjectivity and our 'world view'. It is in analysing 'world views' that we are confronted by the concept of *ideology*, one of the defining theories of Media Studies. Arising from ideology are the concepts of *discourse* and *hegemony*.

The final part of this chapter will consider alternatives to mainstream conventions. These are often defined in opposition to the mainstream and so serve as a useful reminder of such things as continuity editing.

The first two chapters have shown that there are a large number of variables in image analysis. Our understanding of these variables is, in the main, derived from socialization. From the moment we begin interacting with the world we are socialized into codes of language, both verbal and non-verbal, and into society's conventions of behaviour. The primary socialization starts at a very young age and usually takes place in the home; secondary socialization is the more formal education we receive in schools.

Language is often used and understood in an unconscious fashion. This is a testimony to the human brain's sophistication: we are usually unaware of the large mount of information our brain is processing at any one moment. The objective of Media Studies analysis is, in part, to allow us to become aware of the unconscious reading we are making of, in the first instance, media texts, but also – and this is a consequence of the first step – how we also unconsciously read our social environment. This is done by pulling apart, or deconstructing, the constituent parts of communication.

This deconstruction is not, however, an objective, mechanical exercise, because we can never categorically state what any communication means to any one individual. Everyone's way of seeing is a product of her or his values and beliefs, and so any analysis will be made from a specific point of view. This specific point of view means that anyone analysing a text, effectively, has their own agenda; although because our values and beliefs are obviously influenced by the society of which we are a member, it is unlikely that this agenda is unique.

It is important to be conscious of any agenda you are using because it will structure the way you make the analysis. This is particularly important in an exam context, because you can only say so much about a text in a restricted amount of time. However, even in coursework an agenda must play a part; a genuinely exhaustive analysis of a text is likely to be, simply, too exhausting.

The analysis of the Nokia 232 advertisement in the earlier chapters consisted, essentially, of a list of all the elements used in image analysis; it lacked a more specific agenda, unlike the 'examination' version in Appendix 2. Clearly, any agenda you use in an examination context (including coursework) must be a Media Studies agenda. This, however, need not be limiting; while Media Studies demands that you use certain tools of analysis, how you use them should be determined by your own interests and desires.

In this final chapter on image analysis (and you should have realized by now that many of the techniques described apply equally to written and oral texts) we shall consider more advanced techniques of analysis which allow us to link the individual components in a comprehensive manner. Some of the ideas, particularly those of ideology, discourse and hegemony, are difficult and my advice is that you 'wrestle' with them throughout the duration of the course (and after). If you feel you do not fully understand them, even just before your final examination, don't worry; below post-graduate level examiners are not looking for a fully-rounded, academic command of the difficult concepts.

The tools described in the first two chapters lead us to look very closely at texts as if we are pressing our nose against a subject and looking at each component individually. In this way it is easy to see the parts but it makes looking at the whole problematic. The contents in this chapter are intended to show you how to 'pull together' the disparate elements into a coherent whole.

If the detail in this chapter appears to you to be overwhelming, then you are not over-reacting: it is overwhelming! This is why it is important to be systematic about approaches to analysis and to concentrate on one aspect at a time before drawing conclusions; after all, no one would expect us to read a short story or novel instantaneously.

Before we continue, it will be useful to understand why Media Studies does not discriminate against texts which lack cachet – all texts should yield interesting information from a Media Studies perspective.

4.2 High culture versus low culture

Raymond Williams (1976) states that 'culture' is one of the most difficult words in the English language to define. For the purposes of image analysis I am going to use a wide definition that emphasizes the 'democratic' Media Studies view on what is worthy of academic analysis. My definition of 'culture' is 'any artefact created by human beings'; so the Mona Lisa and the *Mahabharata* are examples of culture, as is the rubbish in your dustbin.

From a Media Studies perspective all media artefacts are worthy of investigation, particularly if they are popular. They are worthy of study because they have much to teach us about how societies are organised and how societies create meaning. A study of the ownership of large media corporations can demonstrate how they have an enormous influence upon our lives; for example, News Corporation (Rupert Murdoch) controls 20th Century Fox (film and television), HarperCollins publishers, Star TV in the Far East, four national newspapers in Britain and BSkyB (with concomitant influence upon association and rugby football) among others. An understanding of the political orientation of newspapers is critical for the health of any democracy.

This starting point is, however, diametrically opposed to the 'common sense' view. In common sense terms, culture is often synonymous with art; literature is culture, as is opera and 'classical' music. However, artefacts such as blockbuster novels, soap operas and popular music are often excluded from this definition. Art is defined, in a common sense discourse, as a collection of artefacts which demonstrates 'universal truths'; for example in English Literature the novels of Jane Austen are deemed to speak the 'truth' to all cultures in all times. However, an examination of these 'truth'-bearing artefacts reveals that what the definition really means is that minority, middle-class, art is good and mass (popular) art is bad. Media Studies is not primarily concerned with whether artefacts are 'good' or 'bad', 'high art' or 'pop(ular) culture'; it is interested in what we can learn from them.

This has led some commentators to suggest that Media Studies is undiscriminating, that practitioners of the subject believe that, say, Hollywood films are as 'good' as the 'great works of Literature'. This is a misconception, but Media Studies does operate from the basis that we should study both Hollywood and 'Literature'.

Many students new to Media Studies, however, are imbued with these 'common sense' values. One does not have to be middle class to possess them, as this definition of art has achieved a very wide consensus. While the thought of reading Charles Dickens' *Bleak House* for a literature course may not fill students with joy, they usually accept the value of the exercise. Ask the same students to watch an old Hollywood movie and the response is often one of suspicion. This is unsurprising; there are even teachers who believe going to the cinema, during school hours, is a waste of time because the film could be watched on video.

In Britain, this 'common sense' view is regularly reinforced by bursts of newspaper outrage about the teaching of soap opera in schools. In recent years the British Government has even gone to the extreme of forcing all 13-year-olds to study Shakespeare, because it will be good for them. It is hoped that the study of Shakespeare will teach children morality by giving them access to High Culture. The nation's youth, according to certain quarters of the press, are being brought up on a diet of sex 'n' violence in video nasties. (The fact that one of the original set plays, *Romeo and Juliet*, contains under-age sex, as well as violence, appears to have escaped the legislators' notice.)

In Media Studies, as we have said, all images and texts are worthy of investigation. Some texts, like those of Shakespeare, for example, will yield more to study than others; but we do not subscribe to the view that studying 'high art' is, in some way, better for you. However, this debate about what constitutes culture is really, from the point of view of Media Studies, an irrelevance.

In image analysis what we have to be most aware of are two inter-related facts:

- all images are cultural artefacts and are therefore the products of a particular society at a particular time;
- both the sender and receiver of any image have their own cultural backgrounds (though they may be the same) which have influenced, respectively, the creation and reading of the image.

The next part of this chapter considers various ways we can read texts: the author's intention, the most 'obvious' reading of a text, how a text may be 'open' to other readings, and how we – the reader – influence the 'way we see' the text.

4.3 Authorial intent

There is a belief, particularly in the study – in its more traditional forms – of English Literature, that the task of analysis is to work out the author's, or addresser's, intentions. It can, however, be very difficult to be sure of authorial intent; even if the author has written explicitly about her or his own work, who is to say that theirs is the true reading? Film director Alfred Hitchcock, for example, was notorious for stating that his films were 'merely thrillers', when they clearly also deal with notions such as good and evil. As we saw in Chapter 1, there are numerous variables at work in any act of communication and if we assume that the author's view is the 'correct' one, we might as well dispense with contact and context and, possibly, even the receiver (other than being a recipient of the sender's wisdom).

Certainly, authorial intent is of interest but it must not be allowed to dominate the process of analysis; analysing artefacts is not about trying to decode what the author is trying to tell us. Searching only for authorial intention assumes that meaning does not change through time, so that the text will always mean what the author meant it to mean. This is related to the idea that great works of art, whether they be literature, painting and music (as long as they are not 'popular') express universal values that speak to all peoples in all times. This approach to criticism is antithetical to Media Studies.

F. R. Leavis, and his followers, developed this view to an extent by focusing upon the text rather than the author. However, Leavis' approach tended to ignore the text's historical background, for he believed that the close reading of extracts, even out of their textual context, would allow the text's essential message to be decoded. Students studying 'A' level English Literature in Britain are still tested on this skill as, indeed, are Media Studies students. However, while traditional literature criticism is interested in *what* texts mean, Media Studies is more concerned with *why* texts mean what they do to particular audiences.

In Media Studies knowledge of authorial intent is, in fact, less important than knowledge of the author's (or, in the case of broadcasting and cinema, for example, the institution's) cultural background. If we understand the culture in which the text was created, whether it be from the past, from our own society, or from a contemporary society which possesses values different from our own, we have a better chance of understanding the text's codes.

4.4 'Preferred' reading

Although authorial intent can at times be difficult to ascertain, an addressee's (not the sender's) intention is often contained within the text, either explicitly or implicitly. It is clear that an advertisement's function is to sell a product, a service or a company image, and the way in which advertisers would prefer the audience to read the text is usually made obvious. Texts which clearly have a preferred meaning are 'closed' texts and these texts are usually heavily anchored. Because a text is closed, however, does not mean that alternative readings are not possible.

Other texts are more open. For example, fictional texts usually invite different perspectives, and the reader may have a choice of sympathetic characters with whom to identify, possibly determined by gender.

Some texts, such as instrumental music, are almost completely free from linguistic anchorage (except for its title) giving a greater latitude to the audience's reading. While instrumental music does not have linguistic anchorage, it still possesses codes which are conventional – for example, most minor keys are sad.

Texts, then, are closed, open, or – most likely – somewhere in between. At least this is how the passive reader experiences them. Stuart Hall who, with members of the Centre of Contemporary Cultural Studies in Birmingham, described three possible reader positions:

1. The *dominant* hegemonic position, in which the reader accepts the message given by a text; such a reader would believe that the Nokia 232 is a desirable object because it would make the owner appear to be more sexually attractive and powerful. (The concept of hegemony is considered later.)
2. The *negotiated* position, in which readers understand the dominant position but choose to apply it to their own social context; the Nokia 232 could be acknowledged as desirable but inappropriate to themselves (the readers may recognize that they do not need a mobile phone, or that while the product might make others sexually powerful, it would not actually work for them);
3. The *oppositional* position which, while understanding the dominant coding, rejects the values it is putting forward. Here the Nokia 232 advertisement's message would be rejected, possibly on the grounds that it is perpetuating sexist stereotypes (this reading, of course, would be using feminist discourse).

O'Sullivan *et al.* (1994) added a fourth position which they termed an *aberrant* reading, in which the preferred meaning is not understood and the text is read in a deviant fashion.

Finding the preferred reading of complex texts such as films, novels and drama, can be difficult. Many of these texts do, however, possess an explicit 'moral to their tale' and this is the preferred reading. Complex texts, by their nature, tend to be open texts. This subject is covered in *Narrative and Genre*.

◀ EXERCISE 4.1 ▶

Choose any text, whether it be an advertisement, a song, a film (or extract), novel, short story and so on, and create three different readings using Hall's categories.

It should be noted that a preferred reading does not necessarily concur with authorial intent. The creators may be attempting to convey a particular message which is not apparent, at least to the receiver, in the text itself. This begs the question of where the preferred reading is situated: in the addressee, in the unskilled (at textual analysis), or in the skilled addressee?

As an example of the way the same text can have numerous readings I shall use the classic Hitchcock film *The Birds* (1963). In common with many of Hitchcock's other movies it is primarily, in terms of genre, a thriller. It is set in a small Californian town, Bodega Bay, where, inexplicably, birds start attacking, and killing, the local population. Caught up in this disaster are Melanie Daniels (Tippi Hedren), a playgirl, and Mitch Brenner (Rod Taylor), a lawyer, who are on the verge of becoming lovers.

As already indicated, Alfred Hitchcock was often disparaging about reading any complex psychological meaning into his work but you can get an idea of his intentions from the interviews he made with French 'new wave' director Francois Truffaut (1978, pp. 359–69):

> [The audience] come to the theatre and they sit down and say, 'All right. Now, show me!' And they want to be one jump ahead of the action; 'I know what's going to happen.' So, I have to take up the challenge: 'Oh, you know what's going to happen. Well, we'll just see about that!' With *The Birds* I made sure that the public would not be able to anticipate from one scene to another . . . At the beginning of the film we show Rod Taylor in the bird shop. He catches the canary that has escaped from its cage, and after putting it back, he says to Tippi Hedren, 'I'm putting you back in your gilded cage, Melanie Daniels.' I added that sentence during the shooting because I felt it added to her characterisation as a wealthy, shallow playgirl. And later on, when the gulls attack the village, Melanie Daniels takes refuge in a glass telephone booth and I show her as a bird in a cage. This time it isn't a gilded cage, but a cage of misery, and it's also the beginning of her ordeal by fire, so to speak. It's a reversal of the age-old conflict between men and birds.

For Hitchcock, the emphasis is on the love story but this, as we shall see, is not readily apparent in the text. It appears that the love story is merely the conventional heterosexual romance that accompanies most Hollywood narratives.

Audiences tend to read mainstream cinema in a generic fashion and so it is often genre that structures the preferred reading. I have already described *The Birds* as a thriller but as a genre it is probably most accurately defined as a 'disaster' movie, with science fiction elements. The whole notion of birds 'taking over the world' is clearly a bizarre and catastrophic one for the human race. The films follows the conventional generic pattern where the protagonists fight back against the disastrous circumstances. However, from a conventional point of view the ending is curiously unsatisfactory.

The film concludes with Melanie, Mitch and his family quietly leaving a Bodega Bay that is saturated with birds. This is unsatisfactory, for it breaks convention in two ways: the birds appear to have triumphed, and there is no obvious reason why the birds are allowing the protagonists to escape. There is a hint that the end of the film is the end of the world, but there is no narrative justification for this conclusion, we receive no information that the bird attacks are a worldwide phenomena. From a generic point of view the film appears to simply end, nothing is resolved.

This preferred reading is, of course, completely ignoring what Hitchcock stated was his intentions in making the film. Despite this, I believe that most people would read the film as I have described above; as usual in discussions of audience, it is exceptionally difficult to be certain what audiences are actually thinking.

4.5 Polysemy

It should be clear that signs can generate more than one reading – they are polysemic – which means that audiences are no longer under the yoke of the tyrannous text where Leavis and his followers would like to place us! What we must avoid, though, is total anarchy: while, theoretically, texts can mean anything receivers wish them to mean, if receivers want to persuade others of the validity of their reading they must refer to socially agreed meanings. With this proviso, we are at liberty to make any reading of a text *if it can be justified* by that text. In other words, as long as we can demonstrate in our analysis that the combination of signs that the text consists of could mean what we say, then we are justified in our reading. In order to do this we must consider all the variables of analysis. If we reject the preferred reading then we create either a negotiated or oppositional one in its place.

Numerous readings of texts are possible because of arbitrary nature of signs, what signs mean is determined by a large number of factors. In his investigation of *parole* and *langue* (the speech act and underlying rule system) Saussure concluded that because the speech act was wholly individual it was not a suitable object for study. However, a contemporary of Saussure's, the Russian Volosinov, pointed out that speech is not an individual act, but a social phenomenon. Volosinov concluded that a sign's meaning was created, not by *langue*, but in the dialogic interaction created by social intercourse and this also increases the possibility of polysemy.

Volosinov argued that all communication is structured as a dialogue, even when individuals are talking to themselves. Similarly all artefacts are created with an audience in mind; even writing a diary assumes, at least, the audience of oneself at a future date. Once a sender has an addressee in mind, this fact must, inevitably, influence the signs used to communicate the message. For example, if you were having a conversation about local politics with a someone who lived abroad, you would probably give a great deal more background information than you would to somebody who lived locally. Similarly, this chapter is addressing an audience which has understood the ideas in the first two chapters (if you haven't understood them, then you might not understand what I am writing).

Volosinov described signs as being *multi-accentual*, and it is this property that creates the possibility of polysemy. Signs are not fixed; their meaning is determined by their interaction with the other dimensions of communication. However, as we have seen, in practice anchorage usually suggests a text's preferred meaning.

Who we are influences how we read texts. If you are the type of person who accepts things at face value, you are more likely to accept a text's preferred reading. However if you are a 'questioning' or sceptical type of person, you are more likely to make oppositional readings. The form these oppositional readings take will be determined both by your knowledge and by your ability to use different discourses from those into which the text invites us (discourse will be described later in the chapter).

What follows is an example of a negotiated reading of *The Birds*, drawing heavily on Bill Nichols' (1981) interpretation of the film. My reading attempts to bring together its two apparently disparate narratives; the love story between Mitch and Melanie, and the bird attacks.

The advertising slogan used at the time of the film's release was 'The Birds is Coming', which suggests impending doom. This sense of threat is continued by the credit sequence, with its high-pitched electronic sounds mixed with bird calls, and images of black birds fluttering across the screen. The credits themselves appear to break up under the impact of the birds. However, the first scene opens on a very different note:

The Birds: scene 1:

Pan on Melanie crossing road and walking along pavement.
Soundtrack: ambient sounds of traffic and gulls. Then a human 'wolf-whistle' of sexual appreciation.

Melanie responds appreciatively to the whistle by turning toward the unseen source and smiling.
Soundtrack: two distinct and louder gull cries.

Melanie turns to continue her walk but catches sight of birds massing over San Francisco. She looks puzzled, or concerned, or afraid, then walks into a bird shop.

In my reading the disaster narrative begins at the moment of the wolf-whistle and the 'two distinct and louder gull cries'. (There are two very similar cries at the end of the film, implying a narrative circularity.) Because these initial bird cries immediately follow Melanie's appreciation of the wolf-whistle it can be assumed that, in narrative terms at least, they are linked.

As we shall see in Chapter 5, women in cinema are often represented solely as sexual objects; the 'heroines' of films are offered to the audience for erotic contemplation. In this scene we see the female protagonist for the first time in the shape of the blonde and beautiful Tippi Hedren. The wolf-whistle is from off-screen, although clearly from within the narrative space (or diegesis): I shall argue that the whistle is, metaphorically, from the audience.

Melanie enters the bird shop at the end of the first scene and it is here that the 'love' narrative ensues. Melanie meets Mitch but the prospect of romantic entanglement seems distant as Mitch taunts Melanie with the 'gilded cage' joke referred to by Hitchcock in the interview. The narrative is driven from this point by Melanie's desire for revenge and she purchases two love birds for Mitch's sister (why this would constitute revenge is not relevant to our purposes).

Although this second narrative is a (potential) love story, it is best conceptualized as melodrama. Steve Neale (1980, p. 22) described how melodrama is characterized by 'an eruption of heterosexual desire' and often involves a confrontation between family and sexuality. Bill Nichols (1981, p. 99) summarizes this narrative with the following paradox: 'If I am to win Mitch, I must become part of his family, but if I become part of his family, I cannot win Mitch'.

The barrier that prevents the consummation of Melanie and Mitch's love is Mitch's mother, who sees Melanie both as a rival and as wholly unsuited to marriage with her son.

This love narrative is dominant for the first 23 minutes of the film. The only reference to 'the birds' of the title is the bird cage which Melanie takes to Bodega Bay as a present. At this point the disaster narrative, which is meant to be the defining narrative of the film (after all, audiences expect to be thrilled by a Hitchcock movie, they do not expect a romance), returns briefly when Melanie is scratched by a gull just as Mitch greets her.

Up until this moment, and until the bird attacks begin in earnest, Melanie is the protagonist. Unusually for Hollywood films, it is she who initiates the action and is sexually assertive; as we shall see in Chapter 5 this is usually the preserve of male characters. Nichols describes how she is abstracted from the three-dimensional texture of the diegesis (narrative) by soft focus photography (1981, p. 163); Melanie is the focus of the audience's erotic gaze, hence the 'wolf-whistle' at the beginning of the film.

In my reading, because the audience's expectation of bird attacks is not fulfilled for the first 40 minutes of the film (except for the scratch referred to above) they become antagonistic towards the text. John Ellis (1982, pp. 25–6) describes the act of going to the cinema:

> At the point of sale of an admission ticket it is not the film that is sold . . . it is the possibility of viewing a film or films; it is not cinema as an object that is sold, but cinema as an anticipated experience.

In *The Birds* the anticipated experience is withheld for a major part of the film so that when the bird attacks do begin the audience response is 'about time too'. Because the love narrative, with Melanie at its centre, has taken centre stage for so long, Melanie is perceived as a threat the progression of the narrative which the audience has come to see and this threat is eliminated by the bird attacks. As we shall see, the birds are the mechanism by which Melanie is forced into Mitch's family, not as his wife but as his mother's daughter. As a result, she loses both her sexual confidence and her ability to motivate narrative.

At last the disaster movie commences. And with the fulfilment of expectation comes audience pleasure and satisfaction as the attacks become more numerous and violent. Melanie is usually associated with the attacks, either as victim or as onlooker; indeed in a climactic café scene she is blamed for the attacks:

Why are they doing this? Why are they doing this? They said when you got here the whole thing started. Who are you? What are you? Where did you come from? I think you're the cause of all this. I think you're evil! Evil!!

This speech is filmed directly from Melanie's point of view (she ends the diatribe by slapping the woman) and so it appears that the speaker is directly addressing the audience. This address of the audience makes us realize that, in a way, we are responsible for the attacks. After all, we have been waiting impatiently for them to happen. This complicity of the audience in the attacks is further emphasized during the scene when Melanie is trapped in a telephone booth as the gulls try to smash their way in through the glass, as if they are trying to smash their way through the screen itself.

The final attack on the film is a metaphorical rape of Melanie, alone in the attic of Mitch's house. She is attracted by the whistle of a bird, just as she was attracted earlier by the 'wolf-whistle'. In this scene the representation of Melanie as a powerful, sexually assertive, female protagonist is finally destroyed. She does not scream, there is only the frantic flutter of feathers and Melanie's heavy breathing (she even gasps 'Oh Mitch!'). She is rescued, in time-honoured fashion, by the male and when she regains consciousness can only flail helplessly at the camera – at us, who desired to see the violence of the birds.

Melanie is led away, mute, by Mitch's mother, and the family drives off in a world full of birds. The ending is now no longer incoherent; the reason the birds do not attack is because their task is complete, the love narrative is over, the dominant female has been subjugated.

This is an example – albeit a very incomplete one (there is more evidence in the text to support this view but not the space to describe it) – of an oppositional reading of Alfred Hitchcock's *The Birds*. I believe I have justified my argument from the film and therefore it is a valid reading. The only way you can test it for yourself is to watch the film and make your own reading. (You will find it invaluable to watch the film at least twice in quick succession, otherwise a large amount of detail will be lost.)

A fuller version of my own reading requires the use of psychoanalytic discourse, which will be touched on later in the book; the present one implicitly uses the notion of ideology, which seeks to uncover a common thread structuring the text. In this case the idea of patriarchal, or male-dominated, society is used to decode the film.

There follows a discussion about ideology which is an important part of media theory. However, it is a difficult concept to understand and describe, and recently, because of the term's lack of clear definition, the value of it as a concept has been questioned. Nevertheless, it is still an essential idea to consider because it helps us unify the disparate tools of analysis we have so far described.

Once again, having an agenda for your analysis is shown to be important. Because texts are polysemic, media analyses need an explicit agenda. With an agenda, the student is reading a text from a particular perspective which, of course, limits the polysemic nature of a text. However, an analysis that attempted to cover all the possible readings (which is, in any case, probably impossible) would in all likelihood drive the student, as well as a reader of the analysis, to distraction. As was stated earlier, this agenda should be structured by your own interests and pleasures; while most of us are aware of what these are, how many of us are aware who we are? Therefore, before we consider the concept of ideology, we shall investigate what makes us individuals.

4.6 Intrapersonal communication

Intrapersonal communication, communication that takes place inside a person's mind, is a subject properly investigated in Communication Studies and Psychology. Clearly, however, the media is about communication, and psychology, as we saw in our investigation of non-verbal communication in Chapter 1, does have important implications for the analysis of images and media texts.

It should be clear that there is no one correct reading of any image: there are too many variables involved for even the heaviest of anchorage to guarantee absolutely that the audience will make the preferred reading. It is my belief that while we can all deconstruct a text's codes, and be aware of our context and the influence the contact is having on our reading, the real difficulty in analysis is being aware of the influence you, as the receiver, are having on your own reading. While it is probably impossible, in normal life, to 'step outside' of your body into a self-reflexive position, we can all gain a degree of self-awareness by considering what constitutes our 'self' as defined by current, Western, psychological theory. When we are asked who we are, we usually respond by giving a name. Our name is not, of course, unique to us, because it is almost certain that other people share the same name. Who, then, are we?

◀ EXERCISE 4.2 ▶

Michael Argyle (1983) described the '20 statements test': write down 20 answers to the question 'who are you?'

In truth nobody can give the 'correct' answer to this question (though we will all have preferred readings) but we can describe the central core of how we consciously perceive ourselves; this is called our *self-image*. This core consists of name, bodily feelings, body-image, sex, and age. In addition to this, our job, and/or our achievements in education, social class, religion, and any personal success, will also form part of our self-image.

However, while your name may not change throughout your life, your feelings about your body are almost certain to, possibly even on a daily basis. Even if we could pin our feelings down with any accuracy, we also occupy a number of roles. In the course of one day we can be a daughter or son in the morning, a friend as we travel to school or college, a student when we get there, and – with luck – a lover in the evening. While these roles may be complementary, it is unlikely that they will never generate conflict. Even the person most determined to take Polonius's advice, 'to thine own self be true', is likely to behave differently in these roles; being a daughter/son is very different from being a lover.

In Western society, body image is probably still more important for females, although the increasing incidence of anorexia among teenage males suggests that it is becoming a major influence in their lives, too.

These elements of our self-image contribute to our self-esteem, defined as the degree to which we approve of ourselves. People with a high degree of self-esteem tend to be more confident than those with low self-esteem. Clearly this has a major impact on our behaviour and it can also influence the way we read texts. For example, people who have problems with their body image are likely to look at images of conventionally attractive people – such as the woman in the Nokia 232 advertisement – very differently from those who are happy with their bodies. Individuals who strive for a certain body weight may either admire images of those who have this weight, or despise them. The individual's reading will inevitably be coloured by this perception.

Similarly, people with low intellectual self-esteem may believe that they will never understand semiotics and 'can't analyse images properly anyway'; these individuals are defeated before they have started. The opposite can also be true; people with high intellectual self-esteem may think they 'know it all' and also fail in their analysis because they don't work hard enough. This assumes, of course, that semiotics is worth understanding and the way the subject is being explained to you is in a coherent manner.

As a way of measuring self-esteem individuals often possess an *ego-ideal*. An ego-ideal is an individual, or individuals, with whom a person identifies and whom he or she strives to become like. At an early age these are often parents; in later life people such as teachers (No!) can fill the role. An ego-ideal does not have to be real, the personas of film or pop stars often fulfill the role, and their appearance on adolescent's walls serves as a reminder of his or her aspirations. (While the individual star is a real person, their star persona isn't; in fact, the images of stars are often constructed as ego-ideals.)

Ego-ideals do not even have to be individuals; they may be a role. For example, a person may aspire to be a fashion model or a sports person. However, an ego-ideal is unlikely to affect a reading of an image unless it is present within the text. For example, a reader who aspires to be an athlete is more likely to admire the image of a runner than a reader who does not.

Group dynamics can have a great influence upon our reading of texts. Whenever you are asked to analyse a text in a group it is likely that the opinions of those who are considered expert in the subject will be given more credence than those who are not, even if they do not know what they are talking about. This is not just a case of the expert influencing a group consensus; it can also affect the way individual's perceive texts. Unless you consider yourself an expert, or have high intellectual or Media Studies self-esteem, the 'expert's' opinion is likely to influence your individual reading of the text which, in turn, influences your perception of it.

I have mentioned, in this section, some variables that the self-aware Media Studies student should consider in her or his analysis. However the whole notion of subjectivity is far more complex than I have suggested. We can, more or less, be conscious of all the aforementioned variables, yet, as Freud brought to our attention, we all possess an unconscious that is likely to have just as much effect upon our social self as our consciousness does.

There have been a number of attempts, particularly in film studies, to create a model of subjectivity. These theoretical notions of subjectivity and spectatorship will be touched on later in the book (particularly with reference to Laura Mulvey's ideas in Chapter 5), although they are considered in more depth in the second volume of this series, *Institution and Audience*.

4.7 Ideology

Ideology is one of the central ideas of Media Studies, and probably one of the most difficult to understand. An ideology is a 'world view', a more or less coherent system of beliefs, used to make judgements about society. There exists the dominant ideology, which inflects everybody's perception of the world, but there are also competing ideologies, which may be relics from the past, or new ways of seeing emerging to challenge the dominant ideology's supremacy. At the core of all ideologies is their relationship with a society's power structures.

Ideology is not a monolithic set of ideas; on the contrary it tends to be relatively flexible, which allows it to adapt to the changing conditions of material existence. For example, the dominant ideology of the Western world is expressed in economic terms by capitalism, which seeks to generate profit from investment. It follows that our society should benefit most those who have most money. The dominant ideology of Western society is that of the bourgeoisie, or the owners of the means of production (for example, the owners of factories). This use of the term was coined by Karl Marx in his analysis of captalism; he described how Western society was structured to benefit those with money, capital, at the expense of those without.

The dominant ideology does not solely structure the operations of the economy, it also forms the basis for more fundamental social interaction. For example, the importance of individual freedom (at the expense of the community) is held to be sacrosanct in Western society, as is the importance of the nuclear family (consisting of father, mother and children). Although the importance of individual freedom seems to be self-evident, it is constituted as a myth, in Barthes' sense. As we shall discover below, there are other ways of viewing the world.

Like all ideologies, bourgeois ideology is not simply a monolithic set of ideas. For example, the right-wing version of the dominant, bourgeois, ideology states: the 'free market' should be at the heart of the economic system; public ownership is an inefficient way of managing utilities; the welfare state is something which encourages laziness; criminality is a moral, rather than economic, choice. A more liberal version of the same ideology suggests that it is right for the state to intervene in certain economic matters; that public ownership is good for public utilities; that the welfare state acts as a safety net and prevents poverty; that crime is a product of social conditions such as high unemployment.

The crucial point for Media Studies students is that ideology does not act as a 'window on the world', but shapes our view of the world. As we have seen in our consideration of semiotics, all communication, whether it is, for example, spoken or written language or an advertisement, is structured. A structure must have a foundation, and the foundation of that structure is ideology. So when we analyse the structure of a media text we aim to reveal the ideological basis of that text.

Neither the right-wing nor liberal view on economics, both of which are expressions of bourgeois ideology, have a privileged relationship with the 'truth', or 'reality', they are merely sets of ideas. There is a belief that it is impossible to 'know' the real world, that there are only 'ways of seeing' the world using different ideologies. This conventionalist position posits that there are an infinite number of ways of observing reality. Reality, in this view, is merely the product of the framework, or paradigm, used to observe the world, and no paradigm, or ideology, can give an unadulterated picture of what the world is actually like.

As I have stated, in Western society our view of the world is structured by bourgeois ideology. Looking out of the window, as I write, I can see houses in which families live. These clearly exist in the physical world, but my understanding of them as sign systems, whether at a denotative or connotative level, is determined by the society to which I belong, and this, in turn, is structured by the dominant ideology.

The ideological family

◀ Exercise 4.3 ▶

Analyse an image of a family (advertising often uses such a group) by listing the connotations present; can you isloate implicit assumptions about what makes an 'ideal' family?

In Western society the central social unit is the family and the most common family unit is nuclear, that is, parents and offspring; a grouping which also consisted of aunts, uncles, cousins, grand-parents, etcetera would be an extended family. Families usually inhabit houses which, of course, can also be shared as dwellings by friends or even, occasionally, by strangers; but the dominant social unit is the nuclear family.

It could be argued that the nuclear family is the predominant social unit simply because it is the most 'obvious' one. The reason it is the norm in our society is the belief that nuclear families are the most efficient way to reproduce the dominant values through the process of socialization. This belief, which is a myth, can appear so natural to us that the idea, for example, of people other than the parents bringing up children appears bizarre (unless the original family unit was dysfunctional leading to fostering or adoption). However, even in the Western world there are examples of communal family structures, such as kibbutzim in Israel.

The declining importance of the extended family is a recent phenomenon in Britain, and is probably a result of changing work and educational patterns. Labour-intensive, and location-specific, occupations such as mining and dock work have declined, destroying traditional communities. Meanwhile, higher education has been widened to include greater numbers, which has increased job opportunities for those who are qualified; this, in turn, has aided social mobility. In the 1960s some sociologists argued that this was leading to the 'embourgeoisement' of the working class; that is, people of working-class origin taking the values, but not becoming members of, the middle class.

An example of an opposing view to the consensus can be found in the work of R. D. Laing, and others, who argue that the nuclear family is in fact a 'sick' social unit, which reproduces and encourages neuroses within its members. If this is the case, why, then, is it effective in reproducing bourgeois ideology? Laing suggests that by creating more or less neurotic individuals, society makes its members less aware of their subordinate position in society. (The notion of subordination is dealt with in more detail in the next section, with a consideration of the ideas of Louis Althusser.)

Whatever the validity of that argument, there is no doubt that looking out of the window I am seeing more than a house in which a family lives – I am perceiving a sign system which has attained the status of a myth. As mentioned in Exercise 3.4, this myth is utilized with great efficiency by the advertising industry; it is, however, a myth in crisis. There are an increasing number of children born to parents who aren't married and the number of one-parent families has been increasing for many years. The fact that these changes has yet to compromise the myth of the family demonstrates how powerful myths can be; but it is likely that this will change soon as it becomes even more 'at odds' with the reality of the situation.

Whatever the reason for the centrality of the family to bourgeois society it is clear that, as a sign system, it is anything but a neutral reflection of the world; it structures the way we see the world. The most powerful set of ideological signs which shape our view of reality is language.

◀ Exercise 4.4 ▶

Return to your image of a family used in Exercise 4.3 and, if you did not do so earlier, make an oppositional reading.

Ideology and language

The fact that I can offer alternative views of the world demonstrates that while ideology has a profound influence on my way of seeing, it is not an unalterable influence. However, ideology is not subverted simply by an analysis of connotations, it is very resistant to a deconstruction of its ideas because, of course, the very language we use to deconstruct is itself a product of the dominant ideology. Attempts to circumvent this have often led to obscure jargon, as we shall see later.

Ideology structures language and language structures the way we perceive, and communicate about, reality.

◀ Exercise 4.5 ▶

Choose any object around you and write down any associations it has which you recognize to be consensual. Say what other associations the object may possess and, if possible, discuss why one set of associations has attained a consensus while another hasn't.

Ideology and reality

One of the reasons we tend not to notice the ideological construction of our world is because ideology denies itself as an ideology; in other words, it does not express itself as an ideology but as reality. Ideology appears to be reality because it conceals its own construction, just as the 180-degree rule conceals the join between shots in the classical system of editing film.

Many who have progressed this far on a Media Studies course have found that their 'naïve' view of the world has been compromised, because once it is realized that meaning is a social construct, and not a product of objects, then it is obvious that reality is being mediated by systems of signs: we know a tree is a tree and not a 'plang' because society tells us that it is a tree. Once it is understood that, in turn, society is not a neutral grouping of individuals but a system of competing power relationships and competing ideologies, then it becomes clear that the mediation has a political purpose which may, or may not, be to our benefit.

Of course the description of society given above is itself is an ideological construct. It is an example of an oppositional way of seeing our society which is obviously in disagreement with the consensus. This consensus has not been arrived at by asking people what they think of society, it is a product of people being 'told', through socialization, what to think of society.

I wish to avoid the notion of conspiracy theory that this analysis may suggest. There is no one individual who is independent of ideology and so can pronounce upon it, except, possibly God, if she exists (by giving God a female gender, which is unconventional, we immediately notice that the conventional, bourgeois construction of the Creator is sexist). Although individuals who wield power in our society, whether elected or through their institutional positions, are usually 'better off' than most of us, they are, to an extent, merely fulfilling a role within the power structure.

George Orwell described, in *Shooting an Elephant*, how when he was a police officer in Burma, which was part of the British Empire, he was forced to shoot an elephant against his will. Although Orwell (1971, p. 267), as a policeman, clearly wielded power, unless he used this power in an expected fashion then he would lose it:

> Here I was, the white man with his gun, standing in front of the untamed native crowd – seemingly the leading actor of the piece; but in reality I was only an absurd puppet pushed to and fro by the will of those yellow faces behind. I perceived in this moment that when the white man turns tyrant it is his own freedom that he destroys.

So although Orwell was in a position of power, he could only use this power in an expected fashion – in a sense he was powerless; Orwell had to shoot the elephant despite the fact he did not wish to do so.

The creators of media texts are in a similar situation. Clearly they are socialized into the values of the dominant ideological system and most of them, like the audience of the texts, use media conventions, which reflect the dominant ideology, in an unconscious fashion. Media practitioners are not in a wholly privileged position, they cannot manipulate meaning independently of the dominant ideology, they must use media conventions in some way. Like Orwell, unless they create texts which audiences understand (that is, behave in the expected fashion) then it is likely that they will lose their power to create media texts (that is, lose their jobs).

Bourgeois ideology is only one, albeit the dominant one, of a number of ideologies that exist in our society. Religion is, of course, another ideological construct; however, most of those who have faith believe it is 'real' and not just a particular way of viewing and understanding the world. As we shall see in the history of images later in the chapter, the dominant way of seeing the world in pre-capitalist times was as an unchanging and unchangeable place: religion provided the answers to most questions. In contemporary Western society the world is still seen as a dynamic and developing place where technological innovation is leading us ever on to a higher standard of living despite the growing evidence of climactic breakdown and dwindling resources.

As there is no single person who is, or has ever, dictated the ideological world view, where then does ideology originate? Clearly it must, in the first place, originate in the real world, in the material conditions of existence. How this happens is (fortunately) beyond the scope of this book.

The dominance of religion in the Western world collapsed with the arrival of capitalism. It had survived for centuries by denying the possibility of change and claiming there was no alternative to the *status quo* – clearly an effective way of preserving a dominant status. When it became clear that religion's explanation of the world was partial, then religion either had to adapt or lose its pre-eminence. An ideology that is built upon inflexible premises will find it very difficult to adapt to changing circumstances.

One example of how a new view of reality was dealt with by the Church (the institution of religious ideology) was the case of Galileo Galilei. By using a telescope, invented in Holland, Galileo showed conclusively that the Earth was not at the centre of the universe. By demonstrating that the moons of Jupiter revolved around their mother planet, and not around Earth, he shattered one of the central tenets of religion. (Nicolas Copernicus had realized this 100 years earlier, but the time was not then ready for his ideas.)

The Church's response to Galileo's 'blasphemy' was to force him to recant the truth or die. This was a very weak response, for it attempted to hold on to a past way of seeing, rather than adapting to a new perspective. Because it could not adapt, religion become an inappropriate system of thought. However, it might have been successful in suppressing the 'new truth' were it not for the fact that the currents of the time were conducive to change; this is considered further, with a history of realism, in Chapter 5.

Bourgeois ideology is far more adaptable to change than religion because it is based on the notion of the freedom of the individual. Some alternative ideologies suggest that this freedom is illusory and when the masses realize this, then bourgeois ideology will go the way of religion in Western society.

Alternative ideologies

The impression that there is a monolithic, ideological structure 'running' society must be avoided. Though the dominant ideology will, inevitably, fundamentally structure our way of seeing, we can consciously use alternative ideologies in an attempt to see the world differently. Alternative media texts often use these ideologies to inform the way they represent the world. As we shall see, Cubism was a radical departure from the Renaissance way of seeing.

Raymond Williams (1977) described two types of ideologies which are different from the dominant:

1. residual and
2. emergent.

A residual ideology belongs to a past dominant ideology, one that has been superseded. Religion clearly belongs to a pre-capitalist era and yet still exists, and in some places thrives, in the modern world. In Britain, the monarchy is still extant, representing a former, feudal, power structure.

An emergent ideology is a new cultural development which may eventually supplant the dominant ideology, just as capitalism supplanted feudalism. During the 1960s the 'women's movement' was an emergent ideology that attempted to gain power from the patriarchal bourgeois system. From a perspective of 30 years on, this clearly hasn't yet happened and feminism has a fairly low profile in Western society. Feminism is an example of an emergent ideology that forced the dominant ideology to adapt but not to change fundamentally.

For example, in Britain the Sexual Discrimination Act 1975 made it illegal to pay a woman less for doing the same work as a man.

However, an analysis of the gender of those in political or economic power, shows that men still dominate (and are often paid more for the same work). Feminism still exists as a viewpoint, or discourse; but it may again rise as an emergent ideology, just as it emerged in the 1960s, or following the suffragettes, or campaigners such as Mary Wollstonecraft in the eighteenth century.

◀ EXERCISE 4.6 ▶

Choose an advertising image of a powerful woman. How is this power represented and in what ways, if at all, is that power qualified? (Hint: it is likely that the woman is sexually attractive.)

Both residual and emergent ideologies may be in opposition to or co-exist with the dominant system. In many Western countries the Church poses no threat to the *status quo*. However, during the upheavals in Poland during the 1980s, and in Romania a decade later, the Catholic Church played a major role in the downfall of the so-called communist regimes.

It is possible that 'green' issues may form an emergent ideology. As it becomes increasingly obvious that technological progress, part of the bedrock of bourgeois ideology, has compromized the environment (even the weather forecasts detail ozone pollution and/or ozone depletion) the dominant ideology has to respond to these developments. One way in which this is detectable is in the massive increase of 'environment-friendly' products over the past few years – although, of course, this is also another way to sell a product.

Society is a complex collection of individuals, groups, institutions and culture which is structured, fundamentally, by the dominant ideology. These constituents are often competing for power within society and this competition is most clear in the analysis of discourse.

4.8 Discourse

We described ideology as the foundation of all societies and, clearly, ideology will influence any media artefact created in that society. Because foundations are usually hidden, we can only become aware of an artefact's ideological base when we become skilled readers. Our skill consists of being able to describe the foundation by deconstructing what is visible, that is, the text itself. Ideology becomes visible in texts through the discourses employed.

Discourse, like culture, is a multi-discursive concept. 'Multi-discursive' is a term coined by O'Sullivan *et al.* (1994) to describe concepts which have very different meanings depending upon the context in which they are used. The most straightforward definition of discourse is its use in linguistics as 'a verbal utterance which is greater than one sentence'. Its use in Media Studies is not so simple.

We have seen that our understanding of the world is a result of ideological processes; in discourse, as in myths, we can observe ideology in action. Discourses operate at the level of individuals, in a social context, and are subject to historical change. For example, it is a tenet of contemporary, bourgeois ideology that education is good for you and the discourses of education are subjects, such as English, Maths, Chemistry, Media and so on. However, before an educated workforce was required, education was not deemed to be important for the masses.

At the end of the nineteenth century education was deemed to be intrinsically good: that is, the purpose of education was simply to become educated. In recent years, in Britain at least, this liberal–humanist view appears to be in the process of being replaced by a view that the purpose of education is to service the needs of industry.

Discourse is most obvious at a social level, particularly in a formal context. All institutions possess specific discourses which are expressed in different priorities. For example, the institutions of the law, medicine, politics, and law enforcement have different discourses which involve different ways of looking at the world and even different languages to describe them. Take, for example, medicine. Most of us accept that we 'do not understand' the subject or its language, and give ourselves over to professional advice. We assume, often naïvely, that members of the profession, people who understand medical discourse, do know what they are talking about and we accept their judgements. A doctor may tell us we are suffering from tenovaginitis which we are unlikely to understand until she or he uses the discourse of 'everyday life' to explain we have an 'inflammation . . . of the fibrous wall of the sheath that surrounds a tendon' (BMA, 1990, p. 976).

It is not only institutions that use discourses; every human activity involves a certain prioritization of ideas, and often a particular language, formal or informal, to go with it. For example, we are all members of a particular social class and our 'class discourse' may influence our behaviour. For example, the myth of the working class (usually defined by occupation) suggests they are hedonistic, deferential and instinctive whereas the middle class, mythically, defer gratification, are assertive, and intellectual.

Gender is also a product of discourse. While our sex is obviously a biological variable, gender is a purely social construct. There is clearly nothing biological in male's supposed preference for blue, delight in cars and aversion to child-minding.

◀ EXERCISE 4.7 ▶

List the differences between the genders and then tick those you believe are a result of socialization and not a 'natural' difference.

Discourse is central to our lives; it helps us make sense of information. Each individual has access to numerous discourses, any one of which may be dominant at a specific time. The number of discourses we have is determined by socialization and education: the more knowledge an individual has, the more discourses she or he can enter. While media texts may invite us into a particular discourse, which will result in us decoding the preferred reading, the audience is free to choose whether or not to use the offered discourse. I, for example, chose to read *The Birds* from a feminist perspective.

The same text can always be read using different discourses: for example, a photograph of a naked human being could be looked at anatomically (discourse of biology); lustfully (sexuality); as a photograph (decoding lighting, focal length and so on); or anthropologically (what race is the human?). While each discourse is using the same denotative image, the decoding of it is likely to be very different.

Discourse is not just a way of describing the world, it is at the centre of subjectivity. In fact, the whole notion of individuality is an ideological construct and is expressed within the discourse of subjectivity. Earlier in the chapter we analysed the difficulty of defining oneself. We can, however, define ourselves by analysing the discourses we inhabit.

Take, first, the discourse of subjectivity. In a common sense view, subjectivity is unproblematic, it is simply the way an individual consciousness perceives the world. However, as Louis Althusser (1971, p. 182) demonstrated:

In the ordinary use of the term, subject in fact means: (1) a free subjectivity, a centre of initiatives, author of and responsible for its actions; (2) a subjected being, who submits to a higher authority, and is therefore stripped of all freedom except that of freely accepting his submission.[8]

As the notion of a free individual is one of the central tenets of the dominant bourgeois ideology, Althusser's view immediately casts doubt on this freedom. Before this is dismissed as a mere play on words – the punning of subjective and 'subject to' – it must be remembered that language is an ideological construct. Language and discourse exist before the individual is born, and will exist after the individual's death. As socialized beings we take on this ideological baggage and accept it as 'reality' where, in fact, our individual subjectivity is a discourse.

We have already investigated how bourgeois ideology effaces itself as an ideology; it does this most powerfully within the consciousness of the 'Western' individual:

> The individual is interpellated as a (free) subject in order that he shall submit freely to the commandments of the Subject, i.e. in order that he shall make the gestures and actions of his subjection 'all by himself'. (Althusser, 1971, p. 182)

Because we believe in the freedom of individual consciousness, and presumably Althusser believes women are similarly subjected to ideology, we do not realize that we are reproducing the values of bourgeois ideology in the way we think.

Problems with Althusser's theory arise when we wonder how is it that certain people, like Althusser, are capable of transcending their own subjectivity to understand the operations of ideology. Nevertheless, although we are not automatons at the service of the bourgeois ideology, Althusser's theory serves the useful purpose of shaking our conventional view and, hopefully, analyse images with a greater awareness of the ideological position which we, as individuals, inhabit.

In Media and Cultural Studies Althusser's ideas have been superseded by those of Antonio Gramsci and we shall consider his theory of hegemony later.

Discourse in use

It is important to be aware of the use of at least two discourses in any analysis of a media text: that of the addresser and that of yourself. Any text invites the reader into its own discourse. Occasionally, if the text is specialist and we do not understand its language (discourse) we cannot enter. Usually we understand, from its metalingual, formal and contextual functions, the objectives a particular text might have, whether to entertain (film), inform (news), persuade (advertising) or educate (text book). It is possible for texts to utilize more than one discourse: propaganda, for instance, often intends to persuade in the guise of informing the audience; an entertaining film may contain a message for the viewer – for example, the film *Disclosure* (1994) attempts to raise awareness about sexual harassment yet is primarily an entertainment text; a text book may appear to be educational, while providing information which is partisan.

The other discourse – or collection of discourses – we should be aware of is our own. You should by now be using the discourse of Media Studies to read all texts; in fact you may be finding your enjoyment is being compromised by your conscious reading of a text's structure. This, I hope, is a 'passing phase'; most students 'rediscover' the 'art' of enjoying texts in a non-academic manner with the added richness that an understanding of the subject has given to the reading of texts.

Genre is the most obvious example of discourse in a media text. We usually immediately recognize a text's genre – often during the title sequence – and use this to read what follows.

The task of the Media Studies student is to recognize the discourses present in all media texts. Once this is achieved we can then understand what ideological values is operating within them. Often these will be the values of the dominant ideology, however, as conservative attacks upon television and Hollywood, among other institutions, illustrate.

It could be, of course, that the dominant ideology is hardly present within the text. Alternative modes of representation may be used to 'make strange' our view of the world in an attempt to allow us to see the world from a perspective other than that which has attained a consensus in society. We shall consider such texts at the end of the chapter.

An important discourse that Media Studies students must be conscious of is that of 'common sense'. Human beings do not genetically possess 'common sense', it is a social construct. Although 'common sense' is consensual it must reflect the dominant ideology. Once again, the power of ideology lies in its ability to present itself as 'natural', as 'common sense'. Politicians are consummate users of 'common sense', which usually consists of a series of assertions rather than argument. The next time someone you're arguing with says 'well, it's obvious isn't it', ask them to explain themselves: nothing is 'obvious', everything is constructed.

Earlier in the chapter we investigated, in our consideration of intrapersonal communication, how our reading of images is very much a product of our experience. This, however, is not an expression of our individuality but of the discourses we have available to us; experience determines the types of discourse which constitute our personality. We can, however, consciously use discourses in our analysis of images. Once we have knowledge of a discourse then we can apply it to any text, even if we do not agree with the values expressed in that discourse.

Let us consider what discourses could be used in an analysis of the Nokia 232 advertisement (p. 40).

The Nokia 232 advertisement and discourse analysis

● *Middle-class values* As my analysis has already made clear, this is a lifestyle advertisement: buy the product, enjoy the lifestyle. This preferred reading is structured by the middle-class values which celebrate culture, wealth and the importance of image. Unless we understand the connotations of the copy ('unforgettable . . .'), the classical pillars, or the woman's looks, then we will not enter this discourse and thereby fail to make a dominant reading.

● *Marketing* From a commercial discourse this advertisement forms part of the 'marketing mix'. This mix consists of the product, price, distribution of the product, and publicity. Clearly advertising is part of publicity. Individuals who may use a commercial discourse are those with knowledge of marketing or who are also involved in selling the product advertised.

● *Photographic* The photographic discourse would deal, primarily, with the formal elements of the advertisement such as composition and lighting. The fact it is selling a product could be irrelevant.

● *Media Studies* Media studies is a combination of discourses. Clearly it uses at least part of the photographic discourse, in addition it employs semiotics and knowledge of advertising conventions.

● *Feminist* The discourse of feminism emphasizes the inequality between the sexes in society. Here the emphasis would be upon the portrayal of the woman as a sex object. This discourse would create an oppositional reading.

• *Psychoanalysis*   In brief, Freud suggested that the root of most human behaviour was motivated by the libido, or sexual desire. In analysing texts from a psychoanalytical perspective the emphasis is upon sex symbols. Unsurprisingly, advertising often yields much to this approach as the industry uses sex to sell anything. In the Nokia 232 advertisement the pillar becomes a phallic symbol (representing a penis) and thus the hand placed upon the object becomes much more significant. The problem, alluded to in Chapter 2's semiotic analysis, of using 'little' to sell to men becomes clear with the use of this discourse: having a little penis is not considered sexually attractive and so the large phallic pillar alleviates the negative connotations of the phone's size.

The walk, which in another reading suggested dynamism, now emphasizes the model's legs and the fact that they are apart. The woman's gaze becomes one of sexual desire. The 'lifestyle' advertising equation 'buy this product and get, or be, a woman like this' becomes explicitly sexual.

As a science, psychoanalysis has many critics. As a discourse for analysing media texts, however, it is immensely useful in bringing to the surface what may be latent. Whether you find it convincing depends upon you.

(This is not a comprehensive list of discourses that can be used to read the Nokia advertisement.)

◀ EXERCISE **4.8** ▶

Using any advertisement, write as many discourses as you can that would be appropriate in reading the text. What discourse does the advertisement invite you into (probably determined by 'metalanguage' and 'form')?

Discourse and jargon

The jargon used in discourses is particularly important. Jargon, at its worst, is elitist in that it serves to exclude the uninitiated. However, if the language of analysis is to escape the clutches of the dominant ideology (which it must do if we are to get a 'fuller picture') then words must be used which have connotations outside of the consensus.

The discourse of film studies has been guilty of obscuring more issues than it has illuminated. The problem for the theorist is that in creating a particular language for analysis, you are immediately excluding people who do not know that language. Often it appears that academia is speaking to one very select audience: itself. *Screen*, a magazine of film theory, in the 1970s, was guilty of such preaching to the converted. For example:

> A discursive formation, that is, exists as a component of an ideological formation itself based in particular conditions of production (ideological state apparatuses) and the terms of the discursive formation/ideological formation relation are those of subject and interpellation. (Heath, 1981, p. 102)

It is certainly unfair to quote out of context (and I am an admirer of Stephen Heath's work). However it is clear that unless you understand the concepts used, little communication will take place. It would be wrong, however, to criticize jargon *per se*; at best, it facilitates communication. For example, 'interpellation' is the way an individual is placed, by society, into a discourse: one word used instead of twelve. However, its use supposes a familiarity with the work of Louis Althusser.

It is debateable whether the use of jargon is important. Some believe that it is imperative that you use Media Studies jargon in your own work because it will make your analysis more incisive, and it may convince the examiner that you know what you are talking about; an opposing, and possibly more democratic, view suggests that if Media Studies is to reflect the experiences of the majority then jargon has little or no role, as it breeds elitism.

The consideration of discourse leads us directly to representation. Because discourse articulates an ideological position, it is giving us a particular and partial view of the world. Similarly, representation is the mediation of the world by a media text. What is emphasized and what is omitted in representation is determined by discourse, which is structured by ideology.

Before we proceed to representation (although much of what we have been talking about has been representation) we should consider another central idea of Media Studies: Gramsci's theory of hegemony.

4.9 Hegemony

As has been demonstrated, we do not have unadulterated access to reality, and our perception is influenced by the dominant ideological system. Both ideology and discourse are expressions of a society's power structures. Because there is an imbalance in the distribution of power in Western society (favouring the white, middle classes) clearly there must be groups who are subordinate (for example, the working classes and black people).

Antonio Gramsci, imprisoned for many years by Italian fascists, theorized, in the 1920s and 1930s, that the dominant classes do not wholly wield power through coercion; in fact their most powerful method is gaining the consent of the masses. Because the working classes did not feel particularly oppressed, they consented that the ruling classes should rule them. Gramsci described Western society as a hegemonic alliance between the rulers and their subordinates, in which the right of the dominant class to to rule is accepted.

In democracies political consent is gained through the ballot box. However, in many countries there are only two political parties – occasionally three – to choose from. Despite this apparent choice it is extremely rare for any party to offer a genuinely radical alternative to the consensus. Voters are then left only with a choice of consensus parties which, some would argue, is in fact no choice at all.

In Media Studies the concept of hegemony is useful in showing how, through images and texts, this consent to a dominant ideological position is won. For example, the position of women in western society is generally subordinate, even though legally in most countries they have equal rights. This subordination is, in part, created through the representation of gender in which men are seen to be powerful and dynamic, and women are weak and passive (we shall consider the representation of gender in the next chapter). Although, clearly, many do not agree with the way genders are conventionally represented, the predominance of such patriarchal representations are a powerful socializing agent. The subordination of women is an aspect of patriarchal bourgeois ideology, and hegemony naturalizes this ideological representation. (Hegemony is also useful in the analysis of institutions, though this is beyond the scope of this book.)

Another example of hegemonic representation is revealed by even a cursory examination of American crime television series or films. In many texts criminals are generally from ethnic minority groups and are usually working-class. The representation suggests that these groups are naturally degenerate and this reinforces their subordinate position. If representations of working-class, ethnic minority groups focused upon, say, poor educational opportunities or bad housing, then it is possible that more would be done to alleviate such conditions. As it is, because such groups appear to be degenerate, then their deprived social situation is justifiable.

Hegemony is an extremely powerful tool of social control because the distribution of power in society is often accepted as natural, as, in fact, 'common sense' (which, as we know, is not a natural construct). 'Common sense' should, in fact, be called the 'hegemonic sense'.

So the dominant classes do not merely control the coercive forces of society, such as the police, army and judiciary, but they also exercise cultural leadership. The values of the dominant classes become the norm through the conventions of representation used by mainstream media. It is through the media that the meanings which we use to make sense of our lives are often structured. However, no hegemony can be complete. Emerging ideologies may 'attack' the established order. These alternative discourses can be seen, too, in the media. As mentioned earlier, the developing awareness of 'green' issues is a potential threat to the dominant ideology, particularly if the argument that economic growth should be sacrificed in order to conserve resources gains currency.

Often, by necessity, alternative discourse use different modes of representation from the mainstream One of the most potent ways to break formally the norms of representation is through alternative systems of editing.

4.10 Alternative systems of editing

In Chapter 1 we considered how images in sequence are usually structured so the audience is not disorientated; this is the system of continuity editing. The rhetoric of this system is that it conceals its own construction so what we see appears natural; in fact, we tend not to see the joins between the images.

An alternative to this system could, of course, be to ignore all the rules completely; but this would not be an alternative system, it would be anarchy. In the continuity system the expressive possibilities of editing are usually subordinated to the narrative flow. However, occasionally the graphical relationships between shots are the structuring element. This is true, for example, in Busby Berkeley's Warner Bros. movies of the 1930s and in Leni Riefenstahl's Nazi propaganda piece *The Triumph of the Will* (*Triumph des Willens*) (1935), both of which will be considered in Chapter 5. Montage editing, which is non-classical in structure, also foregrounds the graphical relationships and this will be considered in the next section. (It should be noted that pre-Renaissance and non-Western systems of structuring images may appear alternative to

Western audiences now but are nevertheless conventional, so these systems appear natural to audiences who are used to these conventions.)

The rhythm of editing can also be used to expressive effect. The famous shower sequence in *Psycho* (1960) consists of 70 camera set-ups for 45 seconds of film. Audience disorientation is complete, even though we are aware that the location is the shower, as the frenzied attack is recreated in the 'violence' of the editing.

Because the creation of narrative space is the priority of classical editing, spatial discontinuity can be created by playing upon audience expectation of continuity and subverting it. In Dziga Vertov's *Man with a Movie Camera* (1929) a man's throw of the javelin is immediately followed by a shot of a goalkeeper diving to save . . . a football; our expectation is, of course, that the goalie is about to be pierced by a javelin. In *Un Chien Andalou* (*An Andalusian Dog*) (1928), a surrealist masterpiece created by Luis Buñuel and Salvador Dali, a character opens the door of a first floor flat and steps out on to a beach. The surreal quality of this is again created solely by their not fulfilling the audience's expectation of continuity editing .

Temporal discontinuity can be created by repeating the same event more than once. In *Blue Steel* (1989) the robber shot by the film's female hero is seen to smash through a supermarket window three times, an effect we do not expect to experience in a filmic text. However, the use of a 'slow-motion action replay', often part of the presentation of sporting events on television, has become a conventional part of 'real world' representation.

Other non-classical devices are the jump-cut and the non-diegetic insert.

- *A jump cut*, used to great effect by Jean-Luc Godard in his first film, *Breathless* (1960), breaks the conventions of graphical, temporal and spatial continuity. The two shots that make the cut are of the same subject, but there is little difference between them. Because the difference in the camera's position is small (less than the 30-degree rule) it is experienced more as a 'jump' rather than as a smooth transition.

- *A non-diegetic insert* is the use of images that are not part of the narrative space. For example, in Truffaut's *Tirez sur le pianiste* (*Shoot the Piano Player*) (1960), when a gangster swears on his mother's life that he is telling the truth, a non-diegetic insert shows an old woman suddenly keeling over.

It is unlikely that alternative modes of representation alone can motivate political change. However, what they can do is suggest alternative ways of viewing and discussing society and this *might* lead to political action.

These non-classical systems are often used in *avant-garde* films, whose object is often simply to disorientate the audience by suggesting the possibility of other ways of seeing. There is also alternative (defined stylistically rather than institutionally) cinema, which may use some, or all, of these alternative devices. During the 1920s Soviet cinema threw up a number of attempts to theorize alternatives to the bourgeois camera style which predominated. One of the more dominant theories was that of montage.

Montage

It is, of course, no coincidence that alternative modes of representation should have originated in the Soviet Union, which was opposed to bourgeois capitalism. Foremost among the theorists was Sergei Eisenstein, who used editing, rather than narrative, to structure his films.

Eisenstein's implicitly modernist project utilized montage, which he likened to the Japanese ideogram. His belief was that a montage of images would create a dramatic collision within the audience's perception to create a meaning based on conflict, thus representing a Marxist view of society rather than the consensus, bourgeois view. The dramatic collision would often be created by bizarre juxtapositions of shots, forcing the viewer to consider what they might mean.

In *A Dialectical Approach to Film Form* Eisenstein describes a sequence from the film *October* (1928) which he co-directed:

> Kornilov's march on Petrograd was under the banner of 'In the Name of God and Country.' Here we attempted to reveal the religious significance of this episode in a rationalistic way. A number of religious images, from a magnificent Baroque Christ to an Eskimo idol, are cut together. The conflict in this case was between the concept and the symbolization of God . . . a chain of images attempted to achieve a purely intellectual resolution, resulting from a conflict between a preconception and a gradual discrediting of it in purposeful steps. (Eisenstein, 1979, pp. 117–22)

It is likely that you will find this rather obscure, and if you see the film sequence itself you would probably find it difficult to read; this is because narrative has been subordinated to image, a sign system which we, in the West, are usually not familiar with.

My first experience of watching *October* was one of utter bewilderment (from a modernist viewpoint – see Chapter 5 – this made it very successful because I was completely aware I was watching a text); however it is doubtful if this is what Eisenstein had in mind. The difficulty in Eisenstein's films, for individuals in the West, is their non-conventionality; his cinema is in many ways the antithesis of Hollywood, which stands as the norm in our culture. Until we grow used to Eisenstein conventions, we will have difficulty reading his films.

To make matters worse for Western audiences, Eisenstein's films do not have characters to identify with. This absence is purposeful, for identification with individual, usually heroic, characters is a bourgeois notion. It is usual in Western texts for the main character to serve as the main motivator of the action, as well as a locus for audience identification.

Although Eisenstein attempted to create a film form that reflected Marxist ideology with its emphasis on conflict and the dialectical construction of meaning, it is pertinent to point out that his films were not particularly popular in the Soviet Union at the time. Conventional narrative film was still the box office favourite, with films like *Chapayev* (1934) in which it is very difficult not to identify with the charismatic hero of the title.

It was not until the French 'new wave' cinema of the 1960s that there was a more or less coherent theoretical agenda set out for Western alternative modes of representation. The politicized 'new wave' of the late 1960s, which was a response to the French student revolt of May 1968, was based, in a large part, upon the writings of Eisenstein and other Soviet theorists. The cinema of the politicised 'new wave' became known as *counter cinema.*

4.11 Counter cinema

Foremost among these 'new wave' film-makers was Jean-Luc Godard, who started his directing career, typically for 'new wave' directors, with an affectionate pastiche of a Hollywood genre in *A Bout de Souffle* (*Breathless*) (1960). He formed the Dziga-Vertov (named after the documentarist – see Chapter 4) group, which attempted to make political films in a collective (non-bourgeois) manner. Peter Wollen (1972) used one of these films, *Vent d'est* (*Wind from the East*) (1972), to categorize the basis of counter cinema, contrasted with what he called 'old cinema'.

Old Cinema	Counter Cinema
Narrative transitivity	Narrative intransitivity
Identification	Estrangement
Transparency	Foregrounding
Single Diegesis	Multiple diegesis
Closure	Aperture
Pleasure	Un-pleasure
Fiction	Reality

I will consider each of Wollen's categories, although some of the concept areas, such as narrative transitivity, belong in a companion volume.

Narrative transitivity versus intransitivity

• *Narrative transitivity* This refers to the conventional narrative structure which is at the heart of most Western narratives. Conventional narrative consists of an opening situation (*the thesis*) which is disrupted (*antithesis*) and ultimately resolved (*synthesis*). For example, in *Jurassic Park* the opening situation is a theme park inhabited by dinosaurs; the disruption is caused by them escaping from their confines, thus threatening the main characters; the situation is resolved by the characters' escape to safety and the likely closure of the park. The resolved situation is usually very like the opening one except the characters have been transformed, for the better, by their experiences. Heterosexual love is usually consumated as a by-product of the narrative, although this consummation wasn't required in *Jurassic Park,* as the main adult protagonists were already married.

The narrative disruption in television series, which have a new narrative each week but the same setting and characters, is usually resolved by everything returning to the original situation, so that it can start again from exactly the same position in the next episode.

Within conventional narrative, everything that happens within the world created by the narrative, the diegesis, contributes in some way to the development of the narrative; nothing is redundant. In *Groundhog Day* (1993) the apparently meaningless conversation that Bill Murray has when leaving his bedroom is given significance later when he relives the experience.

• *Narrative intransitivity* You will not be surprised to learn that this is the opposite of narrative transitivity. Counter cinema interrupts narrative flow with digressions and irrelevances which serve to prevent the audience getting 'caught up' within the narrative development. As Wollen says in his article: '[Counter cinema] is within the modern[ist] tradition established by Brecht and Artaud, [who were] in their different ways, suspicious of the power of the arts – and the cinema, above all – to "capture" its audience without apparently making it think, or changing it.'

Identification versus estrangement

Most fictional texts offer the audience a character with whom to identify; in cinema this is very often a star. Counter cinema attempts to prevent this by using distancing techniques such as introducing real people into the diegesis. For example, although Godard did use film stars, he represented them as 'stars' rather than 'stars playing characters'. In this way the audience is made conscious of the constructed nature of the text. In *Tout va Bien* (1972) we are reminded right from the beginning that Jane Fonda is a film star playing a role in a film, whereas in most of her Hollywood movies we are invited to sympathize with her character's predicament.

Again this is a Brechtian technique meant to distance the audience from the text and so prevent any emotional catharsis.

Transparency versus foregrounding

The conventional system of continuity editing strives to hide its operation; counter cinema foregrounds the technique by simply ignoring the 180-degree rule. Once the convention is subverted it becomes noticeable; it is foregrounded.

The camera style of bourgeois cinema also signifies transparency. Taking its cue from Renaissance perspective, described at the end of this chapter, cinema creates an illusion of depth and allows us, by taking different views of objects, to gain a sense of perspective.

However, as Brian Henderson (in Nichols (ed.), 1976) demonstrates, counter cinema attempts to employ a 'non-bourgeois camera style'. It can do this by denying the audience a rich and beautiful image and by flattening perspective within the frame, which emphasizes its two-dimensional nature.

Single diegesis versus multiple diegesis

The narrative world of conventional cinema is a unified place with consistent rules. These usually reflect those of the 'real world' but can also create fantasy worlds as long as they abide by their own stated rules.

In counter cinema the sanctity of the narrative diegesis can be broken at will. For example, showing the film being edited introduces, to an extent, the 'real world' into the filmic world.

Closure versus aperture

The meaning of conventional cinema is contained wholly within the text. Counter cinema, however, can produce meaning through allusion to other texts; indeed knowledge of other texts may be essential for any meaning to be generated at all.

Pleasure versus un-pleasure

Conventional cinema aims to entertain (and thereby generate profit for its makers). Counter cinema aims to make the audience think. All the categories described so far serve, in counter cinema, to alienate the audience, to deny them entertainment, to make them think and, ultimately, to change them.

Counter cinema takes its definition of art from the formalists, who believed art's function was to 'make strange' the world. The world of conventional cinema is a familiar place; even in alien settings there are good and bad guys, and maidens in distress who need that particular man to come to the rescue. The world of counter cinema is ambiguous, it eschews conventional representations and entertainment.

Fiction versus reality

In conventional cinema the fictional world is created as if it were real. BBC television's period dramas are renowned for an attention to detail that signs itself as being 'as it really was'. This is, of course, an illusion; it is a representation. Counter cinema consciously deals with representations and informs its audience of the fact. The belief is that by demonstrating to the audience that it is seeing a representation (showing actors applying make-up, for example), truth is, in some way, being shown.

Wollen demonstrated that counter cinema has its own rules, its own mode of representation in fact, defined by its opposition to conventional cinema.

During the 1970s counter cinema flourished, funded in Britain by the British Film Institute (because of its non-commercial nature many of these oppositional, alternative texts were funded by public money). This source tended to dry up during the 1980s as 'market forces' took over. Inevitably, any text that sets out to create, say, un-pleasure in its audience can only hope to address a small coterie (of masochists?). It is no accident that oppositional texts tend to disappear once commercial logic holds sway, since it is this very logic that these texts oppose.

However, there are numerous alternative texts worth investigating and many of the 1960s and 1970s classics are becoming available on videotape. What follows is a brief consideration of *Tout va Bien* as counter cinema.

Tout va Bien *(1972)*

Tout va Bien was written and directed by Jean-Luc Godard and Jean-Pierre Gorin. It is a fascinating, if difficult, text which deals with the role of the film-maker and intellectual in post-May 1968 France; the significance of May 1968 is described in the next chapter.

The film's opening sequence clearly defines itself as counter cinema in a number of ways. During the titles a clapper-board, and the film's title, is heard continually: we are not going to be allowed to forget we are watching a film called *Tout va Bien*. There follows a voice-over dialogue, between a man and a woman, concerning the requirements of film-making:

> *Man*: 'I want to make a movie.'
> *Woman*: 'That takes money.'
> (sequence of cheques being signed for *Tout va Bien*)
> *W*: 'If we have stars, we'll get money.'
> *M*: 'Okay, we'll have stars.'
> *W*: 'What are you going to tell Montand and Fonda? An actor won't accept a part without a storyline.'
> *M*: 'A storyline?'
> *W*: 'Yeah, usually a love story.'

The institutional basis of film-making is immediately revealed, the fact we are dealing with fiction rather than reality is emphasized. Without money there is no film; without stars there is no money; without a love story there are no stars: it seems the only stories that can be told are love stories, and that is not far from the truth.

Yves Montand and Jane Fonda were big box office attractions in the 1970s and their appearance in a counter-cinema text may well be unique; film stars are usually only found in narrative cinema. Both Montand and Fonda appeared in the film because of their 'left of centre' political convictions. Their presence allowed money – as the dialogue said – to be raised to make the film.

Following the dialogue we see Montand and Fonda, as Jacques and Susan, walking along a river bank talking lovingly to one another. Correction: we see them walking along the same river bank twice, although their voices do not suggest this discontinuity. The editing process is foregrounded, we see the same event twice, although the dialogue suggests it only happened once.

Godard and Gorin do provide us with the love story, against the backdrop of industrial strife in France. Parallels are drawn between Jacques' and Susan's personal and professional crises; he makes advertisements, she is a reporter.

The man and woman's dialogue later explains: 'we shall see farmers, farming, the workers, working; and the middle-class, middle-classing'. Narrative is not hidden as an invisible structuring device, but highlighted, emphasizing the text's narrative intransitivity.

Having a relatively large budget allowed Godard and Gorin to work in a studio. The set for the factory sit-in is a *tour de force:* a tracking-shot takes us from one room to the next and the building is ultimately revealed to be without a 'fourth' wall – this has allowed us to see inside; once again the mechanics of cinema are foregrounded.

The use of film stars immediately sets up the possibility of identification, something which is antithetical to counter cinema. However, we are, at least momentarily, estranged from this by seeing both stars working in the sausage factory when workers explain the poor conditions they have to suffer: stars do not work in factories.

Both management and union leaders engage with the camera in long monologues which, while they wittily satirize both groups, are boring in content; unpleasure is felt!

If you attempted to watch *Tout va Bien* without thinking about the film, then you would probably only experience boredom, despite some fascinating sequences like the interminable tracking shot in the supermarket toward the end of the film. Counter cinema insists that its audience thinks; not to do so leads to a failure to read the text.

It is appropriate, at this point, to give a brief 'history of images' or more accurately, a 'history of western images'. This has two uses:

1. all images have histories which contribute to their meaning
2. when we are analysing images from the past we need to be aware of the codes current at the time of the text's creation; they may well have had very different meanings to contemporary audiences.

This history demonstrates how different world views, or ideologies, lead to different media languages, or modes of representation. As we shall see, the mainstream conventions of the past can be alternative modes of representation.

When we analyse historical images we can create numerous readings: one that was extant when the image was produced (as far as we can ascertain without a time machine); the modern reading; and, possibly, a series of readings from the intervening years. Which of these readings is correct? The following intends to show you that none and all of them are correct.

4.12 A history of Western images

In December 1994, a speleologist discovered a rich hoard of 18 000-year-old cave paintings in the Ardèche, France. These examples of early naturalistic art suggest that images are as much a fundamental part of the human psyche as storytelling. What their spiritual significance was may be answered over the next 30 years as the Ardeche caves are examined; however, we are so distant from these senders that it is difficult to draw conclusions with any certainty. Despite this it is likely that the subject matter, which often consists of beasts which were hunted for food, helped prehistoric humanity to contemplate this crucial task while at rest. (The fact that we do not put images of the local supermarket on our walls suggests that obtaining food is a lot easier now, at least for the more privileged people of this planet.)

It is unlikely that the prehistoric artists imagined that we, thousands of years in their future, would one day be the receivers of these images. Millennia have elapsed since primitive times, and our plethora of cultural artefacts means that we would appear alien to our ancestors. However, with the benefit of history, they would not appear alien to us; we know that, in some way, they are related to us.

Eygptian painting

The Sphinx and pyramids of Egypt are staple tourist attractions. Both, of course, are probably familiar to most of us as images of ancient artefacts. The Western world is probably more familiar with ancient Egyptian culture than it is with modern Egypt, possibly because of the Tutankhamun curse and exhibitions, the regular appearance of the Egyptian mummy in horror movies, and the legend of *Cleopatra* (fostered by Shakespeare's play and one of the most expensive films ever made, the eponymous financial disaster of 1963, starring Elizabeth Taylor).

◀ Exercise 4.9 ▶

Before reading on, find examples of Egyptian art (a good encyclopedia should suffice) and analyse the images. Try to determine what, today, is unconventional about ancient Egyptian images.

You have probably concluded that Egyptian art is non-naturalistic because human beings look strange. Wrong. The ancient Egyptian mode of representation is simply different from our own. Heads were shown in profile; eyes from the front, as was the torso; and arms and legs were shown from the side. The ancient Egyptians were not a deformed race; their mode of representation in the visual arts was to portray different parts of objects from their most characteristic or recognizable angle. This makes sense when we realize that, potentially, we can get much more information from this representation than we can from what appears to us to be a naturalistic perspective.

Greek painting

The ancient Greeks had an idealist view of the world. This means that they represented the world as if it consisted of ideal types, rather than as it actually was. This is similar to the idea, mentioned in Chapter 2, that everybody possesses mental concepts of objects. This idea was articulated by the ancient Greek philosopher Plato. Greek landscape painting was not, as a consequence, interested in the actual environment:

> In the Hellenistic period . . . artists . . . tried to conjure up the pleasures of the countryside . . . These paintings are not actual views of particular country houses or beauty-spots. They are rather a collection of everything which makes up an idyllic scene. (Gombrich, 1989, pp. 77–8)

What was important, for the Greeks, was not a realistic portrayal of the place but the representation of it as an ideal; in this case, the idyllic countryside. It was not even necessary for Grecian artists to visit the place they were representing, and any attempt to draw a map of the area represented is doomed to failure. The idea of a place is portrayed, and this idea is the pictorial equivalent of an individual's mental concept.

This convention was not due wholly to the Greeks' world view. A visual representation of the world as individual human beings might see it could not be created until the mathematical laws that govern perspective were understood. It is probable that the reason the Greeks had an idealistic view of the world was precisely that they did not understand these laws.

Painting in the pre-capitalist era

The pre-capitalist period of history is characterized by a strict class system in which the king (occasionally queen) is subordinate only to God – or to God's representative on earth, the pope. Beneath them in the hierarchy were royalty, representatives of the Church, the land-owners and, at the bottom, the peasantry. The system was strict, with no social mobility (except through the Church).

In the feudal world the dominant view was religious, and placed the Earth at the centre of the universe, God in heaven and Satan in hell. This is a particularly conservative view, which effectively makes society unchangeable; in contrast to this, the modern sense of history is one of progress through time. In feudal times, however, progress was not thought possible, for the world had already attained the best possible state. As in Greek painting, we find that this world view, or ideology, is reflected and expressed in feudal painting.

For example, the size of a person in a painting represented not their size relative to other people in the painting, but their importance in the hierarchy. In his fascinating *The Story of Art*, E. H. Gombrich (1989, p. 147) described 'The Entombment of Christ' from a thirteenth century Psalter:

> The expression of intense feeling, and this regular distribution of figures on the page, were obviously more important the artist than any attempt to make his figures lifelike, or to represent a real scene. He does not mind that the servants are smaller than the holy personages, and he does not give any indication of the place or the setting.

Servants were smaller because they were less important than Christ, and not because they were midgets. As in Greek art, the sense of place was irrelevant, because time and place are not important in a world view that denies change. (In fact, despite appearing completely natural to us, the detailed organization of time did not become important until inter-continental trading began. In order to navigate, ships used the sun by day and the stars at night. Because the sun's and stars' positions vary throughout the year, and are dependent on where you are on the globe, it became necessary to know the exact time in order to work out your exact position.)

It wasn't until the development of capitalism (money-lending and business) in Venice in the fifteenth century that a new world view, that of what is called the bourgeoisie, began to supplant feudalism.

This is not the place in which to try to draw together the historical strands that led to the development of the bourgeois world view which dominates the Western world today. It is sufficient, for our purposes, to to say that the Renaissance, when the 'lost' learning of ancient civilizations was discovered by the Western world in Constantinople, was partly a cause and partly an effect of the development of bourgeois dominance.

Renaissance painting

The bourgeois world view is centred upon the progress of the individual. In feudal times it was virtually impossible for individuals to live a life other than the one they were born into; in a bourgeois society, although accidents of birth are still very influential, social mobility is possible, and this is usually determined by wealth.

Once again the expression of this world view can be found in the work of artists from that era, and because of the emphasis on the individual it was necessary that painting create an individual perspective from which to view the world. The 'multi-angled' views of Egyptian art, the ideal types of Greece, and the symbolism of the feudal era are all inappropriate to a world where the individual's position at a particular time, and in a particular place, are the defining factors.

In the wealthy, merchant city of Florence, in the early years of the fifteenth century, Filippo Brunelleschi discovered the mathematical means of creating perspective. For the first time, a two-dimensional plane could look like three-dimensional space, the illusion of depth was created, and the painting began to look like a 'window on the world'.

Ironically, although Renaissance painting's verisimilitude give the impression that we can look at people and scenes from the past exactly as they appeared at the time, in fact this is an illusion, created by the artifice of the artists.

The conventions of ancient Egypt and Greece are obviously representations to modern eyes. However at the time of their creation the conventions were as 'invisible' to audiences as contemporary conventions are to us. Although images using the Renaissance perspective, also called the Quattrocento perspective, appear to be three-dimensional, in reality, of course, they are not:

> The conception of the Quattrocento system is that of a scenographic space, space set out as spectacle for the eye of a spectator. Eye and knowledge come together; subject, object and the distance for the steady observation that allows the one to master the other. (Heath, 1981, p. 30)

This coming together of 'eye and knowledge' is crucial to the understanding of the modern, bourgeois conception of representation. Knowledge is, literally, in the eye of the beholder, and the beholder is an individual, 'I'.

So Quattrocento perspective is determined neither by the inflexible sense of order that characterized feudal painting nor the idealism of the Greeks. It addresses the individual spectator, and was part of the change in representational conventions which were, in turn, part of the emergent bourgeois ideology that was starting to 'see off' the old feudal ideology.

It is grossly over-simplifying the history of images to leap across a few periods of history and conveniently forget what lies in between. However, we are discussing Media Studies and not Art History, so we bridge 400 years to the creation of photography.

Photography

As Walter Benjamin (1979, p. 851), in his seminal essay 'The Work of Art in the Age of Mechanical Reproduction', says: 'the presence of the original is the prerequisite to the concept of authenticity'.[15] In the age of mechanical reproduction, however, there is no guarantee of authenticity; everything might be a copy, at least to the untutored eye. Mechanical reproduction, then, changed the way people looked at artefacts.

Benjamin saw this lack of authenticity as wholly liberating because it means the 'aura' of the original is eliminated. People are free to examine artefacts in their own particular context, and artefacts of great cultural value are accessible not only to the elite, but to a much wider audience.

Paradoxically, while mechanical reproduction, in Benjamin's terms, destroyed the authenticity of art, in other ways it seemed to guarantee authenticity. With the invention of the camera it appeared, for the first time, that reality could be reproduced without the intervention of human subjectivity, hence the notion that 'the camera never lies'. (Writing had been mechanically reproduced since Gutenberg's printing press, but the meaning generated by words, which are wholly symbolic, is not influenced to any significant degree by what the letters look like.)

Early daguerreotypes, the name given to photographs by the French inventor Daguerre, were of very poor quality compared to those produced by modern technology. Exposure, which took minutes rather than fractions of a second, created images that were almost surreal in character. If moving figures were present during the exposure these would probably not appear at all, and even as technology progressed they would appear only as ghost-like figures, as if super-imposed upon the background.

In fact these early photographs inspired the use of Impressionist painting, a form we hardly regard as 'realistic' today. Aaron Scharf, in his interesting *Art and Photography* (1983, p. 172), demonstrates how the painters Corot and Monet 'represented their subjects, not as the eye would see them but as they might be recorded by the camera'. It is ironic that Impressionism, which is the subjective impression of reality based upon a *mélange* of colours, should be inspired by a mechanical apparatus which common sense still deems objective.

Photographs were also used by artists as an aid to more traditional forms of painting; Courbet, for example, used photographs as the basis for some of his paintings. It is obviously far easier to take a photograph of a scene into a studio than to take the easel and palette outdoors, where the artist is at the mercy of the weather.

Photography did also inspire the use of 'realist' subjects in painting. It was conventional in nineteenth-century paintings to concentrate on 'worthy' subjects which meant, in essence, middle-class people and settings. The advent of photography legitimized the use of virtually anything as a suitable subject, including what was seen as the seedier (working-class) side of life. Such paintings were often derided by the art establishment as daguerreotypes.

As we shall see in Chapter 5, which considers the history of realism in the art of the Western world, mainstream art has a mimetic function, that is, it mirrors life. With the invention of photography it appeared, for the first time, that reality could be represented using technology rather than being 'processed' through the consciousness of the individual, and therefore subjective, artist. This objectivity is illusory, as will be demonstrated in Chapter 6.

Photography appeared to have a privileged access to reality because of its iconic nature (see Chapter 2). Cinema had even greater claims for verisimilitude for, as early film theorist Siegfried Kracauer (1979, p. 7) put it, '[cinema] satisf[ied] at last the age-old desire to picture things moving'.[18]

While Kracauer believed the mechanical aspect of cinema allowed it to fulfil the project of realism, André Bazin (1967, p. 15), an influential theorist who founded the important film journal *Cahiers du Cinéma*, believed the photograph created a metaphysical realism:

> The aesthetic qualities of photography are to be sought in its power to lay bare the realities. It is not for me to separate off, in the complex fabric of the objective world, here a reflection on a damp sidewalk, there the gesture of a child. Only an impassive lens, stripping its object of all those ways of seeing it, those piled-up preconceptions, that spiritual dust and grime with which my eyes have covered it, is able to present it in all its virginal purity to my attention and consequently to my love.

Both Kracauer's and Bazin's views are now only interesting for their historical significance. Neither takes account of the 'world view', or ideology, that constructed the images in the first place or the ideological basis of any readings made of those images.

All images are representations and, as we have seen, one can only fully analyse representations by deconstructing the ideological basis of the artefact as well as the ideological basis of the audiences's reading of the artefact.

It may seem that the history of images up until this point has been the gradual development towards the 'window on the world' which cinema and photography appeared to be uniquely placed to provide. However, in the mid-nineteenth century the glass started to become blurred by Impressionism, and was later shattered by Cubism.

In some ways Cubism is a return to the Egyptian aesthetic, for it acknowledges that paintings are created on a two-dimensional surface and therefore three-dimensional objects have to be 'opened out' in order for us to 'genuinely' see more than one aspect of the image's contents. This shattering of perspective was particularly suited to the *Zeitgeist* of the years following the First World War and is considered, along with Modernism, in Chapter 5. Recent technological developments, such as virtual reality, are featured in Chapter 6.

Despite the fragmentation of perspective by Cubism as part of the Modernist aesthetic, mainstream conventions are little changed from those of the Renaissance, a tribute to the durability of the bourgeois world view that portrays itself as 'natural'. It seems obvious to us that representations of objects should look like the objects that are portrayed, but this belief ignores, of course, that what was obvious in ancient Egypt, Greece, and in the medieval era, now looks peculiar to us. Similarly, our ancestors would be confused by images that appear normal to us.

What should be clearer now is that a historical, or diachronic, investigation of images shows (to a degree – the further back into the past we go the hazier our knowledge usually becomes) that the way an image's codes are a product of a particular era and society. While it is not necessary for us to know the original meaning of these codes in order to make a reading of the image, knowledge certainly adds to our understanding. We can still analyse historical images synchronically, without historical knowledge, and create a meaning, but our analysis of historical images is more powerful if we have some idea about their cultural background.

5

REPRESENTATION

5.1 Introduction

The first three chapters considered media language with a particular emphasis on images. Language must obviously convey something and that something is always, in one form or another, a representation. It will soon be clear that much of the previous chapter has been concerned with representation.

This chapter uses Richard Dyer's typography of representation but, you will no doubt be pleased to learn, there is less theory; the emphasis is on examples and case studies.

5.2 Dyer's typography

In his essay *Taking Popular Television Seriously* (ed. Lusted and Drummond, 1985) Richard Dyer describes a typography of representation:

1. *re-presentation* – this consists essentially of media language, the conventions which are used to represent the world to the audience;
2. being representative of – the extent to which types are used to represent social groups – this is dealt with here in a consideration of stereotypes;
3. *who is responsible for the representation, how the institution creating a media text influences representation* – this is particularly contentious in the representation of gender, as it is often men who are doing the representing;
4. *what does the audience think is being represented to them* – as we saw in our investigation of preferred readings, audiences can make different readings of media texts from the one offered.

This chapter will consider each of these types in some detail; although the second and fourth categories will be dealt with more fully in *Institution and Audience*.

5.3 Re-presentation

As we learned in the earlier chapters, meaning is communicated by conventions. Different media may have different conventions; television will use sound and image codes, while radio is limited to sound. However, many texts, particularly generic texts, have their own conventions which are used regardless of the medium; soap operas have specific conventions of narrative and character representation which hold true whether on radio or television.

Formal conventions are also transferable across media. All mainstream audio-visual texts use the rules of continuity editing outlined in Chapter 1.

In our consideration of image analysis we have concentrated on the tools of analysis, and it is through the application of these tools that we can understand the text's re-presentation of its subject matter, or referent.

Certain objects, and individuals, carry specific connotations. As we shall see below, in our discussion of stereotypes, we learn to associate signs with particular meanings; for example a feather alongside a bow and arrow is likely to connote the native North American. In Peirce's terms, these objects are an index of the 'Indians'.

Individuals, too, have associations which most people of a particular culture know. The President of the USA, for example, whoever he or she is, possesses connotations of power and world leadership. Both the inanimate object and human being are obviously signs, and signs which have specific connotations, or second order signifying systems (described in Chapter 2), when part of a media text, can act as iconography. The red rose discussed in the chapter on semiotics is an icon of romance; it is important, though, not to confuse this form of icon with Peirce's definition; iconography is an index.

In fictional texts, iconography can be used to signify a genre (the Western's ten-gallon hat, revolvers, saloons, sheriff's badges and so on). Certain actors can become associated with a particular genre, just as John Wayne and Clint Eastwood have become icons of the Western (though obviously they have appeared in other types of film).

Iconography is mostly powerfully used in genre texts and will be considered in detail in *Narrative and Genre*. Its use in stereotypes is dealt with in the next section.

Analyse a number of photographs of yourself (contemporary & from the past) and decide whether they are an accurate re-presentation of yourself. If you are doing this exercise in groups, discuss whether you feel other people's photographs are an accurate re-presentation of them. If you are unhappy with the re-presentation of yourself, attempt to re-present yourself using any means available.

5.4 Types and stereotypes

Types

The use of character types has a long history, particularly in literature, which is considered in the next chapter. Types are characters who are defined by what they represent rather than being genuine individuals. The type is signified by an actor's appearance and behaviour and, unlike the stereotype, does not exist in the real world.

Erwin Panfosky (1979, p. 254) described the types derived from the theatre, which were used in early cinema:

> the Vamp and the Straight Girl . . ., the Family Man, and the Villain, the latter marked by a black mustache and walking stick . . . A checkered table cloth meant . . . a 'poor but honest' milieu.

Types were particularly useful in early cinema, which could not use dialogue to establish character and setting. However, the types described above are still recognizable today (although we would perceive the early representations as being crude). In *film noir*, for example, the Vamp becomes the *femme fatale*, often in the pay of the Villain, who takes the Family Man away from the Straight Girl.

Types do not conform to the bourgeois notion of character (which will be described later), they are too simplistic. Stereotypes, on the other hand, offer a more sophisticated shorthand about characters and people in the real world.

Stereotypes

◀ Exercise 5.2 ▶

Write down a list of images and ideas you associate with contemporary New York; then write down everything you can think of about students, and compare your lists with someone else's.

It is likely that your list for New York will include some or all of the following: skyscrapers; yellow cabs; crime; exciting; dirty; poor; rich; violent . . . It is also probable that your construction of this stereotype is not affected by whether or not you have been to New York.

The list you have drawn up about students, however, may differ greatly from the dominant student stereotype, which states that students are: lazy (they stay in bed as late as possible); sexually promiscuous; into soft and hard drugs; dress scruffily; poor; and politically (trendy) left-wing. As you are almost certainly a student you will know that this stereotype is – mainly – untrue. (There is also a stereotype for the 'swotty student' or boffin-type.)

Figure 5.1 is a spread from a media education magazine, *in the picture*, where the editor gave Media Studies students an opportunity to represent themselves. Compare their portrayal with your own: does theirs 'ring true'?

So stereotypes are very common; so common that even the concept of 'stereotype' itself has a stereotype. Tessa Perkins, in 'Rethinking Stereotypes', described the assumptions many people hold about stereotypes, which are that:

1. stereotypes are always erroneous in content;
2. they are pejorative concepts;
3. they are about groups with whom we have little or no social contact; by implication, therefore, they are not held about one's own group;
4. they are about minority (or oppressed) groups;
5. they are simple;
6. they are rigid and do not change;
7. they are not structurally reinforced; . . .
8. the existence of contradictory stereotypes is evidence that they are erroneous, but of nothing else;
9. people either 'hold' stereotypes of a group (believe them to be true) or do not;

10. because someone holds a stereotype of a group, his or her behaviour towards a member of that group can be predicted.

Interestingly, even those of us who possess this stereotype of stereotypes still use them, because they are such an integral way of making meaning in society. Stereotypes are an invaluable aid to understanding the world and all stereotypes must have, in Perkins' terms, 'a kernel of truth'; or they would not have such an influence on our lives. (Truth is not a straightforward concept; it is probably more correct to say that it is necessary that stereotypes 'appear', in the eye of the beholder, to have a 'kernel of truth'.)

Although the media has a very strong influence on the dissemination of stereotypes, it must be remembered that they were not created by the media, they are concepts which are part of everyday life. Walter Lippmann defined the idea of stereotypes in 1922; in *A Matter of Images* (1993) Richard Dyer described four functions of Lippmann's definition, which are:

- an ordering process;
- a 'short cut';
- a way of referring to 'the world';
- an expression of 'our' values and beliefs.

- *An ordering process*   Just as human beings' senses filter out much of what they perceive, stereotypes serve to order our reality in an easy-to-understand form, and are an essential part of making sense of the world and society. The fact that stereotypes offer an incomplete view of the world does not necessarily make them false; there is, anyway, no such thing as a complete view of the world. Having stereotypical knowledge about New York is more useful for audiences watching a news story about the city or a feature film set there, than having no knowledge at all.

- *Short cuts*   Because they are simplifications, stereotypes act as 'short cuts' to meaning. We can characterize New York in a dozen words which will be sufficient for most purposes. We do not, for example, need to research the city thoroughly to understand, say, *NYPD Blue*.

Although stereotypes are a short cut, they can still give us more than just a basic knowledge of the subject being typified. For example, although a 'macho man' is defined primarily by his physical strength, we also learn from the stereotype that such men

features

identity

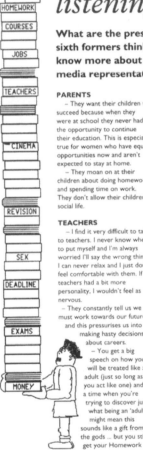

All we need is a good listening to

What are the pressures of being a student? Hanson School sixth formers think that parents, teachers and friends need to know more about the students they pressurise and that the media representation of students is inaccurate.

PARENTS

– They want their children to succeed because when they were at school they never had the opportunity to continue their education. This is especially true for women who have equal opportunities now and aren't expected to stay at home.

– They moan on at their children about doing homework and spending time on work. They don't allow their children a social life.

TEACHERS

– I find it very difficult to talk to teachers. I never know where to put myself and I'm always worried I'll say the wrong thing. I can never relax and I just don't feel comfortable with them. If teachers had a bit more personality, I wouldn't feel as nervous.

– They constantly tell us we must work towards our futures and this pressurises us into making hasty decisions about careers.

– You get a big speech on how you will be treated like an adult (just so long as you act like one) and at a time when you're trying to discover just what being an 'adult' might mean this sounds like a gift from the gods ... but you still get your Homework

Journal checked and it seems that some teachers can't make the adjustment from GCSE to A Level themselves.

– They seem to think that their's is the only subject we take. They don't seem to realise that it all adds up to a heavy workload.

FRIENDS

– "Can I see you tonight?" "But I've got an essay to finish"

– Girls are under more pressure than boys. Boys put on the pressure in a relationship, to have sex when the girl isn't ready, to deny that she is "seeing someone else". But most of all students have to decide on how often they can afford the time to see a boyfriend or girlfriend.

MEDIA

– They portray students as typical, naive teenagers. We want to be treated as individuals rather than classed as a group. We want to develop our own independence rather than be limited in the freedom we possess.

– Newspapers don't promote the image of the student constructively. The reports show students as joyriders, drug abusers and suicide cases. In reality students need to be self-motivated,

independent, reliable and able to cope under pressure. Crucially they need part-time jobs to help finance themselves, proving skills in time management as well.

Figure 5.1

An easy life or a hard road?

In the media, especially the popular press, students have a rough time. The only way to achieve a good image for a student seems to be to commit suicide or arrive at some other horrible fate, whereupon they are commended and become the hardest working, greatest achieving student in the world. For those less fortunate there is the media image of the drug taking, drink crazed idiot who fits his work in between having a good time. We show you both sides of student life, judge for yourself which is nearer the truth...

THE MEDIA PORTRAYED STUDENT?

THE REAL STUDENT?

STUDENT 1

Media Portrayed Student?

6.00 a.m. Arrive home from party totally smashed out of my skull. Smoke a joint and then go to bed.

11.50 a.m. Get up to go to crappy 11.00 Lecture.

12.00 p.m. Arrive at lecture, get out pen and pad and go back to sleep due to terrible hangover.

3.00 p.m. Lecture ends. The bell wakes me up. Photocopy Swotty's notes and go home.

3.20 p.m. Arrive home and write essay on the meaning of life.

3.30 p.m. Make tea.

4.00 p.m. Go to chippy.

5.10 p.m. Watch Home and Away and Neighbours – purely for educational reasons.

6.00 p.m. Ring friends and arrange to meet outside Duck and Bucket. Hang clothes out of window ready to wear later.

9.00 p.m. Get to pub. Buy friend a half, lace it with laxatives for a joke. Friend is violently sick.

10.00 p.m. Gatecrash party and get off with cute girl. Leave her alone when I see her boyfriend.

12.00 a.m. Go to all night rave. Buy a couple of Es to get the party going.

6.00 a.m. Arrive home smashed out of skull. Smoke a joint and go to bed.

STUDENT 2

The Real Life Student?

6.00 a.m. Get up and start getting ready for uni. Maybe do a little work on my essay if there is time.

7.00 a.m. Set off for lecture as the only accommodation I could get is miles away.

8.30 a.m. Arrive and prepare myself for lecture. Skip breakfast and put money towards a pushbike to get me here quicker.

9.00 a.m. Lecture starts. Write copious notes but still not sure I've got everything.

12.00 p.m. Can't afford a proper dinner, salad will have to do.

1.00 p.m. Go to another couple of lectures.

5.00 p.m. Set off to go to my job in a bar as it is easier to get there than to get home.

6.00 p.m. Arrive at work-place and start writing essay. Skip tea which I can't afford and don't have time for.

8.00 p.m. Start pulling pints.

12.00 a.m. Arrive home and get back to writing essay. Go to bed when I have finished.

6.00 a.m. Get up and prepare for uni.

13

are of below average intelligence, have a 'neanderthal' attitude toward women, possess conservative views, and are sexually attractive. To adapt Perkins, the stereotype also refers immediately to his sex, which refers to his status in society, his relationship with women, his inability to think, as well as to men who are not macho. The simple two words 'macho man' are a short cut to a more complex set of assumptions that reflect society's values. As Perkins (1979, p. 139) says, 'stereotypes are simple and complex'.

One of the most powerful 'short cuts' to meaning is stereotypes' use of iconography. For example, yellow cabs are in New York; red buses in London; an intellectual wears spectacles and so on. (Iconography should not be confused with Peirce's definition of an icon; iconography is, in fact, an example of Peirce's indexes – see Chapter 2.) Iconography will be dealt with more fully at the end of this chapter.

- *Refer to the world*   Stereotypes have their origin in the real world. They are social constructs and, as such, are a type of re-presentation. However, stereotypes are also used in fictive texts; stereotypes in fiction are not just social constructs, they are also aesthetic in nature.

When discussing fiction, stereotypes are often contrasted with the novelistic character, or, in E.M. Forster's terms, 'flat' versus 'round' characters. 'Flat' characters are not strictly stereotypes in Forster's description (1976, p. 73): 'In their purest form, they are constructed round a single idea or quality.' Novelistic characters have a greater aesthetic value in Western society because they are seen as more 'true to life', more rounded, than stereotypes. 'Novelistic' characters, which can obviously appear in any fictional text, are considered in the next chapter.

Stereotypes become consensus views, otherwise they could not work as stereotypes. However, we must ask where these views originate, as they could hardly spring up simultaneously among members of the population. Stereotypes are most often used by individuals about people, or peoples, they do not know. It follows, then, that they must have received this stereotype from others. The media, in its various forms, is one of the main sources of information and it is very likely that it is a crucial influence in stereotyping. For example, it is probable that the reported perception that a large proportion of black people is involved in crime is derived, in part, from Hollywood and American television programmes. In fact, suppressed Home Office research has shown that, as a proportion of the population, black people in Britain are less likely to be criminal than are white people.

We have acknowledged that stereotypes have their basis in the material conditions and social practices of society, so it should come as no surprise that stereotypes are an expression of the dominant ideology. Stereotypes serve to naturalize the power relationships in society; they have a hegemonic function, so the fact that women are often stereotyped as subservient to men – whether as 'dumb blondes' (see below) or housewives – legitimizes their inferior position. In this way the importance of the difficult and time-consuming work of running a household is diminished because it is women's work; and women are diminished because they do housework.

Stereotypes are not true or false, but reflect a particular set of ideological values. They are, in fact, mythic (in Barthes' sense) figures, representing social values in a concise fashion. The degree to which a stereotype is accepted as being 'true' or not is dependent upon an individual's knowledge of the group in question.

• *The expression of values* Stereotypes are only effective if they are believed to be a view of a group which has a consensus. Of course, as many of the people who hold the stereotype actually derived their view *from* the stereotype, then the consensus is more imagined than real. Despite this, much of the power of stereotypes exists because they appear to have the status of consensus. What stereo-types represent, however, are not the beliefs based upon reality but ideas which reflect the distribution of power in society; in other words, stereotypes are not an expression of value but of ideology.

The fact that travellers, for instance, are maligned as a lazy, sponging, thieving group of people is an expression of the bourgeois belief in the importance of the home as a stable place where the nuclear family can flourish. Similarly, the 'dumb blonde' stereotype is common, in Western society at least, because it serves the purpose of patriarchal ideology.

The 'dumb blonde' stereotype

The 'dumb blonde' stereotype is an interesting construct and has gained wide currency in the media. Clearly hair colour is not related to intelligence; so where does this stereotype come from? Blondeness may be deemed attractive in British and North American society because of its comparative rarity (a rarity compromised by the sale of blonde hair dyes); in Scandinavia, dark hair is accorded the same exoticism, probably because it's unusual. A blonde is often thought of as being sexually attractive, but why should she be dumb?

It is here that this stereotype's reference to the world takes on ideological overtones. If a woman was sexually attractive *and* intelligent then there is a likelihood that she would be the dominant partner in any relationship a role that bourgeois ideology defines as male.

Similarly, racist stereotypes of black people being like animals has its origins, not in reality, but as an ideological construct. It boggles the civilized mind that Christian people could justify to themselves that slavery was morally right: simple, black people are like animals and thus can be treated as such. Blacks were characterized as Sambos who were docile, lazy, untrustworthy, ignorant and simple. It is likely that much of the discrimination that black people suffer today has its origins in slavery which, after all, was only abolished in USA after the 1861–5 Civil War.

Gillian Swanson (in Lusted, 1991) described the consitutuent elements of the dumb blonde type; they possess:

- strange logic
- innocence and naivety
- manipulativeness
- humour
- a body which is emphazised
- a childlike nature
- adult 'knowingness' and seductiveness.

Clearly many of these attributes are contradictory: adult and child-like; innocent and seductive and so on. We can examine how this stereotype operates in a men's lifestyle magazine, *Loaded*.

Loaded is a 'lad's' lifestyle magazine: laddishness is primarily characterized by an enjoyment of sexist representations of woman, representations which reduce females to sex objects. Other interests which feature highly in 'laddishness' are sport, booze and music. *Loaded* was launched in 1994 and, despite the entry into the market of competitors such as *Maxim* and *FHM*, has established a very healthy circulation of around 250 000 copies a month. This would have been unthinkable in the early 1980s, as there were no general

Figure 5.2

interest magazines for men on the market. *Arena,* launched in 1986, was the first to establish a foothold in the niche and was followed by *Esquire* and *GQ*. The early pace-setters, however, were not defined by their representations of women. *Loaded,* and magazines of its type, almost wholly define women by their sexuality.

Baywatch babe, Donna D'Errico, features on the November 1996 issue; her breasts are clearly the main focal point, particularly because they overhang her name. Her backside is also visible and stuck out, as if invitingly. She is also blonde. Visually, and typical of the stereotype, she is defined by the shape and pose of her body and her 'inviting' expression of parted lips. However, the anchorage suggests sophistication: '*Baywatch* babe on philosophy, science & religion'. Despite the suggestion of childishness in the use of 'babe', there is a suggestion of an intellect behind the breasts, an attribute obviously absent from the stereotype. In order to make sense of this contradiction we must understand *Loaded*'s use of irony as a metalanguage.

The advertising contained in *Loaded* suggests a primarily middle-class (ABC1 as sociologists and advertisers define them) readership. The first five advertisements in the January 1997 edition featured: Guess jeans; Marlboro cigarettes; Nike; Vodazap pagers; base shoes. Analysing the advertising is the best way, short of getting the actual audience figures, of creating an audience profile. The magazine's strapline is 'for men who should know better': the implication being that middle-class men should know better than being sexist. Irony acts as a distancing device: by stating the ridiculous, that the 'bimbo', Donna D'Errico will be profiled from an intellectual standpoint, the magazine is knowingly acknowledging its own sexism which, the rhetoric goes, makes defining women as sex objects okay. In the August 1996 issue a photoshoot was listed in the contents as, 'Bikini clad girls on Hawaiian beaches? Oh, go on then' and sexual innuendo is manifest in many of the headings on the front cover.

The magazine often contains substantial articles on popular culture: the August issue featured particularly good pieces on *The Simpsons* and the cult 1970 movie, *Performance*. Why has the 1990s been the decade when middle-class sexism becomes a successful publishing phenomenon? The tabloid press, characterized by The Sun newspaper's 'Page 3 girl', has been delivering the dumb blonde stereotype, among others, to a working-class audience since the 1970s. I have speculated elsewhere (Lacey, 1996) that this is a result of a crisis in masculinity: females are more successful at GCSE and

'A' level and constitute over half the workforce. Faced with a depletion in their traditional role of being the dominant partner, economically and socially, in relationships it is possible that this rise of the 'lad mag' may be a reaction against growing evidence of male inferiority.

Ultimately, if current trends continue, it could be women who dominate the institutions which make media representations. At the moment, men still predominate and this obviously has an effect upon re-presentations that are made.

5.5 Who does the re-presenting?

Media representations are usually a product of institutions, whether large broadcasting organizations or small independent companies. Even novelists, who are probably the most independent of media practitioners and theoretically only restricted by any generic conventions they are using, are published by large organizations which inevitably have an influence on what they produce.

Analysis of institutions is quite difficult, because our only access to them is usually through the texts themselves where they appear as the addressee. Virtually everyone watches television but very few people get to see the programmes actually being made; even less get to discuss the modes of representation used by the media practitioners. We are usually, armed with our theories and tools of analysis, left only with the text.

In Media Studies it is a commonplace assumption, but a true one, that media institutions are dominated by stereotypical white, middle-aged men, and media production reflects this bias. Western society itself is dominated, politically and economically, by white, middle-aged men so it is logical that the producers of cultural meanings should reflect this dominant group, and hence help create the conditions for hegemony. We have seen how representation and stereotypes serve to reinforce the dominant ideological views, but we must avoid the teleological position that all mainstream media products are, *per se*, sexist, racist, middle-class material, because they aren't.

One way of analysing how the dominant ideological discourses are reproduced by the media is to analyse how media professional's practices and agendas serve to naturalize this value system. (The influence of institutions upon representation will be examined in *Institution and Audience*.)

5.6 Audience and representation

Once again, a full examination of this category properly belongs in another book. However, we have already considered how audiences read texts, and noted that while the addresser's preferred reading, or representation, may be accepted by those in the audience who make a 'dominant' reading, others have the option of 'negotiated' or 'oppositional' readings.

As in a consideration of institutions, our access to information about audience response is severely limited, often to ourselves and friends. Audience research is rarely of much help because it is conducted by media institutions, which have an agenda different from our own; they are usually concerned with quantity of audience rather than understanding how a text is read.

Clearly, our individual response is important and needs to be articulated in any analysis, but wild generalizations should be avoided. It is safer to restrict analysis of audience response to decoding the preferred reading and suggesting both negotiated and oppositional readings.

The influential magazine of film theory, *Screen*, seemed to believe that the text would wholly determine an audience's reading which, ironically given the leftist political position the publication adopted, seems little different from Leavis's belief in the tyranny of the text. In the 1980s an ethnographic form of audience research was favoured. This was derived from anthropology and researchers were meant to immerse themselves within the audience, or culture, being studied. While this is certainly an advance on the, basically, psychoanalytic theories of *Screen*, it is not without its problems. See Morley (1992) for an up-to-date summary of research in the field.

However one way of illustrating how audience readings change through time is to consider texts which were controversial when first seen and compare today's reactions with that initial reading. *Reservoir Dogs* (1992) generated a lot of controversy, particularly in the 'Stuck in the Middle with You' torture scene; how will this film appear to members of the next generation?

Two films from from the post-Second World War years illustrate how much audience readings of texts can change through time. *The Wicked Lady* (1945) was the first British film to be censored in the USA. The narrative was about a bored aristocratic lady, played by Margaret Lockwood, who sought excitement with a highwayman, James Mason. Presumably it was her penchant for black leather, as much as the implied adultery, that led the American censorship to demonstrate his disapproval. Now the film appears incredibly tame, if mildly entertaining. On its release, however, it appeared to be pushing back the boundaries of censorship and clearly thrilled its audience:

> At the age of 12 year I thought it was a great film and voted it the Odeon film-goers 'film of the year' 1947, or was it 1946 (memory's going). Anyway I thought the very beautiful Lady, being bored with her life and wimpy husband, met her match in the handsome highwayman. She was looking for excitement and adventure, and found it in him. While she was very wicked he was, I thought, cruel and mean and didn't really care for her as she did for him.
>
> I like the Pat Roc character, very gracious and refined, just the opposite to the Lady. I think her character loved the husband, was it Griffith John? I may be wrong, but it was a memorable film, remembering it over 47 years shows that. (An old movie fan: Pat Lacey)

Censorship gives us information about society's mores, although, again, this subject is more properly dealt with in *Institutions and Audiences*. Another film that was censored because of its apparent immorality, this time in Britain, was *The Wild One* (1953).

This film, as Richard Falcon's teaching pack Classified! makes clear, is a fascinating case study. It wasn't just censored, it was banned! It only received a certificate, from the British Board of Film Censorship (BBFC, now the British Board of Film Classification), in 1967 when it was 'X' (18) rated. When the video was certified in 1986 it received a PG (Parental Guidance). Clearly the text, *The Wild One*, has not changed over the past 40 years but the BBFC's attitude has. This 'liberalization', however, does not happen in isolation from audiences: how audiences read *The Wild One* now is very different from the past.

Based on a real incident, *The Wild One* stars Marlon Brando as Johnny, leader of a gang of bikers who invade a small town and cause trouble. What upset the censors most was the narrative's refusal to condemn the gang's actions and mete out suitable punishment. This led the Board to fear 'copy cat' actions from Teddy Boys.

> 'Having regard', they told the producers at Columbia, 'to the present widespread concern about the increase in juvenile crime, the Board is not prepared to pass any film dealing with this subject unless the compensating moral values are so firmly presented as to justify its exhibition to audiences likely to contain . . . a large number of young and immature persons.' (Mathews, 1994, p. 128)

Whether the film inspired violence in the USA or not, it appeared to have great influence on young people. The iconography of the film became symbols of rebellion for teenage youth who were being stifled by conformism in Cold War America. As Brando (1994, p. 175) says in his ghosted autobiography:

> [I] never expected [the film] to have the impact it did. I was as surprised as anyone when T-shirts, jeans and leather jackets suddenly became symbols of rebellion. In the film there was a scene in which somebody asked my character . . . what I was rebelling against, and I answered, 'Whaddya got?' But none of us involved in the picture ever imagined it would instigate or encourage youthful rebellion.

As can be seen from Figure 5.3, the iconography now looks more 'gay' than 'youthful rebellion' – another example of how codes are culture-specific.

Figure 5.3

While *The Wild One* clearly had an impact on audiences in the USA at the time of its release, the cultural changes of the past 40 years mean that audiences now read the film very differently; this is acknowledged in Britain, institutionally, by its PG ('parental guidance') certificate. Below are some comments my students made after watching the film in 1995.

'Timid and weak' (Paul Watmough).
'Johnny . . . by today's standards shows extreme sexism in the way he acts toward Mary.' (Alistair McDonald)
'The film *Wild Ones* [sic] is quite tame in comparison with some of today's films. There is not a lot of violence, and no swearing or sex.' (Samantha Ryan)
'I found the film to be . . . entertaining in a humorous rather than violent way.' (Vicky Bastow)
'I felt the things that the gang did were amusing, and felt attracted to their way of life. Perhaps it is because of this attraction to their behaviour that it was banned, as it tends to glamorise rebellion.' (Nicola Wormald)
'The character of Johnny would have undoubtedly provided a role model for '50s youth and, although he leads a motorcycle gang, he appears to be a very sensitive character. His relationship with Mary proves this. I had no unsocial urge to turn over a parked car or run down an old man.' (Jonathan Cockcroft)

The dominant reading of this text is now very different from the one in the 1950s. Not all texts' meanings change so radically: texts such as *The Seventh Seal* (1956), a meditation on death in a medieval setting, is likely to change far less than those which deal with contemporary issues.

When dealing with texts which appeal to a particular audience, a youth audience in the case of *The Wild One*, it is essential to take into account the influence of subculture. Members of different subcultural groups share particular cultural codes and will read texts differently from a mass audience.

Another factor influencing readings is the expectations generated by media coverage. Contemporary audiences' readings of *Reservoir Dogs* are bound to be influenced by the large amount of coverage of the torture scene. It is probable that, in years to come, audiences will read the film differently, possibly with less emphasis on the torture and more upon the film's generic antecedents, just as *The Wild One* now has different readings from those originally made. Away from the 'mediation' provided by the media, future audiences will see the film in a different context.

What follows is an application of the categories Richard Dyer suggested should be used in the analysis of representation to various media texts in the form of case studies. Case studies are an important part of Media Studies for they illustrate the theory with practice, and should form part of all examination answers. Unless theory is applied to case studies then it is impossible to assess whether the ideas are useful in the understanding of media texts. Theory without practice is sterile and would account for some of the difficulties that you may have had with this book so far.

5.7 Institutional case study: British television news

The danger of considering the historical background of texts in Media Studies is that it can become an end in itself. Media Studies is primarily concerned with how meanings are created in modern society and detailed consideration of media in the past is really an exercise in history. Media Studies, however, uses many different discourses and historical background can cast light upon the conventions of representation used today.

Many long examination essays require a historical input, but this must not be allowed to dominate the essay. What follows is a historical background to television news in Britain; it attempts to explain why the British TV news is meant to be 'balanced and impartial', something that distinguishes it from many other nation's news.

Historical background of television news in Britain

In Britain, the BBC was the pioneer of broadcast news. Although the BBC has become the touchstone of public service broadcasting (PSB) it was originally a commercial company, licensed by the government, and created by a cartel of radio manufacturers. The manufacturers needed to have programmes broadcast so consumers would have a reason to buy radios. Despite this commercial origin the BBC soon became, under the aegis of its first Director General, John Reith, an organization dedicated to public education rather than private profit (for more detail on PSB see the forthcoming volume *Institution and Audience*).

The first news bulletins on the BBC used material provided by news agencies. Unless the agency is state-controlled, news agency bulletins are often couched in neutral terms in order to appeal to, and be bought by, a large number of news organizations. This makes it easier for organizations to incorporate agency material into their own news agendas. It was soon clear that this neutrality in news presentation was easily compromised. The reporting of the 1926 General Strike saw the Corporation faithfully following the Government line, even to the extent of refusing to allow the Leader of the Opposition to speak to the nation. In 1927 – as a reward for good behaviour during the previous year? – the BBC was awarded a Royal Charter, which basically allowed Reith to continue his crusade to educate, rather than entertain, the masses. News was also seen as a public service and the emphasis was on honesty rather than entertainment, even to the extent of announcing 'there is no news tonight'!

During the 1930s, the news function was expanded and split from current affairs, a division that is still in place. For the first time the BBC used its own reporters and Richard Dimbleby pioneered 'on the spot reporting'; giving radio news an immediacy that newspapers could never have. The political and economic turmoil of the decade, particularly the rise of Fascism, stimulated reporting from abroad. Events in far away places had a meaning to the general public concerned that there might be another war. It was probably the need for widespread coverage of the Second World War that stimulated a world wide system of reporting, something we now take for granted. Unsurprisingly, during the war the BBC acted as an unofficial 'Ministry for Propaganda', allowing itself to be voluntarily censored by the government. At this time the Nine O' Clock News became a national institution with over half the nation listening to the broadcasts.

BBC television news was first broadcast in 1954; however, it was little different from radio news. In order to give the impression of objectivity it was thought necessary to show a picture of Nelson's Column, and the audience merely heard the newsreader's voice.

Clearly news coverage has developed much in the last 40 years. However the notion that television news is impartial is still commonplace and, indeed, enshrined in British law. The alleged neutrality applies to ITV, as well as to the BBC. This 'impartiality' is possibly unique to Britain. In the USA, for example, it is common for reporters and anchors (the newsreaders) to editorialize, in other words to give their own particular slant on events. This is also common in Europe; in Italy, television stations are even explicitly aligned with political parties.

How, then, do the institutions of British television news re-present reality in this 'neutral' fashion?

Institutional analysis

The analysis of title sequences is often a fruitful source of information about an institution's objectives and values. The title sequence clearly sets the scene for what follows and remains the same each time a programme is broadcast (with revamps every few years). It says a great deal about the way the programme-makers wish to appear to their audience. There follows a description of the title sequence for ITN's News at Ten, which is broadcast on weekday nights on Independent television to the biggest weekday audience for broadcast news in Britain (although its prime time position has been under threat for a number of years).

News at Ten – 31/1/95

Lead in: on screen clock, ticking toward 10pm.

Station announcer: 'Now it's time to join ITN in London for "News at Ten".

music	image	soundtrack, edit and time
1. crescendo – drum roll	horizontal long shot of London at night, with top of Big Ben (BB) in foreground. ITN's logo superimposed.	
fanfare	zoom out and move to very high angle shot of BB's clock face.	
		DISSOLVE (9 secs)
2.	zoom into medium shot of BB 's clock face.	
		DISSOLVE (2 secs)

music	image	soundtrack, edit and time
3.	Trevor McDonald looking at paper on desk	'News at Ten' 'From ITN, with Trevor McDonald' (TMcD)
	camera dollies from left to right to place TMcD almost in centre.	
		CUT (3 secs)
gong		
4.	helicopter shot of flooded landscape	'Quarter of a million ordered to flee Dutch floods.'
		CUT (5 secs)
gong		
5.	'BT boss's flip remarks at Select Committee hearing sparks a new row over high pay.'	
		CUT (3 secs)
gong		
6.	train approaching station	'Private rail operators can cut services by 20 per cent.'
		CUT (4 secs)
gong 7.	supermarket trolley in supermarket, wreaths on shelves	'And how the French plan to cut the cost of dying in Britain. Good evening.'
		CUT (5 secs)

8. as shot 3 . . .

The opening sequence strongly anchors the programme's source as being London; even the station announcer (and the broadcast I saw was in the Yorkshire television region) states the programme is from Britain's capital city. This is intended to give 'News at Ten' authority, emphasizing London's agenda-setting role for national issues.

In addition, the focus on Big Ben, the clock which is part of the Houses of Parliament, is an index (in Peirce's terms) for London and political power. This demonstrates how politics is usually the most prominent discourse in news agendas. The time, of course, is 10pm, giving a sense of actuality; TV news is one of the few types of television that is broadcast live, not pre-recorded.

The use of a fanfare is conventional for the opening of news programmes and emphasizes the opening's heraldic function, that is, heralding news and drama. The dynamic camera movement, the zoom and very high angle shot, also serve to reinforce the drama. Trevor McDonald is anchored at (virtually) the centre of our screen (the cut to shot 4 is on movement, but we can see in shot 8 that the shot came to rest with McDonald in the central position) with another dynamic movement that follows the curve of his desk.

The studio is predominantly blue, connoting the cool, rational consideration of the news, emphasizing the programme's neutral nature. There are numerous television screens, of various sizes, behind the anchorman, connoting high technology. Later, McDonald will look at one of these screens as he interviews journalists; they are, literally, 'windows on the world'. The studio, which is the same for each broadcast, reassures the audience through its familiarity and high tech gloss. As we shall see, much news is 'bad news' and the safe studio surroundings, with the comforting anchor, help distance the audience from traumas around the world.

The voice-over that introduces Trevor McDonald is male, which signifies a voice of authority. McDonald's dress, a suit, signifies formality; his tone of voice and facial expression are both serious. These non-verbal codes suggest that news is important and that the audience should not expect humour, at least not until the final news item. McDonald, as the anchorman, represents the institution, his voice is the 'institutional voice' and what he says will sign itself to be unbiased. McDonald was Britain's first black national news anchor; the norm, though, is still white, middle-class (signed by clothing and accent), male. The anchor is the institutional 'face', the type of individual who is represented as being authoritative enough to deliver the news to the nation.

Internationally, this 'neutral' anchor is unusual in television news. In the USA, for example, the anchors are 'personalities' who can reach celebrity status. US news presenters usually form 'older man–younger woman' teams; like actors, they have agents and, as I have said, comment overtly on news items (editorialize). In many cases, it appears, the anchor is more important than the news. The top anchors can claim massive salaries, which reduces the money that can be spent on news-gathering.

The title sequence, studio and anchor clearly state the institutional agenda: we will show you, in an unbiased fashion, what is going on in the world. In reality, of course, it does no such thing. So what is the real agenda?

British television news agendas

As we have said, agendas are determined by institutions; for example the news agendas of tabloid and broadsheet press are different. In television news there are a number of news values which determine whether an event is defined as 'news for television'.

Selby and Cowdery (1995), in an adaptation of Galtung and Ruge's news model (in Cohen and Young, 1981), describe 11 news values:

1. *Magnitude*: the event has to be 'big', which may be defined in terms of the number of people it influences (like the 'flood story').
2. *Clarity*: the story has to be relatively simple to explain. Arcane matters of economic theory are rarely aired on the news, while the nature of floods is easy to understand.
3. *Ethnocentricity*: the closer the story is to the home audience, the more likely it is to be covered. Later in 1995, in Pakistan, 600 people died in floods which received barely a mention. From 1 September 1993 to 31 August 1994, about 75 per cent of News at Ten was concerned with domestic news. (Cleasby, 1995, p. 9)

   Similarly, ethnocentricity can lead to large numbers of people simply being ignored. As BBC correspondent Mark Doyle (1994, p. 100) describes:

   > When it was announced that most of the foreigners had been evacuated from Kigali [in Rwanda], it meant that most of the white people had gone. On the day the announcement was

broadcast in Europe, I came across about 5 000 Zairean nationals at their embassy, desperate to leave.

4. *Consonance (with the values of the audience)*: stories are presented in such a way that they reflect consensus values (which themselves have often been shaped by the news). So news that Saddam Hussein, for example, had been involved in a humanitarian act is unlikely to appear in many Western broadcasts.

5. *Surprise*: extraordinary stories are more likely to get coverage than commonplace ones. For example, childrens' 'Power Ranger' ice pops were found to contain alcohol.

6. *Elite centredness*: well known people are more likely to be reported on than unknown ones. Hugh Grant's arrest on Sunset Boulevard for 'lewd conduct in a public place', in summer 1995, was only a news story because of his film star status. If the Queen Mother has a cold, this may be reported; if you have a cold, it will not.

7. *Negativity*: most news covered is 'bad news' because 'good news' takes longer to happen and is less likely to be surprising. The abatement of the Dutch floods was hardly reported at all. 48 per cent of all news reports about the developing world in the South by British television news, in the period 1 September 1993 to 31 August 1994, concerned 'conflict and disaster' (Cleasby, 1995, p. 13).

8. *Human interest*: how a news story affects people's lives is deemed important; the vox pop interviews with Dutch evacuees showed the audience a sample of the participant's emotions.

9. *Composition or balance*: in order to maintain audience interest, television news will be structured to give variety. Numerous 'talking head' interviews may bore an audience and so the programme is composed to give a mix of anchor, location footage, computer graphics and so on.

10. *Location reporting*: the reporter is filmed as close as possible to the events. The report about the floods is given from a boat on a Dutch main street.

11. *Actuality reporting*: ideally the events of the story should actually be seen. Stories without pictures get a very low priority in news coverage. The rescue of the British yachtsman, Tony Bullimore, from his capsized boat received massive coverage primarily because it was captured on film.

In addition to Selby and Cowdery's selection there are four more factors:

12. The *inheritance factor*: once a story has hit the headlines, this in itself defines it as news.
13. *Framework*: certain news stories carry expectations of what might happen, and this framework in itself can influence the way a report is presented. For example, a demonstration involving racists is expected to involve violence, and this will be foregrounded in the report even if violence does not dominate the event.
14. *Frequency*: events that happen on a daily basis are far more likely to be reported than those which develop over weeks.
15. *Impartiality*: in Britain broadcasters are obliged, by law, to report impartially. In practice this means giving two sides to any contentious story; political news usually features comment from the Government and an opposition party. It is probably that complete neutrality is impossible; this will be covered in *Institution and Audience*.

Many, if not all, of these values are structured by the dominant ideological discourse of our society. For example, by only dealing with stories which can be represented with 'clarity', the complexity of society as a structure is glossed over. In consequence, social problems (dealt with under 'negativity') are represented as relatively simple, which does not allow a 'full' picture of potential social dysfunctions. When, for instance, homelessness is covered in the news (often a popular Christmas story or motivated by prolonged cold weather) the problem of housing shortage and the Government-imposed financial restrictions upon social housing organizations is rarely addressed. Instead we are often left with the impression that more charitable beds will alleviate the problem.

Ethnocentricity encourages audiences to consider themselves, and their fellow-countrymen and women, before people of other nations. A news agenda which emphasized, say, the notion of Spaceship Earth (a metaphor for the fact that we all have an interest in looking after our planet) is likely to consider certain events thousands of miles away as relevant as those which are local.

Consensus values, by definition, are those of the dominant ideology; and the focus upon elites goes some way to justifying the members of the elite as being important (because they are worthy of news coverage). The *Sun*'s 'scoop', in December 1996, that the Spice Girls would vote for the Conservative Party helped to define – at least for the *Sun*'s readership – that the Spice Girls' opinions were worthy of coverage.

The use of location reporting, in particular, often gives status to 'trivial' information. A device television news often uses is to go live for an update on, 'a breaking' story – one that is happening during the broadcasts. These 'updates' are usually nothing more than a restatement of what's already known, but give the impression that the audience is receiving vital information because the report is being filed from 'on the spot'.

From a broadcasting perspective, the definition of the legal requirement for 'composition and balance' in their reporting as necessitating (only) two points-of-view means that binary opposi-tions (see section 2.5) are used to structure the report. Often implicit within such a structure is 'right' and 'wrong'; the 'right', of course, representing the values of the dominant ideological system.

There should be no sense of a conspiracy in what is described above: the professional practices that lead the dominant ideological discourse to structure the news are institutionalized. The notion of gatekeepers (who are the people, like news editors, who make decisions about whether to 'run' a story or 'spike') emphasizes that individuals in a news organization are less important than the position they fill. To an extent, it doesn't matter *who* the individual in the 'gatekeeping' role is, only what decision he or she makes, and this is invariably determined by the institution's agenda.

News agendas serve as a filter and structuring device between the audience and the events the news represents. Where does the news of these events come from? Many stories come from a 'socially respected source', such as the police, professional bodies, and the Government. These are given greater credibility than, say, a press release from a religious cult. Indeed it is increasingly the case that 'new stories' from 'respected sources' are public relations exercises. For example, the police, when reporting crime statistics, are likely to present this information in a light favourable to themselves. Some organizations issue video news releases (VNRs) and this could be used as part of the news broadcast without acknowledgement. In 1995, the environmental pressure group Greenpeace issued VNRs as part of their successful campaign to prevent the Brent Spar oil rig being dumped at sea.

The ownership of the organization producing the news is also very important, although in the case of broadcast news in Britain the legal requirements of balance are more powerful determining factors. In newspapers, knowing who is the owner and what is their political orientation is essential.

In the analysis of the opening sequence we have used some of the tools of image analysis described in earlier chapters. Many media texts, however, have their own language of representation in which they deploy a unique combination of conventions. The conventions of television news are as follows.

British television news conventions

Television presents its news within the frame of the anchor in her or his studio. The news itself is shown through a mix of interviews, reportage and commentary. Interviews, be they with eye witnesses, vox pop ('the man on the street') or with known individuals like politicians, are 'accessed voices'. The reporter will give 'factual' detail about the story; comment usually comes from a 'correspondent', who will normally give a consensus interpretation of events. (The report and comment may be given by the same journalist but are clearly signed as different; the anchor may ask for their opinion after we have being given the 'story'.) All the main news stories include a filmed report which is usually shot on location. This is often 'signed off' in front of a significant location (stakeout), such as, the White House for US political stories, giving the report more authority.

I have used the terms 'report' and 'news stories' interchangeably because reports are narratively structured. Dramatic tension is often invoked by the use of a binary opposite, for example 'nature versus humanity' in the flood report which led 'News at Ten' on 31 January 1995. This tension is the narrative disruption that needs resolving and without which there is no story. The report may not carry the resolution; it may occur later and be reported in future broadcasts.

Clearly the most important story of the day, as defined by the news agenda, will be the 'lead'. The running order of stories demonstrate the priority the news agenda is giving to them. Political and economic stories are common leads, followed by domestic issues. A foreign story will normally only take the lead if it involves a disaster, preferably with some home nationals involved. Sport, as in newspapers, is commonly positioned at the end. The last story is usually light-hearted in tone which can lead to the rather odd situation of the audience listening to the repeated 'bad news' headlines at the conclusion of the broadcast with a smile on their faces!

Filmed reports themselves are usually a mixture of montage and continuity editing, and will contain reaction shots and other techniques of continuity editing. This transparency of construction reinforces the notion that the news is a 'window on the world'.

Television news uses stereotypes as much as any media. For example, the final headlined story, about the French cutting the cost of dying in Britain, draws upon the stereotype of the French as being somewhat shifty and greedy. The implication is that the traditional British sanctity of dying is going to be subverted by 'profit-making frogs'.

As in all mainstream media texts, the dominant ideology is the structuring feature, always working to create a preferred reading which reflects (bourgeois) consensus values.

Audience readings

In Britain television news has greater credibility than printed news, the BBC more so than ITN, even though more watch the latter. This is probably due to a combination of a press which is too obviously partisan and the strength of the myth that 'seeing is believing'. During the first half of 1995 an average audience for News at Ten was 6.8 million viewers. Clearly, the television news has a great influence upon people's perception of the world.

It is likely that most of this audience make a 'dominant' reading of the representation, though both negotiated and oppositional readings are also, of course, possible. Political stories are most likely to receive readings which are not 'dominant'; depending upon the individual viewer's political orientation. Because news often deals with issues removed from the immediate concerns of the general public, audiences frequently have no first-hand knowledge of stories covered. When stories concerning, say, a particular locality are carried, then an 'oppositional' reading may be made, especially if – as is quite probably – the content is negative. Negative stories are often followed by complaints about misrepresentation. However, as you may have found when you tried to represent yourself, in an earlier exercise, it is impossible to represent anything other than in a partial way. There is no such thing as an absolute truth.

This discussion has only scratched the surface of one particular broadcast. Television news is clearly worthy of much deeper analysis because of the importance it has in shaping audiences' perceptions of the world; it is certainly far more influential than the 'sex 'n' violence' movies which are often blamed for moral corruption.

◀ Exercise 5.3 ▶

Videotape a whole news programme (avoiding any 'one-offs'; where one story dominates the whole broadcast) and apply the 14 categories of news conventions. (A comparison of different stations' news bulletins can also be revealing about news agendas.)

5.8 Institutional case study: *More!*

More! is published by EMAP, a British-based company with a large number of magazine and newspaper titles. The company also runs radio stations. Like all commercial media groups, EMAP is in the business of making profits, which means it must deliver audiences to advertisers. Unusually, *More!* claims to be profitable on sales alone, although, clearly, the more advertising it carries, the greater its profitability.

Vital information about publications is contained in the media packs which are sent out to potential advertisers. For example *More!*'s media pack boasts the circulation for the publication of 414 081 (ABC July–December 1994) and a readership of 1 219 000 (NRS July–December 1994). The circulation figure is supplied by the Audit Bureau of Circulations (ABC) and readership figure by the National Readership Surveys (NRS). These are both industry-funded bodies which operate independently of the industry to assure advertisers of valid figures. The figures are given in six-monthly averages because that presents a more stable picture of sales than monthly figures (although newspapers' statistics are now published monthly).

Readership is always higher than circulation because of the 'pass on' rate; *More!* has 2.94 readers per copy (rpc). The readership profile contained in media packs give us details of the audience to which the publication appeals. For example, the *More!* media pack describes the reader as follows:

> *More!* readers are leaders rather than nesters, funseekers or free spirits; they are independent, concerned, responsible, hard working, competitive and gregarious. *More!* readers like shopping for clothes and are heavy users of cosmetics; they use environmentally friendly products and are sensible about what they eat.

I guess it must go without saying that they are also female although, undoubtedly, *More!* will be 'passed on' to, or pinched by, male readers. Clearly this picture of *More!* readers is meant to appeal to advertisers of consumer goods.

Readership profiles are not just about giving a publication's total sales or describing a typical reader. NRS can provide a breakdown of the readership in terms of class and age. For example, 81 per cent of *More!*'s readership is 15–24-year-old females; clearly if this is an advertiser's target market then *More!* would be an ideal publication to use because there is very little waste (that is, only 19 per cent of the readership is outside the target market).

Other figures are available which help to sell the title to potential advertisers. For example, the Youth TGI (Target Group Index) 1993 shows that *More!* reaches 36.1 per of all 15–19-year-old women. This represents a phenomenal coverage of this group. However, this is hardly prime territory for advertisers, as 15–19 year olds tend not to have a lot of 'disposable income'. Indeed, *More!* carries comparatively little advertising.

The information in the media pack shows us the composition of a magazine's audience, and it is likely that most of this audience is making a dominant reading of the text. The next stage of our analysis is to decode the preferred reading (although, as a thirty-something male, I am probably not the best person to do this).

Generically, *More!* is a lifestyle magazine which, increasingly in Britain, means it is about sex and more sex. Even established lifestyle magazines, like *Cosmopolitan*, have been increasing their erotic content; the August 1995 issue of *Cosmo* featured '40 ways to arouse a man' and '12 pages of erotic explosive intimacy'. The male equivalents, which have been mushrooming in recent years, are slightly more sedate: *Maxim*'s August issue featured 'six hot sex tricks every man should know'. The readership profile of these magazines is older than *More!*'s 15–24 year olds, which may explain why the publication with the younger target audience contains more sex. *More!* competes in the same market as *Sugar* and *Just Seventeen*.

As you can see from the front cover (Figure 5.4) all the stories, with the exception of that concerning Naomi Campbell, are about sex. The design is brash, with a lurid purple background, and eye-catching; the contents are unashamedly about lust (8-page special: 'tackling his tackle, the hard facts about the male member'). The model is not outrageously 'beautiful', and, with her lack of smile, could even appear a bit dopey, thus not setting too high a role model for the magazine's readers. Her attractiveness appears to be more the product of her make-up, emphasizing that everyone has a chance to become attractive. When *More!* featured Pamela Anderson on the front cover she was anchored by the critical 'Pamela, is marriage her biggest boob yet?'. While *More!* is interested in

Figure 5.4

glamour, it is a glamour that most can manufacture, and not the elitist perfection sported by many lifestyle magazines with an older readership profile.

The lifestyle of *More!* readers is not supposed to be glamorous, it is signified as being normal. The fact that a social class profile of the readership is not included in the media pack suggests that it may have a large 'working class' component, which is less attractive to advertisers. (Of course, the glamour associated with magazines like *Cosmopolitan* is probably not in evidence in many of that magazine's readers' lives either.) On a monthly basis *More!*, which is published every two weeks, is more expensive than *Cosmopolitan's* £2.30; however, £1.25 is easier for a younger audience to 'shell out' in one go. Annual subscriptions are probably something the advertising manager only dreams of, while *Cosmo* sells them aggressively.

More!'s content is gossipy, the 'real-life drama' of 'I'm sleeping with my sister's husband', giving it a British tabloid newspaper feel. Film, television and pop stars are also given space, as is fashion. The articles tend to be short in length and the inside pages are as 'busy' as the front cover. It is full of conventional material about icons of glamour and sexuality, presented in easy to read 'bites'.

More! is probably an excellent 'sex education' publication which serves a basic need, particularly when public information on the subject is scant and puritanical (a British Minister for Health prevented the publication of a health education pamphlet on the grounds that it was 'smutty' – I wonder what he thinks of *More!*).

However, *More!*'s representation of young women suggests there is only one subject on their minds. This places it centrally within mainstream media which defines sex as the most important issue in young people's lives. The motto 'smart girls get *More!*' suggests that if you're not having sex regularly, then you're thick.

What does the target audience think of *More!*:

> *More!* is entertaining but I feel it may be irresponsible in its approach to sex. I feel younger girls are attracted to the magazine through curiosity and as so much emphasis is placed on sexually orientated material it will encourage underage and casual sex.
>
> I find the magazine amusing but not really informative. (Fiona Barnes)

> I find *More!* extremely entertaining although, most of the time, the portrayal of teenage life is a little unrealistic. However the advice given in the publication can be helpful. *More!*'s approach to sex is responsible and the advice about sex will probably answer most questions on the

subject and will, maybe, ease the curiosity of the younger readers of the magazine. (Fiona Jordan)

Although *More!* doesn't intellectually stimulate me I find it quite amusing. The articles and weekly (*sic*) features are entertaining. However I feel that as the magazine promotes sex too much and does not consider the effect it might have upon its younger audience. (Samantha Ryan)

It is disingenuous of me to state that these comments are made by the target audience. Although all three women were 17-year-olds it is incorrect to suppose that their views are typical. They were all Media Studies students, who undoubtedly make up only a tiny percentage of *More!*'s total readership.

In order to get a more accurate portrayal of audience readings it would be necessary to take a large sample, ideally thousands of people, drawn from the readership profile of the publication. They would then be questioned about their readings of the text. This may bring us closer to audience readings but is clearly a difficult and expensive task. Although industry bodies, such as ABC, are well placed to do this, they have little interest in doing so, their brief being to supply advertisers with a readership profile and not audience readings. In recent years, however, television companies have started using an Appreciation Index (AI) to try to quantify audience likes and dislikes.

Clearly, the three students quoted above are making a 'negotiated' reading of *More!* and this is constructed, at least in part, by the sub-cultural groups to which they belong (it is doubtful, however, whether Media Studies students can be classed as a sub-cultural group). They find the magazine entertaining, but realize that its portrayal of teenage life, or rather teenage sex life, is unrealistic.

Without adequate 'market research' we can never be sure what readings audiences are making of texts. This doesn't mean that it is a meaningless task to ask friends what they think, although it is probably best done with a well-constructed questionnaire. However, we cannot make generalizations based upon what they say.

5.9 Generic case study: the Western

How a subject is represented to an audience is often determined by the genre and the form of the media text. The Western genre deals with frontier USA, a place familiar to many people through Hollywood productions; the Western was a staple genre during the

Hollywood's Golden Age (approximately the 1920s–40s) and into the 1950s. After a barren period in the 1960s–80s (with the exception of Clint Eastwood films) the Western experienced something of a box-office renaissance in the 1990s with films like *Unforgiven* (1992) and *Maverick* (1994).

The Western genre originated with the novels of James Fenimore Cooper, whose *The Last of the Mohicans* was given the Hollywood treatment in 1936 and 1992, and is primarily characterized by the myth of the frontier. The frontier was a specific place and time, which receded westward from the moment the Founding Fathers landed until the end of the nineteenth century. At the frontier various thematic clashes were enacted. Jim Kitses, in *Horizons West* (1969), described the binary oppositions which structure the Western genre:

The Wilderness	Civilisation
the individual	the community
freedom	restriction
honour	institutions
self-knowledge	illusion
integrity	compromise
self-interest	social responsibility
solipsism	democracy
Nature	Culture
purity	corruption
experience	knowledge
empiricism	legalism
pragmatism	idealism
brutalisation	refinement
savagery	humanity
The West	The East
America	Europe
the frontier	America
equality	class
agrarianism	industrialism
tradition	change
the past	the future

The conflict these engendered was enacted in narratives of revenge, chase, pioneers verses the Indians, and farmers verses ranchers. What follows is a brief consideration of the classic Western, *The Searchers* (1956).

The Searchers

This film is driven by a revenge narrative in which Ethan Edwards (played by John Wayne) and Martin Pawley, his half-breed 'nephew', search for his niece, Debbie, who was kidnapped as a child by Indians. Edwards' brother's family had been massacred when Debbie was captured. The narrative covers the massacre and the years of searching.

Directed by John Ford, who was responsible for many other classic Westerns (such as *Stagecoach* [1939]), *The Searchers* is a Hollywood movie. This does not only mean it was filmed in California, USA, or that it was financed by a film company based in the state. A 'Hollywood film' refers to the style in which the text is created. We can expect, then, that, stylistically, *The Searchers* will be a conventional film.

Like many Hollywood films, *The Searchers* uses film stars. John Wayne was one of the biggest box office stars in the 1940s and 1950s and is associated particularly with the Western. His well-established persona of a rugged individualist who lives by his own code is subverted, somewhat, by the psychologically disturbed nature of Edwards' character. Edward's obsessive hatred of Indians is such that he intends to kill Debbie because she has been 'defiled' (had sex with) an Indian.

By the 1950s the Western genre had reached a 'mature' stage and was starting to question the myths it was propagating. Ford's later film, *The Man Who Shot Liberty Valance* (1962), is a an overt consideration of these myths. The presentation of the Wayne character as psychologically sick casts doubt not just on the heroism he represents in *The Searchers*, but in all of his films.

The film's representation of women is conventional for Hollywood at the time, with Vera Miles' role (Laurie Jorganson) little more than the 'love interest'. The women are the homemakers who wait anxiously for their men to return from the wilderness. It is Laurie's mother who makes a statement about civilizing the frontier; women create a community to which men like Edwards, an individual and therefore an outsider (as revealed in the *mise-en-scène* of the opening, and in the closing shots), can never belong. Community spirit in Ford's Westerns is often symbolized by the singing of 'Let us gather at the river'; in *The Searchers* this takes place at the funeral of Edwards' family, but he cuts it brusquely short.

As with women, *The Searchers'* representation of Indians as savages is true to generic type. It wasn't until such revisionist

Westerns as Ford's *Cheyenne Autumn* (1964), *Little Big Man* (1970) and *Dances with Wolves* (1990) that the genocidal nature of the frontier began to be acknowledged. Anyone wishing to see a true representation of what the West was really like can only conclude that the Western genre is a travesty of the truth. However, this misses the point; the crux of the Western is that it articulates the myths of nationhood which are important in sustaining national identity, particularly in a very young nation like the USA.

Even in the late twentieth century the myths of the frontier and the meeting of wilderness and civilization, characterised so admirably by Kitses' antinomies, still shape North American consciousness; 'Space, the final frontier' . . . However, as Jack Kerouac discovered in his novel *On the Road* (1957), there is in reality nowhere else to 'boldly go', whatever the myths.

Indeed, it has been argued that far from sustaining the USA, the frontier myth actually weakens it because meaning is created primarily through violence:

> It is by now a commonplace that our [American] adherence to the 'myth of the frontier' – the concept of America as a wide-open land of unlimited opportunity for the strong, ambitious, self-reliant individual to thrust his way to the top – has blinded us to the consequences of the industrial and urban revolutions and to the need for social reform and a new concept of individual and communal welfare. Nor is it a far-fetched association that the murderous violence that has characterized recent political life has been linked by poets and news commentators alike to the 'frontier psychology' of our recent past and our long heritage. The first colonists saw in America an opportunity to regenerate their fortunes, their spirits, and the power of their church and nation; but the means to that regeneration through violence became the structuring metaphor of the American experience. (Slotkin, 1973, p. 5)

Ethan Edwards is a portrayal of a person who can only seek redemption through revenge. This individualism is at odds with the organic, agrarian society of the Western settlers. However, the original settlers' ideals of living by the natural law, like Thoreau at Walden, were soon to be:

> overcome by the Jacksonian Democracy of the western man-on-the-make, the speculator, and the wildcat banker; [by] racist irrationalism and a falsely conceived economics [which] prolonged and intensified slavery in the teeth of American democratic idealism; and . . . men like Davy Crockett became national heroes by defining national aspiration in

terms of so many bears destroyed, so much land preempted, so many trees hacked down, so many Indians and Mexicans dead in the dust. (Slotkin, 1973, p. 5)

Westerns, then, do not relate to reality, they create and articulate myths of North American nationhood.

The Western is a particularly 'male' genre, but there follows a consideration of texts which may offer female-orientated representations. The first is a Hollywood movie, which is heavily institutionally determined; the second is the work of a photographer who probably has more 'artistic freedom'.

5.10 Film case study: *Blue Steel*

Like *The Searchers*, *Blue Steel* (1990) is a Hollywood movie and therefore follows the techniques of mainstream cinema defined in Chapter 1. However, it was directed and co-written by Kathryn Bigelow and is an interesting case study for the representation of women.

Jamie Lee Curtis plays Megan Turner, a rookie New York cop who, at the film's opening, graduates from the academy. Her family, though, is noticeably missing from the ceremony. Turner's wife-beating father hates his daughter for becoming a cop. Turner's close friend, Tracey, and her family act as 'stand ins' for the celebratory photographs. Soon after Turner shoots and kills a gun-toting thief. The thief's gun is stolen by Eugene Hunt, a psychopath who is a trader on the New York stock exchange and who witnessed the shooting. As the thief then appears to have been unarmed, Turner is suspended for using 'unreasonable force'. Hunt becomes obsessed with Turner and starts shooting people with bullets on which he has placed her name. Turner then teams up with sensitive detective Nick Mann to catch the killer. Meanwhile, Turner has embarked on an affair with Hunt, not knowing she is also hunting him. Later, Hunt murders Tracey, with Turner in powerless attendance.

One way of determining authorial intent, which helps decode the preferred meaning, is to assume the director is the author of the film: the *auteur* theory. This idea was originally a polemic that attempted to get Hollywood cinema treated seriously by critics. François Truffaut's *politique des auteurs*, from 1954, became a theory after American critic Andrew Sarris introduced the original idea, in 1962, to English-speakers. Those who follow the *auteur* theory look, basically, for common themes and stylistic devices in a director's work; for example, in our consideration of the Western we saw how some of the themes in *The Searchers* were dealt with in other John Ford movies. Ford's visual style is distinctive, too, particularly in his use of Monument Valley as a location for many of his films.

What was originally a polemic has now become a cliché, with many films prefixed with the words 'a film by . . .'. According to current convention everyone is an *auteur*, which is clearly not the case – for some directors it is impossible to isolate unifying themes and/or style.

While the *auteur* approach can be fruitful in decoding a text's meaning it is far too narrow a focus to describe such a collaborative art as cinema. Hundreds of people are involved in movie-making and though most cannot claim a decisive input there are cases to be made that the screenwriters are film's authors, or even their stars. Cinematographers, too, can have a decisive impact: the revolutionary look of *Citizen Kane* cannot be wholly attributed to director Orson Welles, cinematographer Gregg Toland is an important collaborator.

Kathryn Bigelow, the director of *Blue Steel*, has to date, only four other feature films to her credit, *The Loveless* (1981), *Near Dark* (1987), *Point Break* (1991) and *Strange Days* (1995). This is probably an insufficient *oeuvre* from which to be confident of making many *auteurist* statements.

Blue Steel deals with the relationship between male power and violence, and is unusual for a 'cop' film in having a female lead. However, the film is not just a 'cop' movie; it has elements of *film noir* and horror, and even ends in a Western-style shoot-out.

Film noir deals with the dark side of the human psyche, usually with a criminal context, and in an urban, nocturnal (and often rainy) setting. Classic *noir* movies include *The Maltese Falcon* (1941), *The Lady from Shanghai* (1948) and *The Big Heat* (1953). The main female character in *noir*, the *femme fatale*, is usually a sexually powerful creature who corrupts 'good' men and receives her punishment at the film's end. *Blue Steel* reverses this, to an extent, by making the psychotic male – Hunt – the *'homme fatal'* to whom Turner is sexually attracted.

After the credit sequence, Turner is seen graduating amongst hundreds of other similarly uniformed individuals: she is the only female cop we see. The *mise-en-scène* often uses a shallow depth of field, allowing only one individual to be in focus; this is usually Turner, but a black cop is given similar treatment, emphasizing his kindred status: they are both in subordinate positions in North American society.

Narrative conflict is immediately introduced with Turner's absent family. Tracey, who tells Turner how proud she is of her, is a married mother and represents 'normal' femininity. In contrast, Turner's family is shown to be dysfunctional, her father represents patriarchal power which he uses to brutalize women. In a climactic scene Turner arrests her father but takes him home when he breaks down in tears, confessing he does not know why he beats his wife. On their return Hunt has entered the Turner home posing as a boyfriend, emphasizing the male power which Turner, in releasing her father, has just failed to subdue.

Turner's main problem is that she is simultaneously a victim of male power and a member of a repressive agency of patriarchy, the police. (Jamie Lee Curtis's own androgyny emphasizes the maleness of her profession.) When she arrests her father she is using the forces of patriarchy against, in this discourse, 'one of its own'. The instrument of male power is the gun, represented as a phallic symbol; when Hunt and Turner are apparently about to have sex early in the film we find that he is interested only in her gun. The title sequence also plays upon this symbolism, with extreme close-ups of a Smith & Wesson, shot in a blue light, fetishizing the weapon. The insertion of bullets further suggests the equation of male (sexual) power and violence.

◀ EXERCISE 5.4 ▶

Analyse Figure 5.5, taken from the scene where Turner shoots the thief in a supermarket, and 5.6 from *Thelma and Louise* (1991).

Figure 5.5 emphasizes the 'maleness' of Turner's character with the 'classic' gun-holding pose of a cop, her grim expression, and her uniform. Turner's journey through the supermarket shelves, when she shoots the thief, is shown in some detail, emphasizing both her nervousness and her fear. Clearly these emotions are motivated by her status as a 'rookie', although the emphasis they are given may indicate a female sensitivity that allows such 'non-macho' feelings to be displayed.

The setting for this scene is very important. Shopping, conventionally, is a female activity but in this film roles are reversed somewhat, as it is Hunt who holds the shopping basket. Turner's

Figure 5.5

familiarity with such an environment is completely destroyed by her terror as she makes her way toward the thief.

Thelma and Louise is a fascinating 'road movie' where the men, with the exception of the Harvey Keitel character, are either wimps or deceptive. Thelma, played by Geena Davis (Figure 5.6), is holding the gun is a similar fashion to Megan Turner, though clearly she is not a professional. What I find fascinating in this image is the comparison between Thelma's and Louise's expressions: there is a certain vulnerability about Thelma's expression that might be considered feminine; Louise's, however, is aggressive. Does this mean Louise has a masculine expression or is it the way gender is defined in our society that leads us to use such terms? My guess is the latter because, of course, men can have an expression that has 'a certain vulnerability'.

Figure 5.6

Hunt is incapable of the normal, tender sex which Turner and Mann share, and when he rapes Turner he is portrayed as an animal, ferociously copulating. It may seem, then, that the portrayal of Turner as a female victim is rather conventional, despite her being the central character. However, she is shown to be assertive in her relationships with men and she kicks Hunt off her as she is being raped, escapes from hospital to pursue him, and eventually kills him in a shoot-out.

Despite the ability of Turner's character to motivate narrative, an ability usually reserved for male characters, the narrative conclusion subverts any assertiveness she may have shown throughout the film. In order to escape from the hospital she must don a male uniform, and she is finally left speechless and is taken into comforting male arms.

Blue Steel articulates the possibility of females using patriarchal power systems and concludes, in my reading, that any attempt to do this will fail. The woman simply becomes a tool of men; she cannot, ultimately, stand alone against patriarchal power. Could this also be a metaphor for Bigelow's film-making? In order to get finance to shoot a movie she must, ultimately, conform to male values. However, it is a fascinating movie that plays with gender representations and the follow-up, *Point Break*, broke new ground in the action movie.

Cindy Sherman has much greater artistic control over her texts and, possibly as a consequence, is able to create a very different representation of women.

5.11 Photographic case study: Cindy Sherman

◀ Exercise 5.5 ▶

Analyse the image, Figure 5.7, 'Untitled Film Still No. 21, 1978'.

Figure 5.7

The work of New York photographer Cindy Sherman explicitly deals with the representation of females. In her early work she used herself as model for a series of photographs called 'Untitled Film Stills' and, later, simply 'Untitled'. Though a title such as 'film still' implies a frozen moment of a narrative, the lack of title liberates the image by not anchoring it to an explicit, preferred reading. The ambiguity this creates forces the audience to make its own interpretation of the images (although clearly its interpretation will be conditioned by its cultural expectations). In addition, Sherman uses different photographic styles and and wears a range of 'disguises' so that the audience cannot be sure that the images are self-portraits.

Because of this intentional ambiguity, what Sherman's images are representing is mainly constructed in the audience's mind. Sherman's 'philosophy of representation' is as follows:

The central theme is identity, the roles people play, real or forced on to them by society. 'I wanted to show that the characters were as confused and frustrated by the roles they had to play as I was,' [Sherman] says . . . She speaks of 'wanting a man to look at it in expectation of something lascivious, then feel like a violator . . . I guess I'm trying to make people feel bad for certain expectations'. (Barnes, 1994, p. 4)

Sherman's project succeeds because of the variety of guises she uses for her own image, and the variety of settings; these have a range of different and often conflicting connotations. In a culture where we are used to seeing females represented primarily as sexual objects or as mothers, the deliberate ambiguity of Sherman's images resist simplistic categorization and forces the audience to consider other meanings. It is likely that such unanchored and unconventional imagery will create a varied response in audiences; probably revealing their own prejudices and expectations.

This was certainly my experience. Of the few images of Sherman's work I have seen (in *Screen*, 24.6) I find the often impassive expression of the model's faces (it would be wrong to call them all Sherman's) quite hostile, as if they resent me looking. I find myself categorizing the models as attractive or not – and then remember they are the same woman: this simplistic categorization is clearly a 'way of seeing' in which I am heavily implicated.

As a fan of film, the name 'Untitled Film Stills' invites me to 'guess the director' and the scenario. 'No. 21' suggests, to me, a French 'new wave' film set in the USA in the 1940s. The woman appears chic and powerful, connotations garnered from the low-angle shot and urban setting. Her serious expression and focused gaze suggest confidence. She could be waiting for a lover but would not be bothered if he didn't turn up . . . These personal associations are probably derived from my favourite films (unfortunately the lighting means I cannot characterize her as a *femme fatale*).

In fact, all of my readings are essentially personal because of the lack of context and the images' refusal to be anchored. I learn less about the women in the image than I do about the way I see women; if my response is brutally limited then that is my fault: one cannot characterize 'woman' so simply.

Despite this, there do exist preferred readings (clearly, for example, the woman is not subservient) but the text is so open that creating a preferred reading requires a great deal of work.

It is very likely that women will read Sherman's images differently from how men read them. In an article which accompanied the issue of *Screen* cited earlier, Judith Williamson (1983, p. 105) sees Sherman's images as:

> 'Essentially feminine' . . . [but] they are all different. This not only rules out the idea that any one of them is the 'essentially feminine', but also shows, since each seems to be it, that there can be no such thing . . . The identities she acts out may be passive and fearful. But look what she does with them, what she makes [shows] she is in control.

Given 'artistic' freedom, women are likely to make very different representations from the predominantly male perspectives which are presented in mainstream media (we shall see in the next chapter how the very structure of Hollywood film creates a male point of view in the representation of women).

For example, *Oranges Are Not the Only Fruit* (1985), a novel written by Jeanette Winterson, a well-respected feminist writer, was adapted for BBC television in 1990 by the author, produced by Phillipa Giles and directed by Beeban Kidron. Despite the programme's success, Phillipa Giles continues to have problems getting 'female' projects 'off the ground' unless they contained a male-orientated 'narrative thrust'. In media institutions, decision-making executives are, typically, male.

Oranges Are Not the Only Fruit concerns the 'rites of passage' of Jess, who is born into a 'fundamentally religious' family and discovers herself to be a lesbian. In an interesting investigation into audience readings, Julia Hallam and Margaret Marshment (1995, p. 2) argued that:

> The makers had very consciously adopted a strategy that would ensure a supportive response to the issue of lesbian identity. Playing off the representation of one unpopular minority position (religious fundamentalism) against another (lesbianism), they aimed to secure a reading in sympathy with the protagonist Jess and her predicament rather than with the fundamentalist sect who persecute her. If we were right, then viewers who accepted this preferred reading would be accepting a definition of lesbianism directly counter to dominant ideological positions concerning 'normal' sexuality.

Hallam and Marshment's investigation into the responses of 'ordinary women' found this to be the case and concluded that, despite the overall diversity of the readings, they 'remained within a recognizable "we" of common experiences and common pleasures which seemed to owe much to our common positions of women'.

Here we are touching on specifically female discourses which get little airing in the mainstream media. When women are given total control to make, say, television programmes, their texts are, by necessity, pioneering in trying to make themselves heard amid male dominated bureaucracy. *Oranges Are Not the Only Fruit* shows how a text broadcast by a mainstream institution can offer discourses alternative to those of the dominant ideology.

The Open University programme *Women in TV: Taking the Credit* pointed out other texts as being particularly feminine, including *Making Out, Culloden* and *Street Girls*. (NB: The Open University, in Britain, produces some excellent media programmes.)

5.12 Propaganda

Propaganda attempts to persuades its audience to a particular political, or religious, point-of-view. It does this through attempting to convince the audience that its explanation of the world is the correct one and adherence to the views which it is propagating will benefit the individual. In propaganda, as Steve Neale (1977) has shown, the individual is often identified as a national citizen, so by addressing a mass, who are all of one nation or race, the text is addressing the individual.

Propaganda is recognized as being biased, it is representing the world from a partial point-of-view. However, if you are convinced by the propaganda, or it is propagating views you believe in, then it will appear to be representing reality.

Because of the requirement for 'balance' in news and current affairs, party political broadcasts are the only legal form of propaganda allowable on British television. Newspapers are not so bound, so owners are free to vent their prejudices, restrained only by the law and occasional libel suits.

The line between information and propaganda is very narrow. Propaganda is not necessarily lies; it can represent actual events, such as the Nuremberg rally in 1934, discussed below. To distinguish between 'lies' and actuality, it is necessary to analyse the way the information is given to the audience and, if possible, ascertain the intentions of the text's producers. If it appears that the prime function of the text is to persuade audiences to their viewpoint, rather than inform, then it is propaganda.

Persuasion attempts to alter an individual's attitude by an intellectual and emotional process. Salespeople will attempt, at first, to find out what the customer wants and then proceed to demonstrate how their product 'fits the bill'. However, as all good salespeople know, what sells products is the salesperson's personality; if a customer likes him or her, then the product is as good as sold. Similarly, propaganda will use 'facts and figures' to give an argument 'objectivity' and intellectual respectability, but it will also attempt to appeal to the emotions, often drawing upon myths of nationalism, in an attempt to 'side-step' the mind and communicate directly to the 'heart'.

In many ways the influence of propaganda is a product of the mass media, whose technological base makes it possible to disseminate information to large numbers of people. It is not, however, solely a product of the modern age; in the late sixteenth century it was recommended to Pope Gregory XIII that there should be a Cardinal for Propaganda in order to convert dissenting nations to the faith.

Propaganda is only obvious as propaganda to an audience which is aware of its nature. This awareness may be the product of an 'oppositional' reading (as people loyal to a political party are likely to make of their opponent's publicity) or of contextual information (such as being told by a respected expert that a text's message is false). Clearly a propaganda text cannot work as effectively if the majority of the audience of the text is aware of its true purpose.

In war, where truth is often said to be the first casualty, propaganda is a major weapon. Recently in former Yugoslavia television has been in the vanguard of the propaganda battle:

> The Croatian government in Zagreb was still denying that [Vukovar] had fallen. Since there had been no surrender, there could not be any refugees, nor buses full of desperately thirsty people on the road to Zagreb. As proof, that evening, the Zagreb Television news described the heroic, irreducible resistance of the Croat fighters of Vukovar, the commentary given against a montage of artillery salvoes filmed at least three weeks ago, before the journalists of Zagreb TV had packed up and left the town. I then flipped to Belgrade TV, which was broadcasting a sequence of images of children's mutilated bodies – mutilated, it was claimed, by Croatian forces. (Hatzfeld, 1994, p. 215)

Propaganda was also used to great effect by the Nazis in the Second World War.

Nazi propaganda

One of the most effective proponents of propaganda in Nazi Germany was Joseph Goebbels, Head of the Ministry for Popular

Enlightenment and Propaganda (interestingly, Goebbels did not feel the need to conceal his ministry's function). He is often credited with enabling the Nazis to mobilize the German nation into the atrocities of the Holocaust.

The Frankfurt School of media theorists concluded that the co-operation of the bulk of German people, who were not Nazis, was due to the corrupting influence of popular culture and they feared the same would happen elsewhere in the Western world. Their theories were influential for a time, and still have a residue in 'common sense' discourses (dealt with in *Institutions and Audience*).

Hitler appealed to a nationalism based on folklore, tapping into a yearning for the 'good old days' during the economic maelstrom and cultural decadence of the Weimar Republic. He used mass meetings to reinforce his ideological standpoint, impressing his audience with the scale of the meeting, and making the audience feel part of a mass movement.

One of the most famous pieces of Nazi propaganda is Leni Riefenstahl's *Triumph des Willens* (*Triumph of the Will*: see Winston, 1995). This film record of the Nuremberg Rally in 1934 probably earns its reputation today more from its undoubted visual power than from any particular influence it had on its audience at the time. While the rally was certainly important in consolidating Hitler's power – it came only days after the Rohm *Putsch* when he wiped out opposition within his party – it probably had little impact on the German population.

In the Rohm *Putsch*, Hitler had wiped out the leaders of the SA, the Brownshirts, who had continued advocating a populist socialist agenda, something which was anathema to the German establishment.

Brian Winston (1995, p. 75) has shown that the propagandistic aim of *The Triumph of the Will* was to reposition the Nazi Party after it had gained power in the 1933 elections and to gain the support of the Brownshirts:

> The film has, despite its mind-numbing repetitiveness and interminable length, a careful and coherent structure which articulates a quite clear social/public-education purpose ... Virtually every synch word is directed towards the SA problem and the renegotiation of the Nazi Party's populist stance in the aftermath of the putsch.

It is a fascinating, and repelling, document to analyse, for it reveals much about how the conventions of filmic representation can be used for emotional, and propagandistic, impact.

The Triumph of the Will – opening sequence

Sound effects: silent

Music: martial in style

Shot number	Time (mins/secs)	Description
Fade in (FI):		
1	0	Roman-style eagle (Nazi emblem) – swastika Camera moves from low angle to eye level, we see *'Triumph des Willens'* on base of emblem in Roman-style lettering.
Dissolve (D)		
2	22	'The record of the State Party Congress 1934' (Roman-style, as on base)
D		
3	30	'Produced by Order of the Fuhrer'.
D		
4	37	'Directed by Leni Riefenstahl'.
Fade out (FO)		

Music: Wagnerian, ends with a drum roll which continues . . .

FI

5	43	'On 5th September 1934' (Expressionist typography) (After each shot of this introduction the lettering goes out of focus).

FO

Music: drum roll leads into a minor key (more sinister music)

6	51	'20 years after the outbreak of the World War'

FO

Shot number	Time (mins/secs)	Description
FI		
7	1 00	'16 years after the German suffering began'
FO		
FI		

Music: becomes heroic, like Wagner's theme for Siegfried

8	1 13	'19 months after the beginning of Germany's rebirth'
FO		
FI		

9	1 21	'Adolf Hitler flew to Nuremberg again to rally his followers'.
D		

Music: subdued, but still major key (i.e. sounds positive)

10	1 31	Right to left pan, hand-held, cock-pit of aeroplane, and above sun-gilded clouds. AH's point-of-view (POV).

Vertical wipe (virtually invisible)

11	1 43	POV clouds
Cut (C)		

12	1 53	POV more clouds
C		

13	1 59	PO clouds
C		

14	2 09	POV goes into clouds
C		

Shot number	Time (mins/secs)	Description
15	2 14	see 14
C		
16	2 34	see 14
C		
17	2 41	see 14

D (invisible transition)

Music: new theme

Shot number	Time (mins/secs)	Description
18	2 41	POV, high-angle: Nuremburg, church spires through clouds
C		
19	2 47	POV, lower: churches, castle prominent, German and Nazi flags on wall
C		
20	2 55	POV, lower
C		
21	2 54	Lower, medium shot ornate, old building
C		
22	3 00	Closer, Nazi flag on building
C		
23	3 09	Hitler's aeroplane
C		
24	3 14	Aeroplane's shadow on buildings, marching masses on road.
C		

Shot number	Time (mins/secs)	Description
Music: crescendo		
25	3 22	As 23 but closer.
C		
26	3 27	POV 90 degrees angle, people marching (right–left) below
C		
27	3 33	25, aeroplane rises out of frame
C		
28	3 36	90 degree shot, people marching top to bottom
C		
29	3 41	25, aeroplane drops into frame
C		
30	3 44	30, POV, marching on bridge (left–right)
C		
31	3 57	25
C		
32	3 54	Ground-level pan (l–r): Crowd behind barrier, looking into the sun, shading eyes, policed by men in Nazi uniforms. Two stand up just before . . .
C		
33	3 57	Aeroplane landing (r–l)
C		
Soundtrack: cheering		

Shot number	Time (mins/secs)	Description
34	3 59	Medium close-up of smiling Nazis, saluting
C		
35	4 02	Striking composition: top left-hand corner of frame sky, the rest people saluting toward this space.
C		
36	4 10	Close-up (CU) of emotional faces; salutes
C		
38	4 13	Medium CU aeroplane's wheels
C		
39	4 17	Military going to meet aeroplane
C		
40	4 18	See 38
C		
41	4 20	Aeroplane door opening
C		
42	4 23	Aeroplane door opens
C		
43	4 25	Salutes; massive cheer
C		
44	4 27	Hitler comes out and salutes; massive cheering
C		
45	4 30	LS from . . .

The Triumph of the Will *Opening sequence analysis*

The martial style of the music connotes militarism and nationalism. The Nazi emblem draws upon Roman iconography, which also represented a militarist nation. The low-angle shot emphasizes the power Nazis possess. By bringing the shot to eye-level we are brought into a privileged position, a position we are given access to throughout this sequence.

The old-style lettering of the title emphasizes its longevity: it, Nazism, has always been with us, only now is it fulfilling its destiny.

The title given in shot 2 suggests it is a documentary ('a record') and this reality is shown, in shot 3, to have been sanctioned by the Führer. 'Hitler as god' is another of the structuring themes of the sequence.

The music becomes Wagnerian, with connotations of archetypal myths of creation. The music explicitly comments upon the titles at this point, a minor key emphasizing the sinister circumstances of Germany's defeat in the First World War leading to the heroic theme associated with Hitler and Germany's rebirth. A partisan view of history is clearly being created and reinforced by the music's emotional impact. Then the documentary's narrative begins, with Hitler's arrival at Nuremberg.

Shot 10 is clearly a point-of-view shot but we are not sutured (shown the position of the point-of-view) until shot 23, when we see Hitler's aeroplane. This lack of anchoring within the sequence serves to create mystery and a god-like feeling of power as we see the descent from the clouds from Hitler's perspective. Of course everything looks comparatively small from the air, though the buildings are impressive in their grandeur (clearly selected for this). In 1934, few people would have flown, giving the sequence the excitement of a space flight now.

The photography is stunning, the sun-gilded clouds emphasizing nature's beauty and power, myths on which Nazism drew; particularly in its representations of the purity of the mountains.

As we descend from the clouds, among the first buildings we can see clearly, appropriately for a god, are a church and a building that has both the German and Nazi flags upon it, emphasizing the interchangeability of the Nazis and the German nation.

Once Hitler's point-of-view is anchored, in shot 23, his shadow – actually the aeroplane's but we identify it with Hitler since we assume him to be in the aeroplane – is seen both on the buildings and on the minute people marching to greet him. (This is similar to a scene in *The Third Man* (1948) in which Harry Lime points out that it is easy to kill people you perceive as insects.)

At last, after 3 minutes of descent, the aeroplane lands. Just before this crowds are seen waiting in anticipation, shielding their eyes – obviously from the sun, but it could easily be from the Führer's aura.

Cheering starts and the medium close-up of shot 34 brings us close to the masses, who are smiling, saluting Nazis. Shot 35 is a very striking composition which creates the effect of people saluting into the sky, from where their 'saviour' has just landed.

The arrival concludes with our perspective safely within the crowd. Our privileged position is now denied us, leaving Hitler on his pedestal.

It is a powerfully-constructed sequence, but only fascists could find it convincing now, as to us, Hitler has come to represent evil. In 1934 it appears that most people found the film boring. However, the rhetoric of the film's style works by giving us access to a privileged position squarely within the adoring masses that attended the Nuremberg rally. This is the 'you' that Neale defines as a function of propaganda, although rather than identifying 'you' as a national citizen, 'you' are placed as a Nazi.

Goebbels believed that feature films were, by far, a more potent force of propaganda than documentaries, for films were about entertainment and not 'preaching to the masses'. He believed that feature films would imperceptibly influence the audience because they would be unaware that they were watching propaganda.

Goebbels controlled film production by nationalizing the German film industry. Only members of *Reichsfilmkammer* (Chamber of Film) were allowed to make films. However, the notorious propaganda feature films such as *Hitlerjunge Quex* (1933) and *Jud Suss* (1940) did not appear out of a cultural vacuum. Ufa, Germany's premier film studio, had been producing 'mountain movies' since the late 1920s (Leni Riefenstahl, as an actress, starred in many of them). These films emphasized the racial purity of Aryan heroes by associating them with glaciers and mountains. The seeds of Nazi myths, and anti-semitism, were already part of German, and in fact European, culture.

Although *Hitlerjunge Quex* and *Jud Suss* are both clearly propaganda to our non-fascist eyes, they represent different styles of feature film. *Hitlerjunge Quex*, with its heroic, sacrificial tale of the Hitler Youth (a vicious variant of the boy scouts), did not find favour with Goebbels. It was too overtly propagandistic. *Jud Suss*, however, was Goebbels response to the trite and nauseating documentary *The Eternal Jew*, commissioned by Hitler. *The Eternal Jew* left little to its (small) audience's imagination in its equation of Jews with rats; *Jud Suss*, however, used the technique of cloaking contemporary issues in costume drama, and employed conventional feature film narrative to instil the message that Jews were evil and should be exterminated. Audience research at the time – albeit Nazi research – showed that the audience did make the equation.

So the most effective propaganda were texts that appeared to be entertainment and yet carried a specific ideological message which was intended to influence audiences' attitudes. All films, in fact, carry an ideological message. However, Goebbels' films differed in that they were specifically designed to change attitudes; most films seek, usually 'unconsciously', to reinforce the dominant ideological view. It is interesting to compare an overtly fascist propagandistic film, albeit a documentary, with a Hollywood film made in the same decade which explicitly attempted to articulate the liberal values of New Deal America.

The Triumph of the Will, 42nd Street *and the New Deal*

In *The Triumph of the Will* there are numerous long shots of thousands of people moving as one. This creates abstract patterns that only the multitude of cameras – and the fact that much of what we see is from Hitler's god-like point-of-view – can capture. These sequences have great visual power.

The fact that, though National Socialism is undeniably disgusting, the film has moments of incredible aesthetic power has caused problems for a number of film critics and has led some to eulogize Riefenstahl as 'a great film-maker' while acknowledging that the subject matter is dubious. This view has been encouraged by Riefenstahl, who claims she was 'politically naïve' and was only concerned with making films, the content of which was incidental. This position is indefensible, as Susan Sontag demonstrated in 'Fascinating Fascism' (in Nichols (ed.) 1976).

However, it is interesting to see how similar sequences in a Hollywood film can create the same aesthetic effect and yet are, on the face of it, articulating values which are the opposite to fascism.

US President Franklin D. Roosevelt was starting his term in office, in 1933, amid the 'Great Depression'. This originated in the Stock Market Crash of 1929, and was threatening the economic and social fabric of Western society. Roosevelt brokered a New Deal, a liberal attempt to intervene in the economic management of the country. The New Deal involved everybody 'pulling together' and the opportunity for a 'fresh start'.

Hollywood was drastically affected by the recession; takings and production were down, and investment and cash flow had been reduced to a trickle. This is not the place to embark on a thesis linking all Hollywood production to the New Deal, but there did thrive at the time a genre that seemed to reflect Roosevelt's values quite explicitly: the backstage musical.

The American Dream is that everyone, no matter how humble in origin, can be a success through hard work. Anybody can become President, even if, like Abraham Lincoln, it means going from the backwoods to the White House. As we saw in our consideration of the Western, the American Dream is a myth, an ideological construct designed to give society cohesion and make everyone feel they have a stake in the country. Mark Roth (1981, p. 45) demonstrates that the Warner's 'backstage musicals' subtly varied this myth:

> But while the myth is supported by the plot, it is contradicted, or at least significantly modified, by the dance numbers in which we see the individual subordinated to the will of a single person – the director . . . The message is that cooperation, planning and the guidance of a single leader are now necessary for success.

In the backstage musical an individual, through hard work and some talent, gets to become a star. However, to do this in the Great Depression requires a leader, and this leader, the director, represented Roosevelt. The interdependence of individuals in society is represented through the Busby Berkeley dance routines.

Roth also points out that the leads of *42nd Street*, Ruby Keeler and Dick Powell, are particularly untalented, making the audience feel that anyone can 'make it' (Powell did, however, make an excellent Philip Marlowe in *Farewell, My Lovely* (1944)). Keeler plays a chorus girl who gets her lucky break and becomes a star. Their very ordinariness possibly provokes an even stronger form of identification than mainstream cinema normally facilitates, positioning the audience as a 'you' in an almost propagandistic fashion.

The parallels between the New Deal and the 'backstage musical' are made clear in *42nd Street* with the director, played by Warner Baxter, having lost his money on the financial markets. Warner's also explicitly made the link between the film and Roosevelt's attempt at economic renewal in their publicity material:

The next week, the '42nd Street Special' left Hollywood 'on the greatest ride since Paul Revere', carrying 'news of a Revolution in Picture Art!' and 'leaving a trail of millions of ticket buyers for WARNER BROS. NEW DEAL IN ENTERTAINMENT'. (Hoberman, 1993, p. 32)

On the one hand, 42nd Street is a Horatio Alger story as refracted through the Ziegfeld Follies: the virtuous Peggy Sawyer works hard, resists temptation, gets her break, and makes the most of it. On the other hand, the film offers the vision of some new, collective social order, founded on the industrial production of erotic fantasy, the joyous orchestration of the masses, the confusion between making love and making work. Even more than most musicals, 42nd Street presents 'head-on', as Richard Dyer suggests in his essay on the use-value of entertainment, just 'what utopia would feel like'. (Hoberman, 1993, p. 68)

It takes little imagination to see the similarity between the abstract patterns that Berkeley creates out of people in his dance numbers and the dehumanized masses in *The Triumph of the Will* (indeed Berkeley-style routines featured in mainstream German cinema). However, one is a Liberal expression of community and the other a vicious ideology intent on slaughter – an interesting contradiction that suggests that while both texts are being produced with different aims, they are the product of the same aesthetic sensibility.

But are the aims of *The Triumph of the Will* and *42nd Street* so different? As Roth (1981, p. 55) concludes:

The image of a political leader as a large-scale Busby Berkeley is certainly ambiguous. The thrust of such an image is undoubtedly toward collective effort and subjugation of the will of the individual to the overall pattern dictated by the leader. But does this imply the ideal represented for Ruskin by the Middle Ages, or a socialist-communist ideal, or a Hitler–Franco type fascist dictatorship?

It could be that the same aesthetic device, which makes startling abstract and concrete patterns out of people, can only reflect one ideological position. The needs of Hitler and Roosevelt were the same, obedience, even though one was a fascist and the other a liberal. In this sense, both are propagandistic texts but, in Hollywood texts, the values of the dominant ideology are articulated and packaged as entertainment.

It is important to consider, as part of representation, a text's media language, its use of types, the institution determinants of the text, and audience's readings. When you consider that media language includes narrative and genre, it is clear that all the key concepts are part of representation which is hardly surprising because texts must re-present the world to us in some way. The next chapter considers the relationship between representation and reality.

6

REPRESENTATION AND REALITY

In Chapter 4 we considered four ways of approaching the analysis of representation. In this chapter we investigate what is being represented, which – of course – must be some form of reality. We are not concerned, however, with the 'real world' but with the conventions used to re-present the world. We shall consider the conventions of opposing modes of representation, realism (including naturalism) and modernism.

Media texts cannot show reality as it is; by their nature they mediate. (Of course even our perception of the physical world is mediated, if only by our senses.) Realism is a form of representation which has a privileged status because it signs itself as being closer to reality than other forms of representation such as 'genre' texts.

Our starting point will be a brief history of realism, which will serve as a reminder that all representations are the result of conventions produced at a particular time and place which is determined by the dominant ideology. What appeared 'real' in the past is often laughable now; we should never forget, however, that our mode of realism could be a source of mirth for future generations.

6.1 A history of realism

What has constituted realism over the past few hundred years has constantly changed:

> Historical realisms are: the realism that opposed romanticism and neo-classicism (c 1850); the realism that was distinguished from naturalism at a time when the concept seemed in danger of dilution (c 1890, but revived later, e.g. by Lukács); the realism that was affirmed against modernist tendencies (formalism, abstractionism, futurism, etc.), particularly in the Soviet Union (c 1930); the various realisms within modernism (verism, surrealism, hyperrealism, etc.), 'neo-realism' in opposition to 'Hollywood'. (Nowell-Smith, n.d.)

Confused? You are probably meant to be. Clearly realism is a concept embedded within the ideological discourses of a particular time and, as such, is useful in understanding the historical development of aesthetics. However, for the term to have any use we must first define it, not definitively, but sufficiently for the purposes of this book.

Roland Barthes, writing about literature, defined realism as a form that tries to efface its own production. In this sense mainstream cinema, as defined in Peter Wollen's antinomies, is realism. In this definition a modernist text, one that draws attention to itself as a text, cannot be realist. Realism strives for transparency, strives to appear natural.

> In Barthes' view, there is a literary ideology which corresponds to this 'natural attitude', and its name is realism. Realist literature tends to conceal the socially relative or constructed nature of language: it helps to confirm the prejudice that there is a form of 'ordinary' language which is somehow natural. This natural language gives us reality 'as it is': it does not – like Romanticism or Symbolism – distort it into objective shapes. (Eagleton, 1983, pp. 135–6)

Barthes' definition means that realism is inevitably constrained by the particular conventional codes of the time the text is created. For example, old (a floating definition, dependent on how old you are) films can seem 'corny' to contemporary audiences because the codes used are different from those employed today; at the time, however, the film may have seemed the epitome of realism.

So perhaps we can be a little more specific in our definition: a realist text uses codes that efface its own production, but these codes are specific to cultures at any given time. What, then, are our culture's conventions of realism as they are understood now?

Our conventions of realism were shaped in the seventeenth and eighteenth centuries.

Modern realism

Ian Watt, in the excellent *The Rise of the Novel* (1972), has described the philosophical basis of 'realism and the novel form' as a world view which, as we shall see, still holds sway today. Its intellectual origins were in the ideas of René Descartes.

- *Descartes* Descartes' philosophical formulation, *cogito ergo sum* ('I think therefore I am') describes truth as being a pursuit of individuals. This contrasted with the hitherto dominant belief, of the Greek philosopher Plato, that truth was universal and existed independently of individuals. Plato's universe was unchanging and therefore there was no need for individuals to pursue truth, everything was already known.

In the novels, created in such profusion from the seventeenth century, however, we have characters who are the cause and starting point of human actions. It matters little whether characters are stereotypical or 'rounded' as long as they are the cause of a convincing effect. The novel is concerned with psychological moti-vation, with characters acting on the basis of their experience.

Even in novels where fate takes a hand, such as Thomas Hardy's *Tess of the D'Urbervilles, Jude the Obscure* or *The Mayor of Casterbridge*, the emphasis is on the individual.

Before the novel broke with tradition in creating new plots, writers largely re-cycled previously-used stories. Shakespeare, for instance, used old material as the basis of his plays, material which reflected feudal ideology and offered a world view which empha-sized the unchanging nature of the world. Because in feudal times there could be nothing new, the essentials of human experience had already been investigated: all that remained were variations in the ways of telling archetypal tales.

The novel's new emphasis on individual at the expense of story allowed, in Watt's words (1972, p. 15), for 'the total subordination of plot to the pattern of the autobiographical [and this] is as defiant an assertion of the primacy of individual experience in the novel as "cogito ergo sum" was in philosophy'. This autobiographical emphasis is epitomized, as Watt shows, in Robinson Crusoe.

• *'Particular people in particular circumstances'* As truth could be seen to be the pursuit of specific goals by individuals, these individuals obviously had to be particular, rather than general; they had to exist in a recognizable circumstance, or social background. Once again this was in opposition to literary tradition, which, deriving from Greek literature, insisted upon general human types set against a conventional literary background. For example, the Pastoral had an idyllic countryside setting populated with shep-herds and sheep.

Indeed, when considering complex 'novelistic' characters, which are intended to represent real people, we should consider the following qualities (once again best described by Richard Dyer, 1979):

1. *particularity* – the character is unique rather than typical
2. *interest* – the particularity of characters makes them interesting
3. *autonomy* – characters have a 'life of their own', they are not blatantly a function of the plot
4. *roundness* – characters possess a multiplicity of traits rather than one or two which 'types', or flat characters, possess
5. *development* – characters should develop in the narrative; they learn from experience
6. *interiority* – characters have an interior life; this might be shown by giving access to their intrapersonal communication and, again, emphasises their particularity
7. *motivation* – there are clear psychological reasons for characters' actions, often derived from their particularity;
8. *discrete identity* – the character must be signed to exist beyond the text in which they appear, in other words, they usually have a past and a future beyond the text
9. *consistency* – while characters must develop, they must also possess a central core, an ego-identity, that does not change.

These qualities are to be found within ourselves (think back to the '20 statement test' in Chapter 3). However, they are not real, they are a social construct, a particular way of looking at individuality and, as such, represent the bourgeois conception. Alternative representations of individuals are not inherently wrong, they are merely utilizing a different set of conventions.

● *Proper, rather than characteristic, names* In John Bunyan's *The Pilgrim's Progress*, written in 1678 and 1684, the main character is called Christian and meets Faithful and Hopeful. The 'names' are really descriptions of the characters. The places visited are also allegorical in nature, for example: Vanity Fair, Hill Difficulty and the Delectable Mountains. By contrast, the novel used 'normal' names which did not, generally, indicate character.

● *Time* Convincing characters must exist not only in space (a particular circumstance) but also in a particular time. The philosopher Locke described how personal identity was reliant upon memory, which is consciousness through time. Once again this contrasts with Plato's universals, where time has no role in the creation of meaning, for the ideal types are fixed and universal.

In the modern novel we demand that the setting, whether historical or contemporary, sign itself to be accurate. If an author introduced motor cars in a novel set in the eighteenth century, we would instantly spot the anachronism. However, BBC television's 'classic' serials are not always historically accurate, despite their reputation for verisimilitude – occasionally a prop will be chosen that wasn't contemporary with the setting because modern audiences believe it was extant in the period of the text. Similarly, we can accept futuristic, science fiction settings as being accurate (which, of course, we cannot know) as long it is conventional.

As mentioned earlier, the actions of a novel's characters must be motivated by their experience (their past); this emphasis on the temporal is, once again, at odds with the feudal belief in an unchanging, and unchangeable, world.

The time-scale within novels is often carefully constructed, whether it is a saga that crosses generations, like *Wuthering Heights* or a book that deals with the minutiae of mental experience such as *The Mezzanine* by Nicholson Baker. We expect the novel's time scale to reflect our own experience.

Shakespeare, by contrast, can cause modern academics problems when they try to pin down the time-scale in some of his plays. In *Hamlet* the eponymous prince appears to be in his early twenties until we are suddenly told, indirectly by the gravedigger, that he is thirty. Othello marries, travels to Cyprus, and then murders his wife in a jealous fit, all in three days! While Shakespeare was certainly concerned with 'psychological realism' as we understand it, the time-scale was not important to him. Indeed, he can happily include clocks in Julius Caesar, despite knowing they did not exist at the time. These anachronisms were not seen as such; indeed the word anachronism was not used until thirty years after Shakespeare's death.

Although Watt describes realism in the novel, mainstream texts also follow these conventions. Like Peter Wollen, in his definition of counter cinema, it is useful to consider antinomies as part of our definition of realism. So far we have followed Barthes' definition of realism as a text which effaces its own production. The opposite of this is modernism.

Modernism

Superficially, modernism refers to texts which are modern, often belonging to a specific period early in the twentieth century. However, the elasticity of the term is such that the length, beginning and end of this period are highly debatable.

A more useful definition is that modernist texts, in contrast to realism, parade the fact that they are texts. For example, James

Joyce's *Ulysses* (1968, p. 289) highlights its use of words, which all novels must use, with unconventionally structured sentences and strange combinations of letters:

> Tip. An unseeing stripling stood in the door. He saw not bronze. He saw not gold. Nor Ben nor Bob nor Tom nor Si nor George nor tanks nor Richie nor Pat. Hee hee hee hee. He did not see.
> Seabloom, greasebloom viewed last words. Softly. *When my country takes her place among.*
> Prrprr.
> Must be the bur.
> Fff. Oo. Rrpr.

In cinema, too, *Citizen Kane* begins by showing Kane's life in the form of an authentic-seeming newsreel (the cinematic equivalent of our television news), but then sets about deliberately casting doubt on its authenticity by drawing attention to the fact that 'newsreels' cannot possibly give a completely true picture.

In Chapter 3 we investigated the cinema of montage as an alternative to the continuity editing that dominates cinema in the West. This, too, was part of the project of modernism. Eisenstein and Dziga Vertov (discussed in Chapter 4) both drew attention to their texts as artefacts. Their subject matter, the modern city and the masses within it, is also a common modernist theme.

Clearly the conventional forms of any given era are likely to be considered the 'realistic' forms. Modernist texts draw attention to themselves as texts through being formally unconventional.

Modernism's concerns of the city and the urban environment are shown in T. S. Eliot's quintessential modernist piece, *The Waste Land* (1974, p. 65):

> Unreal City,
> Under the brown fog of a winter dawn,
> A crowd flowed over London Bridge, so many,
> I had not thought death had undone so many.

Eliot's mixture of colloquial phrases ('HURRY UP PLEASE ITS TIME'), erudite allusion and German phrases all serve to draw attention to the poem as a text, as does the mixture of traditional lyric, surrealism and satire. The theme of his poem, the intellectual aridity of Western civilization, is also a modernist concern. When he wrote it, apparently sophisticated civilization, with its dazzling technology and massive conurbations, had just indulged in the obscenity of the First World War.

The year of Eliot's poem, 1922, is an important date in modernism. *Ulysses* was published, as were novels by D. H. Lawrence and Virginia Woolf, and Brecht's first play, *Baal*, was staged.

Brecht developed the theory of 'epic theatre', in which he constantly reminded the audience that they were watching a play, not reality. This had the effect of 'alienating' them and making impossible the catharsis of Aristotelian (Greek) theatre. Catharsis, in which the audience is emotionally purged by the experience of watching a play, is still the defining factor in nearly all entertainment today. Brecht characterized 'epic theatre' as one which turned its spectators into observers rather than implicating them in the action. His objective was to rouse them to action, and, as Brecht's plays dealt with social inequality, he hoped the audience would be moved to fight for social justice.

Modernism was probably not solely the product of the social upheaval engendered by the First World War or the Soviet Revolution in 1917. Einstein published his General Theory of Relativity in 1915 and received the Nobel Prize, for earlier work, in 1921. In effect, Einstein did away with the certainties of Newtonian physics by emphasizing that physical measurement was determined by the position of the observer; two observers in different positions observing the same object could arrive at different results. If science, which many still believe to be the objective way to observe reality, cannot be relied upon to give a coherent view of reality (Einsteinean physics throws up many paradoxes which, obviously, draw attention to themselves) then surely the project of realism was doomed.

Modernism was the expression of a 'paradigm shift', a fundamental change in the social perception of reality. The certainties engendered by the Age of Enlightenment were no longer apparent and the teleological progress of Western civilization was thrown into question by contemporary events.

Although the examples given so far are primarily from literature, Watts' categories, and the description of modernism, apply equally well to all kinds of media texts. Realism is a term that has been used, for example, to describe specific forms of cinema and, indeed, is one of the defining tenets of narrative cinema.

6.2 Realism and narrative cinema

The term 'narrative cinema' refers, in the main, to fictional cinema, although most documentaries have a narrative structure too. (The use of realism in documentary will be considered later.)

It's often suggested that the circumstances surrounding the birth of cinema – with two of its pioneers making very different films at the same time – set up a tension between realism and fantasy which is still with us. On the one hand, there was the documentary record of everyday life recorded by the Lumière brothers; on the other, the fantastic artifice of Georges Méliès. The iconic nature of the film image simultaneously appears to present reality in a recognisable form, yet also makes the fantastic believable, even if to the modern audience, who are used to *Terminator 2*-style pyrotechnics, Méliès' effects now seem contrived and even risible.

From a scientific point of view, film appeared to offer a more powerful perception of reality than even human beings were capable of. Eadweard Muybridge's series of photographs of galloping horses showed, for the first time, that artists had been portraying them incorrectly (the photographs showed all four feet are off the ground at one point). Films through microscopes showed to a mass audience the world as humans do not normally perceive it. Stop-motion photography, often used in nature documentaries, can show how a flower grows, and infra-red photography allows us to see in the dark.

Narrative cinema, including most narratively-structured documentaries, is constructed in a similar way to the conventional novel described in Chapter 4, with the emphasis upon individual actions, and a specific time and place and so on. This cinema, in its fictional form at least, was most potently developed in Hollywood. Once again, it is useful to contrast the mainstream with oppositional discourse; Soviet Socialist Realism was an attempt to negate what was seen as the insidious tendencies of bourgeois cinema, exemplified by Hollywood.

Soviet Socialist Realism

Probably the first national movement that based itself on realism was Soviet Socialist Realism, the doctrine of which was set out by Zhdanov in 1932. The basic idea was that reality would be represented not as it is, but as it will become in a socialist state:

> Realism in this sense means art that sets out to present a comprehensive reflection and interpretation of life from the point of view of social relations; 'Socialist' means in accordance with the policy of the Communist Party. Socialist Realism is therefore based on a direct relationship between the artist and the process of building a new society; it is art coloured by the experience of the working class in its struggle to achieve socialism. (Vaughan James, 1973, p. 88)

What this meant in practice, as stated explicitly in the declaration on socialist realism made at the 1928 Congress on Film Questions, was that the film form used should be understandable by millions. Clearly the modernists, Eisenstein and Vertov, did not fit into this definition. In practice, socialist realism film form was very similar to that of Hollywood, although the content was very different; for example, documentaries in support of Stalin's Five Year Plan.

While the remnants of this credo can still be seen in some totalitarian states – the idealism present in the numerous portraits of Saddam Hussein, for example – it is arguable that Hollywood serves a very similar function. Though, of course, Hollywood does not serve communist ideology, it represents the values of bourgeois ideology.

Italian Neo-Realism

Another national cinema that thrived, artistically if not financially, was in post-Second World War Italy. The premise of Italian Neo-Realism was that cinema should represent human reality, and this was signified by shooting on location rather than in studios (which were not available anyway).

Interestingly, the actual films produced now seem, in some aspects, peculiarly non-realistic: location shooting meant the sound-track had to be dubbed later, and this was usually done by professionals rather than the actual performers (to non-Italian speakers the 'jarring' effect – it is rare for such dubbing to be unnoticeable – this creates is often lost, as we are too busy reading the subtitles). Stylistically there is no common thread, rather the films gain unity from their anti-fascism.

Bicycle Thieves (1948), directed by Vittorio di Sica and written by Cesare Zavattini, is probably the classic Neo-Realist film.

Realism is a set of conventions which set out to portray 'reality as it is'. However, behind the rhetoric there is an ideology that is structuring the world view. As we have seen, the roots of modern, Western realism are found in the Renaissance, when the emerging ideology of the bourgeoisie was first making an impact. The emphasis on the individual in literary artefacts was a result of the shift from feudalism; as was the individual address facilitated by the Renaissance perspective, described in Chapter 3. The notion of ideology enables us to see links between different art forms, here literature and painting, and show how these are expressions of a particular ideological system. Clearly this is a very powerful and holistic way to understand texts and society. However, we must avoid the reductionism which makes a simple leap from the apparently all-encompassing dominant ideology, whatever that might be, to all media texts, for there are always exceptions to the rule. It is common, though, for mainstream texts to reflect dominant power structures.

There follows a consideration of two texts which have different ways of representing reality.

6.3 *The Jungle* and *St Joan of the Stockyards*

Émile Zola, one of the most famous exponents of naturalism, used the term in his preface to the second edition of his novel *Thérèse Raquin* in 1867. However, the term is not easily defined and has metamorphosed as different theorists put their own 'spin' on the idea.

Essentially, though, naturalism dealt with the materialist, rather than idealist, world. It often took working class life as its subject, such as the miners in Zola's *Germinal* or the railway worker in *La Bête humaine* (memorably adapted as a film by Jean Renoir). In some ways naturalists saw themselves as documentarists, objectively presenting a contemporary 'slice of life', and they did not eschew subjects such as sexuality which 'respectable' literature and theatre refused to deal with. Because conditions caused by the on-going industrialization of the times were often inhumane, one consequence of concentrating on working-class life was that naturalism had a didactic edge which was usually anti-bourgeois in nature.

Naturalism does not only describe a text's content. Many authors who saw themselves as naturalists experimented with form, such as the 'camera-eye' of John Dos Passos' trilogy *USA*. In general, however, naturalism and modernism characterize opposite tendencies in art: one attempts to show the 'world as it is', the other is concerned to highlight the 'text as it is'.

The two texts I am using for the purposes of comparison, a novel and a play, represent these opposing modes of representation. Upton Sinclair's *The Jungle* was first published in 1906 in the USA and is credited with forcing government legislation to improve health and safety in the Chicago stockyards (where animals were processed into meat). Brecht's play has the same subject matter – the failure of unfettered capitalism to function to the benefit of society as a whole, in those stockyards. While Sinclair uses a 'naturalist' technique, Brecht uses his 'epic theatre', modernist, approach.

Jurgis, the central character of *The Jungle,* is a twentieth-century Candide (Voltaire's naïve character who investigates the world but fails to learn from his experiences, and retains a faith in goodness that is patently out-of-step with the world). Sinclair used the character as a 'camera eye' – not the subjective eye of John Dos Passos in *USA,* but an objective lens through which the audience observes Jurgis' progress through Chicago society. He has very little character other than his stoicism. The use of an objective camera eye is part of naturalism's project to represent the world through surface detail. The meandering, picaresque structure of *The Jungle,* with its use of 'accidental' encounters, is also intended to signify 'ordinary life'.

The documentary-style attention to detail of the stockyards is also naturalist; although, unlike many naturalist projects, the details are not mundane everyday life – at least not to most of us – but refer to a particular industry, time and place. The details are so shocking that they do not need dramatic embroidery for Sinclair (1936, p. 120) to make his point:

> Worse of any, however, were the fertilizer-men, and those who served in the cooking rooms. These people could not be shown to the visitor, for the odour of a fertilizer-man would scare any ordinary visitor at a hundred yards; and as for the other men, who worked in tank fulls of steam, and in some of which there were open vats near the level of the floor, their peculiar trouble was that they fell into the vats; and when they were fished out, there was never enough of them left to be worth exhibiting – sometimes they would be overlooked for days, till all but the bones of them had gone out to the world as Durham's Pure Leaf Lard!

The Jungle is also a naturalist text in its didactic intent. Sinclair's picaresque adventure ends with the radical statement (1936, p. 411):

> 'We shall have the sham reformers self-stultified and self-convicted; we shall have the radical Democracy left without a lie with which to cover its nakedness! And then will begin the rush that will never be checked, the tide that will never turn till it has reached its flood – that will be irresistible, overwhelming – the rallying of the outraged working men of Chicago to our standard! And we shall organize them, we shall drill them, we shall marshal them for the victory! We shall bear down the opposition, we shall sweep it before us – and Chicago will ours! Chicago will be ours! CHICAGO WILL BE OURS!'

Brecht's intention in *St Joan of the Stockyards* was similar to Sinclair's. However, Brecht believed that naturalism offered only a static portrayal of the world which, he believed, took away the individual's power of political intervention; everything seems unchanging and unchangeable. Brecht rejected the Aristotelian notion of identification with the hero which sought to purge the audience of their emotions; his approach attempted to show the power relationships in society. For Brecht it was these power relations and not the surface detail of naturalism that represented reality.

In *St Joan of the Stockyards* the central character is Joan Dark, a latter-day Joan of Arc who is a lieutenant in the Black Straw Hats, a Salvation Army-type of religious group. Joan believes in the inherent goodness of humanity and attempts to convince Pierpont Mauler, the meat king, of the error of his ways. Joan's effect on Mauler is simply to make him even more rich and powerful: when, in apparent remorse, he sells all his stock he manages to avoid a crash in price; he is then begged to buy back stock to help the market and so gets back everything he sold for a fraction of the price.

To describe a play by merely referring to the printed text is to lose many of the artefact's channels of communication. A director can bring the same words to dramatic life in numerous different ways. However, we can comment on the play as a written text.

Joan is similar to Jurgis in that she is naïve. However she learns from her bitter experiences and reaches the conclusion that:

> ' . . . The truth is that
> Where force rules only force can help and
> In the human world only humans can help.'
> (Brecht, 1991, p. 108)

As can be seen from the characters' names, we are dealing with types (the corrupt major of the Black Straw Hats is called Snyder), Brecht avoids any sense of 'novelistic' characters. The use of poetry, rather than everyday speech, serves to heighten the language's power and calls attention to its artifice.

While Sinclair draws us into his narrative through identification with Jurgis, Brecht distances us by 'scrapping the "well-made" limitations of the Aristotelian unities and substituting a montage based (as in the new visual arts) on cutting and selective realism.' Both authors had the same agenda, to expose the horrors of the Chicago Stockyards, and both were trying to represent a reality. Both texts are very powerful and only ideologues would object to either on the grounds of their formal aspects. Reality can be represented in many different ways: it is unlikely that any of them can tell us the whole truth.

6.4 Formal realism in documentary

Documentaries have a privileged place in the discourse of realism because they declare themselves to be non-fiction and, by extension, the truth. This is different from the claims to realism 'put forward' by fictional texts. Fictional texts lay no claim to be representing actual events, but rather things which could happen.

However, the sign systems, narrative structure and performance within documentaries are very similar to those used in fiction. Documentary is different from fictional discourse in its rhetorical pronouncement that it is representing *the* world rather than *a* world. Bill Nichols (1991, p. 111) makes a useful distinction between these modes of documentary discourse:

> Documentaries . . . do not differ from fictions in their constructedness as texts, but in the representations they make. At the heart of documentary is less a story and its imaginary world than an argument about the historical world.

Nichols further develops this argument as 'placing evidence before others in order to convey a particular viewpoint, [and this] forms the organizational backbone of the documentary' (1991, p. 125).

In the following description of documentary, the similarity of fictional and non-fictional discourse will be demonstrated in more detail. Bill Nichols (1991, p. 132) has described how:

> four modes of representation stand out as the dominant organizational patterns around which most texts are structured: expository, observational, interactive, and reflexive.

To this typology we can add drama-documentary (or drama-doc).

The expository mode

Expository documentary is characterized by a 'voice-of-God' narration, or intertitles, which directly address the viewer. The voice-over is God-like because it anchors the meaning of the images, explicitly states the text's preferred meaning and reduces the possibility of polysemy.

As we have seen in the last chapter, reports on television news also use the voice-of-God to ground the meaning of the broadcast within the institution's news agenda.

So the images of expository documentaries merely illustrate what the narrator is saying and appear to emphasize the 'objectivity' of that commentary; the images seem to show the voice-of-God is speaking the truth. For example, in wildlife documentaries we are usually invited, by the commentary, to interpret animal behaviour in anthropomorphic terms and often have little difficulty in imagining squirrels having a domestic dispute or a snake slyly sneaking up on its pray. Of course, squirrels have no concept of domesticity and snakes are not sly.

Interviews may be included in expository documentary, but are always subordinated to the voice-over which, in effect, is speaking on behalf of the text. Clearly any dissenting interview voices can be edited out.

These documentaries are often structured by a conventional narrative, and are usually centred around a problem which needs solving. They also uses dramatic techniques to heighten the suspense and so draw the audience into experiencing the text as entertainment.

John Grierson started this form of documentary in Britain during the 1930s. His project was in many ways similar to that of another Scot, his contemporary John Reith, the first Director-General of the BBC. Both had a mission to educate the masses: Reith developed the Public Service Broadcasting ethos, Grierson made documentaries.

Grierson's first film, the silent *Drifters* (1929), was made for the Empire Marketing Board, an organization dedicated to promoting trade and engendering a sense of unity in the British Empire. Although *Drifters* is not an advertisement in the sense of selling a product or service, as Barnouw (1993, p. 88) notes:

> Final scenes depict quayside auctioning of the [herring] catch and project the herring business into international trade – 'a market for the world.' Grierson must have had the Empire Marketing Board in mind in his final subtitle: 'So to the ends of the earth goes the harvest of the sea'.

Grierson's most well-known film is *Night Mail* (1934) which narrates the progress of a mail train from England to Scotland. Beautifully photographed and dramatically edited, it is a wonderful advertisement for the Post Office. The 'received pronunciation' of the voice-of-God voice-over, however, jars slightly on the modern audience, particularly when contrasted with the local accents of the workers: the implicit equation is that the middle classes possess the voice of authority.

Armed with the knowledge that synchronous sound was not possible until the 1950s, the Media Studies student will realize that all the sounds which appear to originate from the diegesis, the narrative world, are in fact post-dubbed (added later). The scene of sorters working on the train proved impossible to film because of the train's motion and so was recreated as an eerily still environment in the studio. Clearly the practicalities of filming a documentary were not going to get in the way of representing 'reality'.

The observational mode

The observational mode describes what is more commonly known as 'fly-on-the-wall' documentary, *cinéma vérité* ('truth' cinema), Free Cinema or direct cinema. There is some confusion over definitions, and Nichols dispenses with the terms in favour of the 'observational' and 'interactive' modes.

The defining aspect of the 'observational' mode is that the camera is as unobtrusive as possible, although not usually hidden. (Hidden cameras are usually used for humour or for investigative purposes, the latter often 'expository' in form.) Ideally participants should 'forget' the camera's existence and behave 'normally'. BBC's *The Living Soap* and MTV's *The Real World* both attempted to reveal student life 'as it is'; although the 'soap' aspect of the BBC project suggested the influence of a fictional discourse, soap opera.

The 'observational' mode is very close to the 'window on the world'; it is as if the audience is allowed to see an unmediated reality. The techniques used to create this illusion are:

- indirect address to audience (speech is overheard and not directed to camera);
- synchronous sound (not post-dubbed);
- relatively long takes (shots) demonstrating nothing has been 'cut out'.

Any music must be diegetic, that is, originate from the scene being filmed. Continuity editing is used if a scene consists of a number of shots. This is clearly to ensure that the audience does not become disorientated, but as continuity editing is primarily a form of fictional representation then in such documentaries we are experiencing a spatial construction which represents the world as if it were fictional.

Because it is unusual to use more than one camera it is easier to show events in one take. Once you attempt to use different positions within a scene it can be very difficult to get aural continuity. One way around this is for the documentary-maker to request participants to do an action again – as is very common in news reports and interviews – but is obviously totally against the 'observational' nature of this mode.

Careful cutting can be used to create fictional space. The opening of the Maysles brothers' *Salesman* (1969) shows a salesman failing to sell a Bible. The scene is constructed in eleven shots, with the dialogue usually beginning and ending at the same time as the shot ends, although there is one cut in the middle of a sentence which suggests some post-dubbing.

Clearly the ability to follow the action and record the sound simultaneously (synchronous) could not happen until the light-weight technology of the hand-held camera became available. Today's camcorders are the descendants of years of progressively smaller equipment.

The 'observational 'mode stresses 'an empathetic, nonjudgmental, participatory mode of observation that attenuates the authoritative posture of traditional exposition' (Nichols, 1991, p. 42).

Ironically the 'observational' mode can seem authentic and there-fore more authoritative than the 'expositional' mode. Film-makers do not need a voice-over commentary to anchor the meanings of images. However, the existence of the camera in a social situation immediately turns people into social actors. While it is possible that people will 'act naturally' in front of a camera – although most of us feel self-conscious – once behaviour has been recorded then it is available for analysis to an extent that 'real life' never can be. (Any discussion of how one behaved in a situation must rely upon memories which can lead to much disagreement, whereas looking at an image will at least guarantee agreement at the level of denotation.) An 'observational' documentary does not show 'real people', it shows 'social actors'.

In *High School 2* Frederick Wiseman, the maker of many famous 'observational' documentaries such as *Hospital*, creates a picture of an inner city American high school through a mix of classroom scenes and teachers' interviews with students who have problems. The opening of the film shows students arriving at the school, creating a 'day-in-the-life-of' narrative framework although what we see, clearly, must have been filmed over many weeks.

Filming within an institution obviously requires the co-operation and permission of participants. Full access to 'reality' can be compromised by those people refusing to be filmed.

Wiseman produces a representation of the teachers as caring, liberal individuals; this cannot be the truth, but merely one repre-sentation of the school. If the young black male who states that he would respect the school more if there were more black teachers had made the documentary, then his portrayal of the institution would have been very different.

Deadline, broadcast in Britain by Channel 4 in March and April 1994, used 'observational' techniques in observing how a local television news organization, Yorkshire Television, operates. It was not strictly observational because the 'actors' would occasionally address the camera directly to explain what was happening. This was a result, in part, of the fact that the documentary's subjects were media literate and sometimes because an offscreen voice would request an explanation. Some scenes shot for the documentary were cut at the request of Yorkshire Television – and some requests were rejected – which again compromises the notion of 'objectivity'.

The interactive mode

The 'interactive mode' acknowledges the presence of the camera and crew; it does not try to efface itself, as do the 'expository' and 'observational' modes. This mode was in many ways the dream of Dziga Vertov, the Soviet film-maker of the 1920s discussed in Chapter 4. He created the idea of the Kino-Pravda and later Kino-Eye: a 'wall newspaper [coming] out weekly or monthly; [illustrating] factory or village life' (Willims, 1980, p. 25). Vertov's work, though, is more an example of the 'reflexive' mode, because it was not until the late 1950s that his ideal became practical with the development of light-weight equipment which would make synchronous recordings.

Easily portable equipment meant that post-dubbing was no longer required and allowed the film-maker to speak directly to his or her subjects. The documentary-maker could become involved in the scene, and could indeed interact with what was being filmed. Because of this, 'interactive' documentaries focus on the exchange of information rather than creating a coherent view – an objective of 'expository' documentaries.

For example, in *The Thin Blue Line*, directed by Errol Morris, various witnesses give their views of events concerning the murder of a policeman. They often contradict each other. It is as if the audience are left to make their own decision about the truth; although, obviously, the construction of the images – particularly in the framing and editing – is likely to create a preferred reading. Despite the fact that Morris does not intrude as an interviewer, the audience is constantly reminded of the existence of multiple viewpoints because they are placed in the position of an investigating journalist questioning the main participants for the story. This is in sharp contrast to the 'voice-of-God' omnipotence offered by the 'expository' mode and the 'matter-of-fact' neutrality of the 'observational' mode. Morris only makes his view clear at the end.

It could be argued that this mode is somewhat more 'honest' than previous modes because no attempt is made to disguise the presence of the camera and crew, which, after all, must be present in order for a film to exist. But while the 'interactive' mode acknowledges the presence of film-makers, there remains the question of how far this interaction influences what is being documented. After all, the fact that the rhetoric of all documentaries – that we are seeing the world as it is – is in reality unattainable, holds true for this mode. For example, in *Shoah*, how much are Claude Lanzman's promptings of Holocaust victims to talk about their experiences, a result of the need for drama, rather than a documentarist's need for information?

Many 'interactive' documentaries use the form of the interview, a hierarchical discourse with the interviewer setting the agenda, which immediately cast doubt on the 'reality' represented. Anything can be proved by asking 'loaded' questions (and choosing whom to interview). Similarly, although the vox pop form of interviewing signifies itself as authentic, who, if anyone, checks up on the 'truth' of what is said?

So it is clear that the interactive mode is as constructed as those described earlier. Like the 'observational' mode it appears to allow 'reality' to speak for itself, but simply because the mode acknowledges the film-maker's presence it does not give it access to unmediated reality. The director still chooses where to place the camera, how to light the scene, and what to leave on the cutting room floor.

The reflexive mode

The aim of the reflexive mode is not only to represent its subject but to demonstrate itself in the act of representing; in other words, the mode draws attention to its own codes. A documentary about, say, an election campaign, is also a documentary about making a documentary about an election campaign! In a sense this is the direct opposite of the expository and observational modes, both of which attempt to convince us that we are not watching a carefully-constructed documentary but rather have access to a 'window on the world'. The reflexive mode problematizes what we are seeing by acknowledging the medium.

Man with a Movie Camera (1929), Dziga Vertov's most famous work, is an excellent example of the reflexive mode. It is an ebullient and invigorating city tour, a mix of Moscow, Kiev and Riga, in which the hero, (although Vertov professed to eschew such bourgeois conceptions), is the eponymous observer of events. Vertov's self-reflexivity (a modernist characteristic) consists of a number of techniques which draw attention to themselves. Vertov is even self-reflexive about the cinema experience: his film opens by showing an audience entering the theatre and watching the film begin. Other sequences emphasize the constructed nature of the film by: showing the cameraman filming events we see on the screen, sometimes as a reflection is a window or using eyeline match editing; animating inanimate objects using stop-motion photography; superimposing an eye on the camera's lens (the kino-eye indeed).

Avant-garde film and video maker, Jean-Luc Godard, wrote directly on to the images he was using. This simultaneously drew attention to the construction of the text (as the writing appears, we see the text being created) and also cast doubt on the anchoring of the images by showing the actual act of anchorage.

Whereas the interactive mode emphasizes the relationship between the documentary-maker and her or his subject, the reflexive mode is more concerned with the encounter between the documentary text and its audience. There is, of course, a danger that by drawing too much attention to its own mode of construction, a documentary may cause the audience to lose sight of its subject; the medium can obscure the message. That said, at least this mode makes the clear statement that representing the world cannot be other than problematic, and that to suggest otherwise is a form of lie.

In addition to Nichols' modes, there is drama-documentary which is, usually, formally structured in the same way as narrative cinema.

Drama-documentary

Drama-documentary (drama-doc) attempts to recreate, as accurately as possible, events that actually happened. It is a form that often attracts controversy because no matter how painstaking the recreation, it is a representation and therefore can never be exactly the same as the actuality. Complaints about drama-documentary usually concern the text's lack of authenticity.

Documentary-dramas, on the other hand, are dramas shot in the style of a documentary (use of hand-held cameras, interviews and so on. The classic of this genre is Ken Loach's and Tony Garnett's *Cathy Come Home* (1966).

Drama-documentaries such as the films *JFK* (1991) and *In the Name of the Father* (1994) are thought, by some, to distort greatly the events on which they were based. As a consequence of such criticisms, a group of drama-documentary-makers constructed a self-regulatory charter:

(a) 'no version of events or conclusions should be offered as definitive if they cannot be substantiated through responsible journalistic methods';
(b) 'the nature of the programme must be spelt out to the audience very clearly before it begins';
(c) characters should not be portrayed having sex, smoking, drinking, swearing even, to enliven storylines unless such scenes can be substantiated';
(d) programme-makers must inform people named in programmes that they are about to be screened'. (White, 1994)

The use of dramatic techniques in documentary is not limited to drama-doc. However, its explicit use of fictional styles highlights the dramatic component. While the above charter seeks to avoid sensationalism, documentaries – in any of Nichols' modes – can sensationalize their subjects in much less obvious ways.

6.5 Documentaries and reality

Life is not a conventional narrative unless you class life itself as a disruption (you're born, live, then die). However, conventional narrative is predominantly used to structure documentaries. In some cases, such as following the progress of a trial in a law court, such narrative seems appropriate: the crime defendant is accused of may represent the opening situation, the trial, the disruption, and the verdict the resolution. In many cases, however, conventional narrative invites us into a fictional discourse, when what is being represented is reputed to be non-fictional.

This is not to accuse documentary-makers of lies. Any form of representation requires an agenda, even if it is often dictated by institutions. In a fascinating article, journalist Robert Fisk describes the compromises made in the documentary series *From Beirut to*

Bosnia broadcast in Britain on Channel 4 in 1993. Fisk had reported on the Middle East and Balkans for 17 years, in *The Times* and the *Independent*, but found the technology of television and the director's conception of the documentary's audience problematic:

> the technology of television would both trivialise and authenticate the world in which I had lived for 17 years. Even in a Palestinian hospital, a clapper-board – a real Hollywood-style chalk board with a black-and-white 'clapper' on top – had been clacked in front of wounded men. (Fisk, 1993)

Michael Dutfield, the experienced director of the documentary, characterized the audience as his '82-year-old mum'; in other words, long and complicated political explanations had little role in the film.

The problems inherent in representation were shown when interviewing an elderly Shia Muslim woman:

> when [she] was ready to tell [her son's] painful story on film, Michael did not like the sofa upon which she was sitting. It was second-hand, the only piece of bright colour in the room. 'It gives the wrong impression,' Michael said. 'She's poor but it makes her look rich. And she's not rich.'
>
> I objected to this. If the sofa gave the wrong 'impression', then so be it . . . This woman's sofa was part of her identity. I loudly complained that to move the sofa would be like making a Hollywood film rather than a television documentary, a remark that at once angered Michael's cameraman, Steve. 'Come over here and look through the lens, Bob,' he said softly. I peered through it and understood at once. What was in reality a rather shabby second-hand sofa was transformed by the camera's lens into a heavily-embroidered, satin-covered chaise-longue. (Fisk, 1993)

So in this case the substitution of the sofa arguably created a more accurate representation than if the actual one had been used. However, in Fisk's view the conventions of television, with its use of a particular technology and mass audience, certainly compromised the representation of the area. As Fisk (1993) said: 'It was not the theatricality I identified in documentary film-making [that troubled me] . . . but the refusal to acknowledge it'. An acknowledgement would have made *From Beirut to Bosnia* self-reflexive.

Entertainment of the audience, including Dutfield's 82-year-old mother, is one of the requirements of most television texts. The genre of 'reconstructions', where real-life dramas are recreated using actors or the original participants, is the most evidently entertainment-based form of documentary. The agenda of most reconstructions is to be dramatic and therefore the dominant discourse is narrative. It matters little if the reconstruction is about a rescue from a fire, or a race against time for an antidote to a snake bite, what is important is the dramatic resolution. The fact that these events actually happened serves to make the text even more dramatic than fictional representations. Of course the techniques used in reconstructions, such as cross-cutting between events, are those of narrative cinema.

Reconstructions are a relatively recent form of television drama. The most recent technological innovation has been in the use of small-format video, enabling amateurs to make their own documentaries: video diaries.

Video diaries

Video diaries have become possible because of recent technological innovations. Just as 'observational' documentary was not practicable until the development of lightweight equipment, the ability of amateurs to create professional-looking videos arrived with S-VHS and Hi-8 formats. Indeed, many people now record significant moments of their lives with camcorders in a new variant on the family album.

Video diaries are a form of 'access television', which means that non-media professionals can take control of producing and editing representations; as the title suggests, video diaries are a particularly personal representation.

This liberalization of the media, however, is not as straightforward as it seems. Jenny Gibson, series editor of the BBC series *Video Diaries*, stated:

> It's our job to identify [something very off-putting] and try to turn the diarist to take a less egocentric approach to something and less pushing of aspects of their personality which are difficult or confrontational. The other thing is they may be very much in love with a very contrived material, terribly in love with some parts that we know are a total contrivance. (Keighron, 1993, p. 25)

So despite the diarist's control of camera and editing, there are clearly institutional pressures which may compromise their individual ideas. Only one in fifty applications to create a diary gets beyond the 'waste bin'. Clearly, it would be impossible to make all the proposals, so some gatekeeping is necessary – but the agenda of the gatekeeping organization, in this case the Community Programme Unit, will have a great influence on what is shown. In addition, the simplicity of filming and the relative cheapness of video means that far more footage is shot than will ever be shown. An average of 150 hours of recording are cut down to one hour for broadcast. And even if an individual is completely satisfied with the end product, it is highly likely that representations used, in terms of form, style and content, will be to some degree conventional and largely articulate the values of the dominant ideology.

Although these six categories cover most documentaries ever made, there are always texts which do not conform to conventional outlines. For example, the form of two documentaries directed by Godfrey Reggio, *Koyaanisqatsi* (1983) and *Powaqqatsi* (1988), is heavily influenced by the use of time-lapse photography and slow motion.

Powaqqatsi is structured by montage, there is no voice-over, and chronicles to plight of the developing world (in contrast with its predesessor *Koyaanisqatsi*, which portrayed the pointless speed of urban life). The images are linked graphically by the repetition of people as 'beasts of burden' labouring under sacks of sand, water carriers or fuel. The specially composed score by Philip Glass mixes different musical vernaculars giving a voice to non-Western sounds and peoples. As the conclusion of *Powaqqatsi* nears, the subjects of Reggio's camera are found to stare more frequently at the audience with a gaze that can be best described as accusing.

Although Reggio's movies occasionally seem similar in form to that most Western of art forms, the pop video (except accompanied by minmalist music), the power of his imagery (and the accompanying soundtrack), with the subtlety of his rhetoric (the audience is forced to work for meaning) make him a documentary film-maker who has made political and stylistically avant-garde texts mainstream.

The problems of using conventional modes of representation to make oppositional political statements was the focus of much of the theoretical work done in the aftermath of May 1968. It was at this time the first attempts were made to describe how mainstream texts' 'ways of seeing' are inexplicably entangled with conventional forms. May 1968 has had a profound influence on Media, Film and Cultural Studies. What follows is a brief history of the events and an introduction to some of the more complex ideas associated with the critical thought that followed. The next section is probably one of the most difficult parts of the book and you certainly do not need to know what follows in order to do well in examinations beneath undergraduate level.

6.6 May 1968 and theories of representation

The events of May 1968 in Paris, France, had far-reaching implications, originally for film theory and later for media and cultural
studies. The origin of the student and worker uprising in that month
was the March 22 Movement, which organized the occupation of
university buildings after the arrest of some students protesting
against the Vietnam war. The confrontation between students and
university authorities escalated on 3 May after police were brought
in to arrest 'trouble-makers'. Students gathered in the Latin Quarter
to protest against the arrests and were met with police using
truncheons and tear gas.

The students received much support from the general public and
their lecturers' union, who were similarly concerned about the
authoritarianism of the university authorities. Although, on 10
May, called the 'Night of the Barricades', the students were violently
routed by the riot police, in fact they achieved a moral victory.
Liberal public opinion was scandalized that young people could be
beaten for simply protesting. By 13 May, the labour unions had
joined the protest, uniting – for a short time – students and workers;
up to half a million people took part in a demonstration. In addition,
there were large-scale demonstrations all over France.

In fact, it seemed as if the whole of France was involved in anti-
government protests which spread throughout May. The arts, in
particular, became extremely politicized in a way that had not
happened, in Europe, since the Soviet revolution.

By 24 May, approximately 10 million workers were on strike and
the de Gaulle government was on the verge of collapse. A day later,
journalists on the state-controlled broadcaster, ORTF, joined the
strike:

> The pro-Government bias of the television and radio networks during
> the first few weeks of May was, in a sense, too obvious to be of very
> much use to the government. The huge discrepancy between what was
> actually going on in the streets and factories and workplaces and what
> was allowed to appear on television, was too apparent. The lesson of
> May, from the point of view of the government, must therefore be that in
> a relatively 'advanced' society, based on the principles of mass education
> and mass literacy, what is almost more important than the control of the
> mass media is the creation of public confidence in those media, and the
> skilful negotiation of the susceptibilities – and the code ethics – of
> professional journalists. (Harvey, 1980, pp. 8–9)

After negotiations between the government and unions failed to gained popular support, de Gaulle called a general election. What was potentially a revolutionary situation was negated by a non-revolutionary political device and on 30 June the government was returned to power with a large majority. During June most of the strikes were called off, although there were many violent situations and some protesters were killed.

Despite the fact that the political status quo returned in France, the legacy of the politicization of the arts, film in particular, is still with us. Gone were the old certainties of representation which had, largely, held sway since the Renaissance; in its place was a radical agenda that attempted to make sense of the ideological world.

Ironically it was *Cahiers du Cinéma*, the magazine that André Bazin had founded, that was at the forefront of deriding his own traditional view of realism:

> The real nature of *Cahiers'* and *Cinéthique's* objections to the 'impression of reality' or the 'depicting of reality' in the cinema is that this impression is offered from the point of view of the ruling class – in other words, that it is an instance of dominant ideology. It is objected to on the grounds that it 'presents the existing abnormal relations of production as natural and right', that it 'is never anything other than a method of permitting the audience to live an imaginary life within a nonexistent reality'; that it registers 'the vague, unformulated, untheorised, unthought-out world of the dominant ideology'. What the cinema offers is not the marvellous, refreshing reality of Bazinian aesthetics, but an impression or an account of social reality which is supportive of existing social relations, and which assists in the reproduction of those relations. (Harvey, 1980, pp. 8–9)

Whereas early film theorists such Kracauer and Bazin assumed an unproblematic relationship between film and reality, post-1968 aesthetics, politicized by Marxist philosophy, was ideologically based.

There followed a switch in emphasis. The conventional use of realism was no longer concerned with how an individual text reflected the world, but how a text was structured by society's dominant ideology. In Britain, one of the pioneering examples of this form of criticism was the 1972 BBC television series (also published in book form), by John Berger, called *Ways of Seeing*.

John Berger's 'Ways of Seeing'

In Chapter 3, the ideological basis of the Renaissance perspective was described. Berger dealt with the ideological content of European oil painting. In his analysis of Gainsborough's painting 'Mr and Mrs Andrews' he showed the intimate relationship between landscape painting and capitalism:

> The point being made is that, among the pleasures their portrait gave to Mr and Mrs Andrews, was the pleasure of seeing themselves depicted as landowners and this pleasure was enhanced by the ability of oil paint to render their land in all its substantiality. (Berger, 1972, p. 108)

Berger also describes how the portrayal of women in European oil paintings serves to subordinate them to the male gaze:

> One might simplify this by saying: men act and women appear. Men look at women. Women watch themselves being looked at. This determines not only most relations between men and women but also the relation of women to themselves. The surveyor of woman is herself male: the surveyed female. Thus she turns herself into an object – and most particularly an object of vision: a sight. (Berger, 1972, p. 47)

In his analysis of the nude, Berger shows how the conventions of female representations in oil paintings are prevalent in today's pornographic magazines. Women are wholly defined as sexual objects, objects available for male pleasure.

Ideological criticism, like conventional, pre-1968, realist criticism, shows artefacts to be a mirror held up to society. However, in the post-1968 world, what is reflected is not common sense views of the world, but the power structures of that world.

In the early 1970s *Screen*, the journal of the Society for Education in Film and Television (SEFT), started publishing translations of *Cahiers'* post-1968 theories and further developing the neo-Marxist, psychoanalytic, and semiotic ideas that characterized the French publication. *Screen* published Laura Mulvey's seminal article 'Visual Pleasure and Narrative Cinema' in Autumn 1975.

Mulvey and the representation of women

Although Mulvey's thesis has since been modified – not least by Mulvey herself – it is still a touchstone of ideological criticism. Like Berger's analysis of European oil paintings, Mulvey showed how the male gaze structures narrative cinema.

The form of narrative cinema has been defined, through its economic dominance, by Hollywood. Any film-maker attempting to make a mainstream narrative film is, regardless of where they are in the world, in effect making a Hollywood movie. Mulvey (1985,

p. 309) contrasts this with independent cinema (formally defined) which can use and create different modes of representation (similar to Wollen's definition of counter cinema in Chapter 3).

> The magic of Hollywood style at its best . . . arose, not exclusively, but in one important aspect, from its skilled and satisfying manipulation of visual pleasure. Unchallenged, mainstream film coded the erotic into the language of the dominant patriarchal order.

As in European oil painting and pornography:

> In a world ordered by sexual imbalance, pleasure in looking has been split between active/male and passive/female. The determining male gaze projects its phantasy onto the female figure, which is styled accordingly. In their traditional exhibitionist role women are simultaneously looked at and displayed, with their appearance coded for strong visual and erotic impact so that they can be said to connote to-be-looked-at-ness. (Mulvey, 1985, p. 309)

As Roland Barthes, in one of his essays in *Mythologies*, described the stripper's dance is an integral part of creating the spectacle, legitimizing the male gaze by defining the strip as a performance in a way which the display of a woman simply taking off her clothes could never do.

Mulvey goes on to describe how the use of women, particularly the central female character, serves to freeze narrative flow while the spectators, and characters within the film, contemplate her eroticism:

> Traditionally, the woman displayed has functioned on two levels: as erotic object for the characters within the screen story, and as erotic object for the spectator within the auditorium, with a shifting tension between the looks on either side of the screen. (Mulvey, 1985, p. 310)

As one of the defining tenets of Hollywood cinema is narrative flow, or transitivity, these pauses of erotic display are potentially disruptive. Mulvey shows how the often-used character of the showgirl whose narrative function is one of display, alleviates this tension by narratively justifying looking at women. This device also allows the spectator's look to be unified with that of the characters within the screen story. Despite this:

> the moment of sexual impact of the performing woman takes the film into a no-man's-land outside its own time space. Thus Marilyn Monroe's first appearance in *The River of No Return* and Lauren Bacall's songs in *To Have and Have Not*. Similarly, conventional close-ups of legs (Dietrich, for instance) or a face (Garbo) integrate into the narrative a different mode of

eroticism. One part of a fragmented body destroys the Renaissance space, the illusion of depth demanded by narrative, it gives flatness, the quality of a cut-out or icon rather than verisimilitude to the screen. (Mulvey, 1985, p. 310)

Once again there is the potential that these close-ups may break the narrative flow. Their ideological function, however, is to portray femininity as something abstract and mystical. While men are filmed as part of their environment, the eroticized close-ups of women serve to define them not as individuals, but as fragmented beings who exist only for the male gaze.

The function of the male hero, who drives the narrative through his actions, is to be the bearer of the spectator's look:

so that the power of the male protagonist as he controls events coincides with the active power of the erotic look, both giving a satisfying sense of omnipotence. A male movie star's glamorous characteristics are thus not those of the erotic object of his gaze, but those of the more perfect, more complete, more powerful ideal ego. (Mulvey, 1985, p. 310)

Hollywood narrative invariably concludes with the male protagonist 'getting the girl'. By means of identification, the spectator possesses her too. The positioning of the spectator in the male protagonist's point of view is especially evident the first time we see the female lead of a film. We invariably begin by seeing the male hero looking, and then, with an eyeline match cut, see the woman he is looking at.

◀ EXERCISE 6.1 ▶

Make a note of whether this happens in the next ten 'Hollywood-style' movies you watch.

Annette Kuhn (1985), drawing on Mulvey's ideas, demonstrates how male and females are shot differently by looking at cross-dressing films. Her analysis of the first appearance of Marilyn Monroe (Sugar) in *Some Like It Hot* is particularly illuminating. The awkward walking of Jack Lemmon (Daphne) and Tony Curtis (Josephine), in drag, is contrasted with the fluid movement of Sugar: as Daphne says: 'Look at that! Look how she moves! It's just like Jello on springs. Must have some sort of built-in motor or something. I tell ya, it's a whole different sex!'

The gag is reinforced by filming the characters' walks in the same way but before we see Sugar, we see Daphne and Josephine looking, and then see what they are looking at: Sugar.

on the one hand, Josephine and Daphne, pretending to be women, seem to receive the same sort of visual treatment as the 'real' woman, Sugar. At the same time, however, the shifts of point-of-view between the camera on one side and Josephine/Daphne on the other mark these characters as masculine. (Kuhn, 1985, p. 72)

Mulvey's analysis is very much influenced by psychoanalysis. While psychoanalysis is undoubtedly an important tool in ideological criticism, its roots in the theories of Sigmund Freud are, however, problematic to say the least. Freud's theories are asocial (that is, they do not take society into account), and although they aspire to scientific status, they are also highly idiosyncratic. Despite this, Mulvey's polemic is still important because it was responsible for a new critical way of seeing mainstream texts.

What happens if the male body is at the centre of the narrative, which is often the case in Westerns, musicals or action movies? Steve Neale, in 'Masculinity as Spectacle', published in *Screen* (November–December 1983; reprinted in Cohan and Hark, 1993), attempted to relate Mulvey's ideas to the representation of heterosexual males. Neale (1983, p. 8) points out that:

'male' genres and films constantly involve sado-masochistic themes, scenes and phantasies or that male heroes can at times be marked as the object of an erotic gaze.

Neale refers to Paul Willemen's contention that 'spectacle and drama in [director Anthony] Mann's films tend both to be structured around the look at the male figure' and:

The (unstated) thesis behind these comments seems to be that in a heterosexual and patriarchal society, the male body cannot be marked explicitly as the erotic object of another male look: that look must be motivated in some other way, its erotic component repressed. The mutilation and sadism so often involved in Mann's films are marks both of the repression involved and of a means by which the male body may be disqualified, so to speak, as an object of erotic contemplation and desire.

In musicals, the dancing of actors such as Gene Kelly and Fred Astaire insists that their body be looked at and, like the appearance of the female lead, the performance stops the flow of the narrative: they are, literally, show stoppers.

As Steve Cohan (1993, p. 60) points out, Astaire is 'feminized' in his performance of 'Let's Kiss and Make Up' in *Funny Face* (1957):

In this case . . . it is the female star who looks on and a male star who performs for her benefit, and the two close-ups of [Audrey] Hepburn watching . . . feature her smiling to signify the pleasure she takes in looking at Astaire.

Despite this apparent equality of gender representation, Astaire is a spectacle of performance rather than eroticism; Hepburn's look is an appreciation of action rather than passion. At the end of the number: 'the dance closes without a reverse shot of her looking, as Astaire takes his bow in acknowledgment of the audience's spectatorship more than hers' (Neale, 1980, p. 22).

Like musicals, melodramas can be defined, generically, as narratives 'inaugurated by the eruption of (hetero)sexual desire into an already firmly established social order' (Tasker, 1993, p. 93). So in the opening of All That Heaven Allows (1955), directed by Douglas Sirk, Jane Wyman, playing older, slightly dowdy widow Cary Scott is seen watching the gardener, Rock Hudson's glamourous young 'hunk'.

Other exceptions to Mulvey's idea can be found in the 'action' movie. Possibly the most successful genre of recent years, the action movie's biggest stars, Sylvester Stallone and Arnold Schwarzenegger, are primarily defined by their bodies. The action movie of the 1980s and 1990s has also introduced an interesting variant on the traditional representation of gender: women as heroes. This possibly originated with the science fiction adventure Alien (1979) where Ripley (Sigourney Weaver) is the only survivor of a crew attacked by the eponymous creature (Ripley was, however, originally intended to be male). She subsequently defeats aliens in films which followed, demonstrating her leadership skills to be superior to those of the males in the narrative.

The Terminator (1984 written, produced and directed by James Cameron) featured Sarah Connor (Linda Hamilton) as a waitress (a traditional, low-grade, female job) who has to contend with a virtually indestructible cyborg. By the end of the film she has acquired a military discipline which is even more pronounced in the sequel, Terminator 2: Judgment Day (1991). In a fascinating gender reversal, Arnold Schwarzenegger, the original terminator, is transformed into a caring, father-figure, while Sarah becomes a gun-toting, muscular individual, bordering on the psychotic and virtually incapable of motherly affection.

The conclusion of Terminator 2 offers hope for the future ('No fate'): is this hope because women are gaining more power in society? After all, the film does appear to offer an apparently comprehensive condemnation of machismo. Will the new nurturing man together with the new aggressive woman save the world? Susan Jeffords (1993, pp. 260–1) thinks not:

> It is . . . John Connor and not Sarah Connor or the Terminator who holds the real power of these films, and marks himself as the hero of Hollywood sequels, for it is he who survives the destruction of the 'old' masculinity, witnessing teary-eyed the Terminator's destruction. As he stands above the melting Terminators, audiences are to recognize in John Connor not only the father of his own and the human future, but the new masculinity as well.

John Connor is shown, early in the film, to be criminal. However, he does stress to his Terminator that 'you just can't go around killing people' as his mother is intent on going around to the Dyson's house and terminating the scientist.

> But in one of T2's most remarkable inversions, the film manages not only to reveal the 'new' masculinity / father, but to excuse the 'old' one as well. For though the Terminator must sacrifice itself in order to prevent a destructive future, the film's plot makes it clear that *it's not his fault*. Because the mechanized body from the movie's past has been shown, largely through the oppositional framework of the script, to be a 'good Terminator,' its elimination is constructed to be not vengeful but tragic. The Terminator had to sacrifice itself, not because it was 'bad' or harmful or even useless but because others around it misused its components. Comparably, audiences can conclude that the aggressive and destructive 1980s male body that became the target for both ridicule and hatred may not have been *inherently* 'bad,' but only, in some sociologically pitiful way, misunderstood. And who, finally, does Terminator 2 suggest *does* understand this obsolete but loveable creature? None other than John Connor, the 'new' man himself. (Jeffords, 1993, p. 261)

According to Jeffords, then, the representation of Sarah Connor is not a radical departure from the 'damsel in distress'. She fails to save the world by killing Dyson and it is left to men (like the one her son will become) to make the world a less aggressive place with the emphasis placed on fathering.

In our consideration of *Blue Steel* in the last chapter, *Thelma and Louise* was mentioned in passing. A fascinating road movie, with 'action' elements, the women's journey takes them out of the grasp of patriarchal society:

> Drawing on a long history of representations of freedom and self-respect, the film traces the women's increasing ability to 'handle themselves', a

tracing that follows their ability to handle a gun. Thelma can barely bring herself to handle her gun, a gift from her husband Darryl, at the start of the film – picking it up with an expression of distaste, in a rather 'girlish' fashion. As the narrative progresses, she acquires both physical coordination, which denotes self-possession, and the ability to shoot straight. When the two women shoot out the tanker, they happily compliment each other on their aim. (Tasker, 1993, p. 139)

Despite their ability to 'handle themselves' and guns, which in Hollywood terms is a male characteristic, Thelma and Louise have nowhere to go in contemporary society, hence they drive off the edge.

There are more progressive representations of women in mainstream cinema and on television, but they remain exceptional. Mulvey's description of the way Hollywood cinema tries to make us see, while not being the definitive formula it appeared on publication, is still a powerful tool for unravelling some of the ways women are represented in mainstream audio-visual media.

This chapter has attempted to consider various types of representation with particular focus upon realism and modernism. Clearly, each type is a set of conventions and 'realism' just happens, at a particular time and place, to have greater credibility in its representation of reality than other forms of representation. The task of the Media Studies student is to 'unmask' the ideological workings of a media text, whether it signifies itself as realist or not.

7

TECHNOLOGY

Technology is the medium through which a text is communicated and it clearly mediates between the sender and receiver. As we saw in the history of realism, the apparent objectivity of the camera is illusory. Cameras mediate reality by re-presenting it. How this is done, however, is determined by conventions which are obviously created by people. Despite this, the camera does not lie; machines cannot lie. Any distortion of what might by considered 'objective truth' is caused by human intervention. This intervention has been the subject of this book.

As was stated in the Introduction, technology is an important aspect to consider alongside the key concepts, for it is technology which creates the form into which conventions can be created. An inherent problem in writing books for Media Studies is that they are out-of-date before they are published. To an extent, that has mattered little in the previous chapters – they have been, essentially, 'looking-back'; they contain histories and résumés of the major theories that inform the subject. This chapter, however, attempts to look forward.

It is probable that technological advance has always seemed to be exponential, so my feeling that the rapid changes of the 1990s are unprecedented is probably a somewhat egocentric perspective. However, the rapid development of computer technology in recent years has revolutionized media production and given the general public (at least those not caught in a 'poverty-trap') access to high-powered computers. Computer technology has affected our lives in two ways:

1. it has given us access to media produced by more sophisticated technology, such as giving us 'better' special effects in films, multimedia texts, and more flexibly designed publications;

2. it allows us, using home-based computers, to create our own media texts (even if with limited distribution) or communicate simply and cheaply with many people in the world on the Internet.

This chapter attempts to suggest some ways this technology will affect media images and representation in the future.

Technological development is often portrayed as being wholly beneficial in nature; there is a consensus that technology makes our lives easier. This viewpoint was characterized in the 1960s by British Prime Minister, Harold Wilson, as 'the white heat of technology'. However, by the 1970s a major side-effect of technological development was becoming apparent – pollution.

The creation and use of the atom bomb had already called into question the notion of the benign nature of technology, but the impact of pollution in the West, causing, for example, global warming and nitrate poisoning, made it clear that, for many, technology is a double-edged phenomenon. On the one hand, doing the laundry is now highly automated but on the other the doubling of cars on the road in the last 20 years has made Britain less safe and more polluted.

From our point of view we are concerned with media technology which is, as I have said, the medium itself. Are the side-effects of media technology potentially damaging to our health?

7.1 Image and representation

This book has already made the point that because a medium necessarily mediates between the audience and reality, it must be a representation, and means we must isolate the conventions used. Technology does not create these conventions, it acts as a vessel to hold and communicate them. Clearly the Western genre can be communicated by a variety of technologies, or media, although it may be necessary that its conventions be modified by the medium. Visual iconography has little place on the radio, though 10-gallon hats and six-shooters can obviously be described on the pages of a novel.

So technology is the medium, the form, through which communication passes. Cinematic technology has developed from black and white, silent, hand-cranked images, through the introduction of sound and colour, to the development of wide-screen and stereo-sound. Presumably the future holds a three-dimensional system that does not require spectacles. The technological development of the medium has undoubtedly made images seem more 'real' to successive audiences, however:

> The development of audiovisual technologies has been driven not so much by a realist project as by an illusionary one. That is to say, the illusion of the real has had to be made more convincing and the spectacular has had to be made more 'realistic'. The second-hand has had to become first-hand, the vicarious has had to be made vivid. (Hayward and Wollen, 1993, p. 2)

The most recent development in technology is digitisation. Digitisation, in brief, is a product of computer technology and transforms information into numbers. A photograph taken by a conventional camera is an analogue representation, that is, it looks like what it represents (in Peirce's terms it is an icon); a digital camera, however, will transform the object it is representing into a string of binary numbers (Peirce's symbol). The power that digitisation imparts is due, in the main, to the ease in which it can be manipulated. Digitised information is mathematically-based, and numbers are more easily manipulated than physical material. Any mistakes made in the digital world can easily be undone, just as you can more easily cut an offending paragraph on a word processor than on a typewriter.

Digital images can also be transmitted using telephone lines, cellular links, or satellites, to wherever they are required. For example, an Associated Press photographer took pictures of President Clinton on a boat off Martha's Vineyard; 15 minutes later a selected image was in New York ready for use:

> He removed a pocket-sized hard drive from the side of his camera, slipped it into a docking station attached to a PowerBook, and reviewed all 30 of his shots on the laptop's screen. After selecting his favourite image, he fine-tuned its colours, wrote a caption, and then, using a cellular phone, transmitted both image and caption to a central computer at AP's New York headquarters. (Leslie, *Wired*, 1.02)

By contrast, analogue images, which are material-based, require physical processing. Photographic negatives, for example, need dark-room development and then printing. Unlike analogue images, however, in which physical alteration of the image is limited to superimposition and air-brushing, a digitised image can be completely changed. National Geographic magazine actually moved two Egyptian pyramids closer together so they would fit on the front cover. During the filming of *The Crow* (1994), the lead, Brandon Lee, was killed. In order to finish the film, Lee's digitised image was placed in seven scenes and 52 shots. In the SF action movie *Judge Dredd* (1995), nearly 100 digital effects shots were used to create stunts that were too dangerous to film. *Toy Story* (1996) was the first feature film to consist wholly of computer generated imagery. However, moving one of the world's wonders, and apparent resurrecting of a dead actor, does not signal the triumph of the illusionist.

The fact that technology is more 'powerful' now, because of digitisation, doesn't make its 'illusionist project' any more effective. Indeed it is just possible that, with the spread of subjects such as Media Studies, and the concomitant increase in a media-literate population, as well as audiences' greater familiarity with computer-technology, the 'illusionist project' may be on the wane. As more people become aware that the media is dealing with representations and not reality, and that the potential for image manipulation is very high, they are less likely to accept images at face value. For example, *Texas Monthly* received negative publicity for seemingly digitally enhancing images on the cover of its magazine in 1990:

> Computer technology has so confused the public that in a least a couple of instances, publications have been wrongly accused of digital manip-ulation. In 1992, *Texas Monthly* . . . ran an unaltered cover photograph showing a controversial Texas government official sitting on top of an oil derrick; since the photography looked implausible, the immediate suspi-cion was that it was falsified. (Leslie, *Wired*, n.d.)

In a sense, it matters little whether an image is digitally manipulated or not, what is important is what it represents. The status of the photographic image as the bearer of truth is now truly compro-mised, but it was always a status that it should never have possessed.

For example, Robert Capa's famous photograph, for the Magnum agency, of a soldier shot during the Spanish Civil War, and published in *Life* with the caption 'Death in Spain', may have been staged. In September 1996 new evidence emerged suggesting it was genuine. But even if the event was fabricated, it is doubtful whether this makes it a less powerful a representation of the war; no doubt many people did die in this pose. Footage from the Second World War was also faked for the purposes of propaganda. Roy Boulting, director of *Desert Victory: The Battle of El Alamein* told *The Sunday Times* in 1995:

As a film-maker, the idea of not being able to show a great moment of history was too much. We re-enacted without in any way distorting. Sometimes, fiction is the ultimate truth. Overall, the film was about 95% factual. (Hellen and Alderson, 1995)

And new technology does not abolish selection and censorship. One of the most famous and disturbing images of the Vietnam war, that of a burning, naked, young girl running down a road, after being napalmed by South Vietnamese aircraft, was almost never distributed by Associated Press because of her nudity. The barbaric 'truth' of this event, which this image encapsulates, was almost censored.

As I said at the beginning of this chapter, it is wrong to say, however, that the camera lies; as technology, it is neutral. The 'lying' can only occur through human agency and digitisation undoubtedly makes this easier. Rather than search for allusive, and probably illusive, truth, however, the media student is better off analysing the codes of representation and their ideological basis.

Computer technology will probably revolutionize the media. The production of newspapers, for example, already seems somewhat antiquated in an electronic age. The massive use of paper, difficulties in distribution, and declining markets make them prime candidates for an electronic revolution. The future of 'news' publishing will almost certainly be 'online', with subscribers receiving the information which interests them. Teletext services, in Britain at least, currently offer a service with little detail, but their ability to relay news, particularly sports news, as it happens gives an indication of how limited traditional newspapers are becoming. Indeed, newspapers' news-bearing function has been greatly compromised in recent years by the growth of broadcast news, with tabloids increasingly becoming entertainment-based publications specializing in gossip, and broadsheets increasing their feature-based articles.

Many newspapers in the USA are already online, and in Britain the *Daily Telegraph* and the *Liverpool Echo* were among the first available in cyberspace. Current online newspapers offer electronic versions of their newspapers and have the facility to update news as it happens. Early online newspapers offered only text and lacked layout and images of traditional newspapers. However, publications like *Mercury Center*, the electronic version of the *San Jose Mercury News* offers the traditional-looking newspaper and everything its material counterpart doesn't have room for, such as news wire services, official reports and press conference transcripts. In other words, the raw material of the newspaper is included, allowing readers to become, to a degree, their own gatekeepers.

In terms of entertainment, virtual reality – a computer simulation which will interact with the user – is probably the next 'big step'. Virtual reality arcades are already in existence, but there is no reason why it should not form the basis of future home entertainment systems. The home entertainment systems of the future will probably also incude digital versatile discs (DVD), which will allow whole films to be compressed on to one standard-sized CD. This allows the possibility of the same machine being used for music, vision and multi-media texts. Another development being piloted is video on demand (VOD) where, theoretically, any text, from a recent film to a 1960s television programme, can be downloaded from a central provider. This could also extend to other media: instead of buying a new CD, for example, one could simply download it, at (of course) a cost, on demand. EMI piloted such a system in 1997.

These systems require high-capacity telephonic networks (in effect, fibre-optic cables) to be economically feasible. The Internet, which currently boasts over 30 million users (and growing) has been used as a medium for a rock concert, the Rolling Stones, and a film (the first was *Party Girl* in June 1995). The Internet can also access various art galleries in the world, which may, because of the greater access we have, in a digitised form, like photography, alter our relationship with art. The Net is also a superb research tool, for example the Internet Movie Database has, information on about 50 000 films.

It is crucial that you, as a Media Studies student, keep as up-to-date as possible on developments in computer technology; the best way to do so is through reading some of the large number of magazines associated with new technology.

In fact, technology, with the advent of multi-media publications and the potential for virtual classrooms, could revolutionize education. Multi-media, which usually uses CD-ROMs, combines sound, moving images, and text; instead of, say, looking up a reference to *Thelma and Louise* in a book, it is possible to see and hear extracts from the film as well as receiving written material. This can be cross-referenced to other films by the same stars or director, which can then also be accessed immediately. Books, like the one you're reading, are almost obsolete; they still have, just, the advantage of portability.

There are, however, copyright problems in creating multi-media texts. In a book such as this one, permissions fees are incurred for the reproduction of copyright images. A multi-media version of this text would not be content with a description of, say, the opening of *The Triumph of the Will* or the sequence from *Blade Runner* analysed in Appendix 1; it would be essential to show these texts. The cost of this would, to put it mildly, be prohibitive. It could be that only large conglomerates such as Time–Warner, which already hold the rights to a colossal amount of material, could afford to publish multi-media material.

Convincing arguments (Stannard, 1995) have been made suggesting that digital technologies will alter our conception of language and literacy. Digital technology allows the construction of hypertext where information is linked in a non-linear fashion: the click of a mouse can lead you to related topics on a CD-ROM and also combines sound and image. CD-ROM technology is often sold as being 'interactive' though these claims are exaggerated, clicking a mouse does not mean the reader is actively engaging with the information provided. However multi-media technology is certainly offering information in a new and exciting fashion.

Many of you will be reading this book for examination purposes and a major technological change may be in education. The common route which academic students take to university may well disappear in the next few years, to be replaced by online learning in the home. The classroom of the future will probably not be made of brick, it will be virtual:

> At the University of London, BT has invested in Relate . . . a project to bring remote teaching into the forefront of the communications revolution. Instead of simply putting a lecturer on screen, Relate creates a virtual classroom – which allows questions and answers, and teachers and students to scribble notes and diagrams for each other on a shared electronic blackboard. (Plant, *Wired*, n.d.)

It is my guess that such virtual worlds as the classroom of the future, and the potential for communication of the Internet – and related systems – means we will have to redefine our relationship with the world. Understanding the mechanisms of image and representation will help us create these new definitions. If we do not create them, someone else will.

Appendix 1: Storyboarding

The interrogation of Leon from **Blade Runner**

The opening of *Blade Runner* (1982) is enigmatic. It has a setting, which is clearly in the future, where small aircraft are flying above a city, but shots of this are interspersed with extreme close-ups of an eye, and a man smoking in a room, neither of which, at first, are clearly anchored in narrative space. As the sequence progresses, it becomes clear that we are approaching a large, pyramid-like structure and a zoom draws us toward a window where a room with large fans on the ceiling can be seen. The interrogation of Leon, a suspected android, contains the film's first dialogue and is the first sequence with clearly defined space and narrative. The man in the room, smoking, is revealed to be Holden. The following analysis is an application of the elements described in this chapter, although, obviously, not every element is relevant to this sequence.

A storyboard of the opening shots in the scene is provided to help those who do not have access to the film (it would obviously be better to watch the sequence). The storyboard also illustrates the essential details required to portray the *mise-en-scène*.

Shot 1a Establishing shot: high angle, see partitions between offices.

Leon (L) enters frame top right-hand corner.
Holden (H) medium-long shot smoking.
Blue light from slatted windows on left.
Large overhead fan revolving in centre.

Intercom: 'Next subject, Kowalski, Leon, engineer, waste disposal, file section, new employee, six days'.

Shot 1b   crane shot down to waist height.

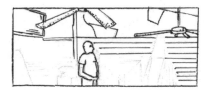

sound effect: knock.

H: 'Come in'.

Shot 1c   H sits down. L enters right, moves into a close-up (CU), torso only, dominates frame, on left. H, comparatively small, on right.

ambient sounds: high technology beeping; hum of machines; voices on intercoms.

21 seconds   CUT TO

Analysis   This crane shot establishes the narrative space and allows us to see Leon enter the scene. The high angle serves to diminish Holden, and the emphasis on the fan, part of *film noir* iconography, suggests Holden's ultimate fate: he appears to be cut through by it.

The crane shot moves to a sitting, eye-level position, a height from which most of the scene is shot. The position of the camera (1c) diminishes Holden at his desk in contrast to Leon's bulk. Leon is appropriately – he is an android – dehumanized by this shot as his head is not visible. He dominates Holden, again suggesting the violence to come.

Shot 2   CU Voigt–Kampff (V–K) test machine switched on in front of H.

1 second   CUT

Analysis   The close-up of the Voigt–Kampff test machine, which will ascertain whether Leon is human or not, emphasizes technology, an essential part of futuristic science fiction iconography. The rapid editing, the shot lasts only one second, relates to the business-like manner of Holden, who just wants to get on with his job.

Shot 3   CU L in profile (emphasizing his 'weak' chin), hostile stare, bright back light differentiating him from bright blue background (b/g).

1 second   CUT

Analysis   The cut from the machine to Leon shows him to be the subject of the investigation. The bright back-lighting almost makes his profile a silhouette, dehumanizing the android. The profile emphasizes his 'weak' chin and balding head, signing that he is an unattractive individual.

Shot 4   as Shot 2   V–K aligning itself

2 seconds   CUT

Shot 5   H point-of-view (pov) of V–K, medium CU (MCU), L sits behind.

2 seconds   CUT

Shot 6 CU of V–K, which is monitoring L's pupil dilation. H's pov.

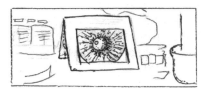

L: Okay if I talk? . . .

2 seconds   CUT

Analysis This continues the emphasis on technology. Holden's reliance on technology in fact acts as a barrier to understanding, and the machine is placed just in front of Holden's face in the *mise-en-scène* throughout the sequence. In contrast, Deckard's, played by Harrison Ford, methods of tracking down replicants are more 'old-fashioned'. As the V–K machine moves into position in front of Leon, the red light looks threatening.

Shot 7 Re-establishing shot

H checking V–K. Medium shot (MS) of L & H either side of table. Moving fan, quite oppressive.

L: (looking around) I'm kinda nervous when I take tests.
H: (looks up) Please don't move.

4 seconds   CUT

Analysis After a series of close-ups, this shot re-orientates the audience, reminding us of the relative positions of the protagonists. We also see Holden still obsessively setting up the machine. The fan lurks ominously above the characters.

Shot 8 as Shot 2 V–K, CU bellows.

L: I'm sorry.
4 seconds   CUT

Analysis The V–K machine appears to be rather incongruous, outdated technology, suggesting it is a rather ludicrous device. This also fits in with the art direction of the film, which creates its futuristic feel, in part, by using fashions from the past. Rachel, played by Sean Young, wears clothes that could have been worn in a 1940s *film noir*.

Shot 9 Table-level of L & V–K MCU

L: I've already had an IQ test this year, I don't think I've ever had one of these . . .

H (interrupting): Reaction time is a factor in this so please pay attention . . .

6 seconds   CUT

Analysis The device is now ready and this 'two-shot' of it and Leon illustrates the confrontation that is about to take place between them.

Shot 10 shot/reverse-shot of Shot 9; H & V–K MCU.

H: Now answer as quickly as you can.

L: Sure.

H: 1187 (unclear, names a location)

5 seconds   CUT

Analysis This a shot/reverse-shot of Shot 9; the last three shots have served to anchor the narrative space strongly.

Shot 11 as Shot 9

L: That's the hotel.

2 seconds   CUT

Shot 12 as Shot 10

HL What?
L: Where I live.
H: Nice place?

3 seconds   CUT

Shot 13 as Shot 9

L: Yeah sure, I guess. That part of the test?
H: No, just warming you up that's all.

7 seconds   CUT

Shot 14 as Shot 10

L: It's not fancy or anything.
H: (look up irritated) You're in a desert . . .

4 seconds   CUT

Analysis The dialogue has been inconsequential. The exchanges in shots 11–14 serve to heighten the tension: something must happen soon. Leon's apparent stupidity is contrasted with Holden's irritability. The audience knows, because this is a mainstream film, that something is going to happen.

Shot 15 low angle (low ∠), CU, L's face; key light on forehead, very shiny.

Movement even closer as test begins.

H: . . . walking along in the sand when all of a sudden . . .
L: Is this the test now?

2 seconds   CUT

Analysis After a series of shot/reverse-shots, Shot 15 is a dramatic intervention, the low angle giving a sense of urgency, as the test has started, that had been absent from the preceding shots. The shiny light on Leon's forehead makes it appear that he is sweating with the tension. The low angle also serves to make Leon look powerful and menacing.

Shot 16 CU H. Key light emphasizes profile. V–K in front.

H: (leaning forward) Yes, you're in the desert walking . . .

1 second   CUT

Analysis The close-up of Holden, profile emphasized as it is with Leon, showing their rivalry visually, also increases tension as it signs that we must look carefully, something is going to happen. This close-up, however, is from a normal angle: Holden is less threatening than Leon. The importance of the exchange is further indicated by the fact that Holden is leaning forward: he, too, is looking carefully. The editing is rapid, adding to the tensions.

Shot 17 CU L, camera moved to right closer, less of a low ∠

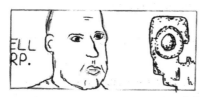

H: . . . along in the sand when all of a sudden you . . .
L: What one?

3 second   CUT

Analysis Leon is stalling as much as possible, he is 'playing dumb' and so reduces the tension of shots 15 and 16. The tension in the *mise-en-scène*, however, is not totally dissipated as the angle, while slightly higher, is not normal.

Shot 18   as Shot 16

H: (irritated) What?

1 second   CUT

Analysis   The brief shot shows us Holden's irritation.

Shot 19   as Shot 17

L: What desert?
H: Doesn't make any difference what desert, it's completely
 hypothetical.
L: But how come I'd be there?
H: Maybe you're fed up . . .

6 seconds   CUT

Shot 20   as Shot 16

H: . . . maybe you went to be by yourself. Who knows? (Leans
 backward and then forward to emphasise what he is saying).
 You look down and see a tortoise . . .

5 seconds   CUT

Analysis   Shots 16–20 form a shot/reverse-shot pattern, Holden is
trying to get the interrogation going, Leon is stalling. Holden
manages to start his question again, in this shot, which leads us to
a repeat of Shot 15 when the interrogation began.

Shot 21   as Shot 15

H: . . .It's crawling toward you.
L: Tortoise, what's that?

4 seconds   CUT

Shot 22   as Shot 16 (s/r-s)

H: (takes a drag on his cigarette as if considering whether L is
 having him on) Know what a turtle is?
L: Course.
H: (shakes head) Same thing (looks down).

6 seconds   CUT

Shot 23   Eyeline match. V-K monitor. Slightly closer version of Shot 6.

L: Never seen a turtle.

2 seconds   CUT

Shot 24   as Shot 16

H looks up, obviously having seen something significant – L has just lied.

2 seconds   CUT

Shot 25   as Shot 15

L: But I understand what you mean.

2 seconds   CUT

Shot 26   as Shot 16

H: You reach down and flip the tortoise on its back.

2 seconds   CUT

Shot 27   as Shot 15

L: Do you make up these questions Mr Holden?

2 seconds   CUT

Shot 28   as Shot 16

L: Or do they make them up for you?
H: The tortoise lays on its back, its belly baking in the hot sun . . .

6 second   CUT

Analysis   Shots 22–8, with the exception of Shot 23, are another shot/reverse-shot pattern. Here the sinister low-angle of Leon, originally seen in Shot 15, is combined with Holden's intense questioning. The 'jousting' between the two is further emphasized by the rapid cutting and the equal length of time they get.

Shot 23 is an eyeline match. The shot returns us to the space defined in Shot 6 but is closer to the V–K machine, emphasizing the significance of what Holden is seeing. Shot 24 acts as a reaction shot: Holden has clearly just realized that Leon is not all he appears to be (he has lied about never seeing a turtle).

Shot 29   CU L, left frame

H: (rapidly, voice has slight echo) . . . beating its legs, trying to turn itself over, but it can't, not without your help. But you're not helping.

L: (staring) What d'ye mean I'm not helping?

s/t: rapid heartbeat sound.

7 seconds   CUT

Analysis   After a series of rapid shots, the tension is now generated through comparatively long shots and the soundtrack. The audience knows that Holden is aware that Leon is probably an android, the narrative tension is now concerned with what he is going to do about it.

In this shot Leon is clearly losing his 'cool', which is made clear by the rapid heartbeat on the soundtrack. In this shot, emphasized by the widescreen proportions, Leon is in the far left of the frame, giving it an unbalanced look; a state of mind that Leon is experiencing.

Shot 30   as Shot 23

H: I mean you're not helping.

1 second   CUT

Shot 31   CU of H, right of frame

H: Why is that Leon?

2 seconds   CUT

Analysis   A return to rapid cutting, in Shots 30 and 31, ends a short passage of high tension that is about to be temporarily dissipated. Shot 30 reminds us that Holden is aware that Leon has lied.

Holden, like Leon, is placed, in Shot 31, at the extreme of the frame – this time on the right – but this composition is more balanced, due to the position of the V–K monitor.

Shot 32   as Shot 29

L twitches and looks uncomfortable; leans forward slightly to be more in the middle of the frame.

s/t: heartbeat, like an engine, weird whining sound like an electronic bug.

7 seconds   CUT

Analysis   In this shot the soundtrack contributes to the tension, suggesting that the 'wiring' within Leon is going wrong.

Shot 33   MCU H, low angle

H: They're just questions Leon. In answer to your query they're written down for me. It's a test. . .

8 seconds   CUT

Analysis   Although this is a low-angle shot, it does not quite give Holden the dominance possessed by Leon, the angle is not as low. This probably signifies the power Holden feels as he has realized that Leon is, almost certainly, an android; this power, however, is illusory.

Shot 34   as Shot 15

H: . . . designed to provoke an emotional response.

3 seconds   CUT

Shot 35   as Shot 33

H: (false smile) Shall we continue?
L: (nods)

2 seconds   CUT

Shot 36   as Shot 15

H: Describe in single words only the good things that come into
   your mind . . .

L leans forward.

9 seconds   CUT

> *Analysis*   Shots 34–36 return us to the powerful Leon of Shot 15,
> counterpointed by Holden's belief that he is the one in control.
> This is emphasized by Holden's supercilious smile as he asks
> whether they should continue.

Shot 37   as Shot 7 (re-establishing shot)

H: . . . about your mother.
L: My mother?
H: Yeah.
L: (leans forward) Let me tell you about my mother.

9 seconds   CUT

> *Analysis*   After the series of close-ups Ridley Scott, the director,
> reminds the audience of the narrative space and sets up the final
> part of the sequence.

Shot 38   MS L, centre frame, V–K on right.

L fires gun under table, flash and his chair goes backward.

s/t: gun fire

$\frac{1}{2}$ second CUT

> *Analysis*   An exceptionally short shot emphasizes the violence: a
> lot which we cannot see clearly happens in a short space of time.

Shot 39   CU of coffee cup being hit by bullet

s/t: breaking crockery.

$\frac{1}{2}$ second CUT

> *Analysis*   Continuing the 'violent' editing, however, rather than
> showing us Holden's 'broken' body, we see and hear the breaking
> of crockery. This acts as a 'stand-in': we have no doubt about what
> has happened to Holden.

Shot 40   high ∠ , medium long shot, H, centre frame

Turns with impact and smashes through wall on chair.

s/t: music starts.

1 second   CUT

> *Analysis*   The high angle makes us look down upon the crumpled mass that was Holden.

Shot 41   MS L standing up. Shoots again.

2 seconds CUT

> *Analysis*   An 'impossible' shot in terms of continuity. One second earlier Leon had been blown backwards in his chair by the blast of his gun; now he is standing up and carefully aiming at Holden. The 'superhuman' transformation is exactly that: Leon is not human and, in, some ways, is better than humans.

Shot 42   Next room through, which H is blasted into.

1 second   CUT

Shot 43   CU H's head smashing on desk.

1 second   CUT to outside

> *Analysis*   The violence of the scene's conclusion ends abruptly with a cut to outside the building.

(Storyboard by Carla Graham and Merle Bentley)

This analysis has attempted to describe how Ridley Scott, and his scriptwriters, have facilitated narrative flow through cinematic codes. In order to do this I have had to put the codes into the narrative context; the codes in themselves, as observed in Chapter 2, do not really possess meaning, meaning is generated by their relationship with other codes. For example, the low angle shot of Holden, introduced in Shot 33, could mean, in isolation, that he is dominant. However, as we have seen, in the context of the sequence he is clearly, ultimately, subservient to Leon and this was signified at the time by the fact that the angle was not as low as those used to portray Leon.

In analysing this sequence I have used the narrative agenda of *Blade Runner,* or at least my understanding of that agenda. The main theme of the film, which concerns the nature of humanity, and its generic structure – a mix of science fiction and *film noir* – are shown to inform the sequence.

Appendix 2: Analysis of Unseen Text

What follows is examples of how you might analyse written text in the constraints of a terminal examination.

Telegraph & Argus

The first thing that catches the eye on this front page of Bradford's evening newspaper (Figure A.1) is the photograph of children smiling. The *T&A* looks like a typical local newspaper which offers a variety of information (national news and television listings) with a local emphasis (particularly in sport).

It is usual, in newspapers, for images to illustrate the accompanying story: story first, image second. In this issue the lead story's headline, 'Transplant heartache', is an example of newspaper's language – or their *langue* – because it is neither a sentence nor a phrase; however, despite this apparent lack of grammatical accuracy, we can make sense of the headline because we understand the convention that headlines are meant to be pithy and eyecatching.

At first, the syntagm of the headline and image is confusing: the negative headline contrasting with the positive image of the children. The apparent contradiction is avoided with the image's caption, 'staying strong', which anchors the image and sets the story's agenda: 'the children are staying cheerful through adversity'. A commutation test on the headline suggests some alternatives, such as 'Transplant fear'; in this case the image would definitely jar because the image does not signify fear.

The children, smiling and cheek to cheek, signify love and happiness: the tilt of the boy's head; they're holding hands; the girl's hug; the close cropping of the image excludes virtually all the background. All this contributes to the creation of a positive image which is constructed to appeal, particularly, to a female audience because the emphasis is on emotion.

Figure A.1

The image also, arguably, draws upon the myth of 'childhood innocence', making them seem even more vulnerable. In terms of the story, the fact the children are Asian is immaterial, they reflect the relatively large Asian population in Bradford. By emphasizing a positive aspect of a potentially tragic situation, the newspaper gives the human interest story a heartwarming 'spin'. However, if the report is read carefully it can be seen that, in fact, there is no story:

> Romesa, [aged] nine, . . . is doing well a year after her third liver transplant.
> But dad Mazhar Hussain and mum Parveen Mazhar fear it is only a matter of time before their son Kabeel, four, has to endure the same transplant agony.

There is no 'hook' for this story: Kabeel is not about to have the transplant; there appears to be no shortage of hospital beds or, indeed, livers; there is no requirement that money be raised to send Kabeel to a specialist and so on. Clearly the children are exceptionally unfortunate, and maybe, in their sunny dispositions, have a lesson for those of us who do not have such problems, but there is no reason why this should be a newspaper story. Presumably it was a quiet news day and something has to fill the front page.

The 'Tonight in brief' column suggests a story that could have been a better lead: 'Police step up security for Bhutto'. The visit of the Pakistan's prime minister, given the large number of Muslims in the city, may well have merited even more prominent treatment. It is possible that the editor felt a relatively heavyweight political news story would be out of place as the lead of an evening newspaper, although he has still given it prominence on page 3. Any potential complaints that the Bhutto story did not lead because of racism would be diffused by the appearance of the Asian children.

The *Telegraph & Argus* was, as the legend on the strapline says, 'voted Britain's best-designed evening newspaper' in 1994. The newspaper's name has a font that signifies itself to be 'slightly old-fashioned', drawing on the myth of 'tradition' (that is, traditional things are better because they come from the 'good old days'). However, any sense of being 'out-of-date' is immediately dispelled by the prominence given to the multi-media equipment that can be won. This has as much visibility as the headline and shows that this newspaper, in common with others, is selling itself with 'special offers' as much as with its news content. In recent years the local press has come under increasing economic pressure, particularly from a number of sources including the 'free sheets', an expanding television local news, the growth of local radio, and the late 1980s/ early 1990s recession which hit advertising revenue particularly badly.

The page is colourful and clearly composed with three vertical lines segmenting the page which separates the contents from the lead story. A very inviting text.

Nokia 232

The message of this advertisement (see p. 40) is: 'buy a Nokia 232 mobile phone for the female in your life and she will appear as attractive as this woman'. The product is aimed at women but the advertisement's appearance in a men's magazine means that, in this context, the aim is to get men to buy the product for a woman. In this case, in fact, it is more important for the woman to look good than the product as it is she who is, metaphorically, being sold.

The Nokia 232 is clearly aimed at women because its main selling point is its size. 'Little' things are not usually a 'turn on' for men, although technological gadgets are. The selling point is anchored by the copy which is juxtaposed with both the woman and the product. The copy line, which our eyes are immediately drawn to by the key lighting on the woman's face, also brings together the product and woman because it refers to both. A connotation of the copy line is 'sexy' and the model has been chosen for her conventional good looks. She is gazing directly out of the frame at the audience, her smile shows this gaze to be confident.

The setting is rather abstract, classical pillars and bust. Although the setting could be a museum, this is not heavily anchored. The Barthesthian myth of the classical era includes the connotations of: purity; beauty; wealth; intellect; tradition; long-lastingness; technology. The syntagm of this classical sign and the woman (she has her hand on a pillar) suggests that she too possesses these qualities which, in turn, become part of the product. The bust's head is angled in a similar way to the woman's, and her hair is like that of the statue's.

The low-angle of the shot gives the woman a powerful position to look down on us, and her evident movement, emphasized by the frame's tilt, give her a dynamic pose. The woman is not only sexy (and therefore desirable), she is powerful too. The power derives, however, from her sexuality, she does not appear in any role other than an 'unforgettable little black number'.

The three diagonal lines draw our eyes away from our initial encounter with the woman's face, and the copy, down to the bottom of the frame, taking in the classical signs. At the bottom left the product name is present with the company's motto. The motto emphasizes the lifestyle quality of the product as well as harking back, for the media-literate, to McLuhan's famous phrase 'the medium is the message'. This product is not being sold on price, it is being sold on its fashionable status.

If you buy the product you buy a lifestyle which is sexy and powerful. However, because this has a specific male address created by the context of *Esquire* (clearly the advertisement could have appeared exactly the same in a woman's magazine such as *Cosmopolitan*), what is being bought here is less the lifestyle than the woman, the woman is being reduced to a male accessory. While it is unlikely that men will be attracted by the product, they are almost certainly, given *Esquire*'s readership profile, going to be attracted to the woman. The equation is: 'buy the product for your woman and she too will be sexy and powerful which, by default, will make you sexy and powerful'.

BIBLIOGRAPHY

Achbar, Mark (ed.) *Manufacturing Consent: Noam Chomsky and the Media* (Montreal and New York: Black Rose Books, 1994).

Althusser, Louis, *Lenin and Philosophy* (New York and London: Monthly Review Press, 1971).

Altman, Rick (ed.) *Genre: The Musical* (London: Routledge & Kegan Paul, 1981).

Alvarado, Manuel, Robin Gutch and Tana Wollen, *Learning the Media* (Basingstoke: Macmillan, 1981).

Argyle, Michael, *The Psychology of Interpersonal Behaviour* (London: Penguin, 4th edn, 1983).

Asimov, Isaac, *Biographical Encyclopedia of Science and Technology* (London: Pan, 1975).

Barnes, Rachel, 'Desperately seeking an identity', *Guardian*, 24 October 1994.

Barnouw, Erik, *Documentary* (New York: Oxford University Press, 2nd rev. edn, 1993).

Barrett, M., P. Corrigan, A. Kuhn and V. Wolff (eds) *Ideology and Cultural Production* (London: Croom Helm, 1979).

Barthes, Roland, *Mythologies* (St Albans: Granada, 1973).

Barthes, Roland, *Image–Music–Text* (Glasgow: Fontana, 1977)

Baudrillard, Jean, ' "The Perfect Crime" ', *Wired*, 1.02

Bazin, André, *What is Cinema?* vol. 1. (Berkeley and Los Angeles: University of California Press, 1967).

Benjamin, Walter, 'The Work of Art in the Age of Mechanical Reproduction,' in Gerald Mast and Marshall Cohen (eds) *Film Theory and Criticism* (New York: Oxford University Press, 2nd edn, 1979).

Bennett, Tony, Susan Boyd-Bowman, Colin Mercer and Janet Woollacott (eds) *Popular Television and Film* (London: British Film Institute, 1981)

Berger, John, *Ways of Seeing* (London and Harmondsworth: BBC and Penguin, 1972).

Bradbury, Malcolm and James MacFarlane (eds) *Modernism* (Harmondsworth: Penguin, 1976)

Brando, Marlon with Robert Lindsay, *Songs My Mother Taught Me* (London: Century, 1994).

Brecht, Bertolt, *St Joan of the Stockyards* (London: Methuen, 1991).

British Medical Association, *Complete Family Health Encyclopedia* (London: Dorling Kindersley, 1990).

Byars, Jackie, *All That Hollywood Allows* (London: Routledge, 1991).

Cawelti, John G., *Adventure, Mystery and Romance* (University of Chicago Press, 1976).

Cleasby, Adrian, *What in the World is Going On?* (London: 3WE [Third World & Environment Broadcasting Project], 1995).

Cohan, Steven, ' "Feminizing" the Song-and-Dance Man' in Steven Cohan and Ina Rae Hark (eds) *Screening the Male* (London: Routledge, 1993).

Cohan, Steven and Ina Rae Hark (eds) *Screening the Male* (London: Routledge, 1993).

Cohen, Stanley and Jock Young (eds) *The Manufacture of News – Social Problems, Deviance and the Mass Media* (London: Constable, rev. edn, 1981)

Collins, Jim, Hilary Radner and Ava Preacher Collins (eds) *Film Theory Goes to the Movies* (New York: Routledge, 1993).

Doyle, Mark, 'Captain Mbaye Diagne', *Granta*, no. 49 (Harmondsworth: Penguin, 1994).

Dyer, Richard, 'Minnelli's Web of Dreams', *The Movie*, no. 58 (1981).

Dyer, Gillian, *Advertising as Communication* (London: Routledge, 1988).

Dyer, Richard *A Matter of Images* (London: British Film Institute, 1993).

Dyer, Richard, *Stars* (London: British Film Institute, 1979).

Eagleton, Terry, *Literary Theory* (Oxford: Blackwell, 1983).

Eisenstein, Sergei, 'A Dialectical Approach to Film Form', in Gerald Mast and Marshall Cohen (eds) *Film Theory and Criticism* (New York: Oxford University Press, 1979).

Eliot, T. S. *The Waste Land* (London: Faber & Faber, 1974).

Ellis, John, *Visible Fictions* (London: Routledge & Kegan Paul, 1982).

Evans, Harold, *Pictures on a Page* (London: Heinemann, 1978).

Falcon, Richard, *Classified!* (London: British Film Institute, 1994).

Fisk, Robert, 'Through a Lens, Fuzzily', *Independent on Sunday*, 5 December 1993.

Forster, E. M., *Aspects of the Novel* (Harmondsworth: Pelican, 1976)

Fowler, Roger, *Language in the News* (London: Routledge, 1991).

Gibson, Ben, 'Powaqqatsi', *Monthly Film Bulletin*, vol. 55, no. 655 (August 1988).

Gombrich, E. H., *The Story of Art* (London: Phaidon, 15th edn, 1989).

Gration, G., J. Reilly and J. Titford, *Communication and Media Studies* (Basingstoke: Macmillan, 1988).

Gregory, R. L., *Eye and Brain* (London: Weidenfeld & Nicolson, 1966).

Hall, S., D. Hobson, A. Lowe and P Willis, *Culture, Media, Language* (London: Hutchinson, 1980).

Hallam, Julia and Margaret Marshment, 'Framing experience: case studies in the reception of "Oranges are Not the Only Fruit"', *Screen*, vol. 39, no. 1 (Spring 1995).

Harvey, Sylvia, *May '68 and Film Culture* (London: British Film Institute, 1980).

Hatzfeld, Jean, 'The Fall of Vukovar', *Granta*, 47 (Harmondsworth: Penguin, 1994).

Hawkes, Terence, *Structuralism and Semiotics* (London: Methuen, 1977).

Hayward, Philip and Tana Wollen, *Future Visions* (London: British Film Institute, 1993

Hayward, Philip and Tana Wollen (eds) 'Introduction: Surpassing the Real', in Philip Hayward and Tana Wollen (eds) *Future Visions* (London: British Film Institute, 1993).

Heath, Stephen, *Questions of Cinema* (London: Macmillan Press, 1981).

Hellen, Nicholas and Andrew Alderson, 'Exposed: how cameras retook the Somme, Berlin and D-Day', *The Sunday Times*, 11 June 1995.

Henderson, Brian, 'The Long Take', in Bill Nichols (ed.) *Movies and Methods* (Berkeley, and Los Angeles: University of California Press, 1976).

Hoberman, J., *42nd Street* (London: British Film Institute, 1993).

James, C. Vaughan, *Soviet Socialist Realism* (London and Basingstoke: Macmillan, 1973).

Joyce, James *Ulysses* (Harmondsworth: Penguin, 1968).

Keighron, Peter, 'Video diaries: what's up doc?', *Sight and Sound*, vol. 3, no. 10 (October 1993).

Keys, David, 'A gallery opens – after 18,000 years', *Independent*, 20 January 1995.

Kitses, Jim, *Horizons West* (London: Secker & Warburg/British Film Institute, 1969).

Kracauer, Siegfried, 'Basic Concepts', in Gerald Mast and Marshall Cohen (eds) *Film Theory and Criticism* (New York: Oxford University Press, 2nd edn, 1979).

Kruger, Stephen and Ian Wall, *The Media Manual* (London: Mary Glasgow, 1988).

Kuhn, Annette, *The Power of the Image* (London: Routledge & Kegan Paul, 1985).

Lacey, Nick, *Media Studies – Exam Success Guide* (Doddington: Philip Allan Publishers).

Leslie, Jacques, 'Truth, Justice and the new Photo(shop) Realism', *Wired*, 1.02.

Lovell, Terry, *Pictures of Reality* (London: British Film Institute, 1980).

Lukàcs, Georg, *Studies in European Realism* (London: Merlin Press, 1972).

Lusted, David (ed.), *The Media Studies Book* (London: Routledge, 1991).

Lusted, David and Philip Drummond (eds) *TV and Schooling* (London: British Film Institute, 1985).

MacCabe, Colin, *Godard: Images, Sounds, Politics* (London and Basingstoke: Macmillan, 1980).

Manchester, William, *In Our Time* (London: Andre Deutsch, 1993)

Mast, Gerald and Marshall Cohen (eds) *Film Theory and Criticism* (New York: Oxford University Press, 2nd edn, 1979).

Masterman, Len, *Teaching the Media* (London and New York: Routledge, 1985).

Mathews, Tom Dewe, *Censored* (London: Chatto & Windus, 1994).

McGuigan, Jim, *Cultural Populism* (London: Routledge, 1992).

Monaco, James, *The New Wave* (New York: Oxford University Press, 1976).

Monaco, James, James Pallot and Baseline, *The Second Virgin Film Guide* (London: Virgin Books, 1993).

Morley, David, *Television Audiences and Cultural Studies* (London: Routledge, 1992).

Morris, Desmond, *Manwatching* (London: Cape, 1977).

Mulvey, Laura, 'Visual Pleasure and Narrative Cinema', in Bill Nichols, (ed.) *Movies and Methods*, vol. 2 (Berkeley and Los Angeles: California University Press, 1985).

Neale, Steve, 'Propaganda', *Screen*, vol. 18, no. 3 (Autumn 1977).

Neale, Steve, *Genre* (London: British Film Institute, 1980).
Neale, Steve, 'Masculinity as Spectacle', in Steven Cohan and Ina Rae Hark (eds) *Screening the Male* (London: Routledge, 1993).
.net issue 9, August 1995.
Nichols, Bill, *Ideology and the Image* (Bloomington, Ind.: Indiana University Press, 1981).
Nichols, Bill, *Movies and Methods*, vol. 2 (Berkeley and Los Angeles: University of California Press, 1985).
Nichols, Bill, *Representing Reality* (Bloomington and Indianapolis: Indiana University Press, 1991).
Nichols, Bill (ed.), *Movies and Methods* (Berkeley and Los Angeles: University of California Press, 1976).
Nowell-Smith, Geoffrey, 'Why Realism?' (unpublished?).
Orwell, George, *The Collected Essays*, vol. 1 (Harmondsworth: Penguin, 1971).
Osborne, Harold (ed.), *The Oxford Companion to Art* (Oxford University Press, 1970).
O'Sullivan, Tim, Brian Dutton and Philip Rayner, *Studying the Media* (London: Arnold, 1994).
Panofsky, Erwin, 'Style and Medium in the Motion Pictures', in Gerald Mast and Marshall Cohen (eds) *Film Theory and Criticism* (New York: Oxford University Press, 2nd edn, 1979).
Peak, Steve, *The Media Guide 1995* (London: Fourth Estate, 1994).
Perkins, Tessa, 'Rethinking Stereotypes' in M. Barrett, P. Corrigan, A. Kuhn and V. Wolff (eds) *Ideology and Cultural Production* (London: Croom Helm, 1979).
Pinker, Steven, *The Language Instinct* (London: Penguin, 1995).
Place, J. A. and L. S. Peterson, 'Some Visual Motifs in Film Noir', in Bill Nichols (ed.) *Movies and Methods* (Berkley and Los Angeles: University of California Press, 1976).
Plant, Sadie, 'Crash course', *Wired*, 1.01.
Plato, *The Republic* (New York: Basic Books, 1968).
Price, Stuart, *Media Studies I* (London: Pitman, 1993).
Reader, Keith, *The Cinema* (Sevenoaks: Hodder & Stoughton, 1979).
Renov, Michael (ed.), *Theorizing Documentary* (London: Routledge, 1993).
Roth, Mark, 'Some Warners Musicals and the Spirit of the New Deal', in Rick Altman (ed.) *Genre: The Musical* (London: Routledge & Kegan Paul, 1981).
Scharff, Aaron, *Art and Photography* (Harmondsworth: Penguin, 1983).
Selby, Keith and Ron Cowdery, *How to Study Television* (London: Macmillan, 1995).
Sheffield, Mary (producer), *Women in TV: Taking the Credit* (Milton Keynes: Open University, 1983).
Sinclair, Upton, *The Jungle* (Harmondsworth: Penguin, 1936).
Slotkin, Richard, *Regeneration Through Violence* (Middletown, Conn.: Wesleyan University Press, 1973).
Sontag, Susan, 'Fascinating Fascism', in Bill Nichols (ed.) *Movies and Methods* (Berkeley and Los Angeles: University of California Press, 1976).
Stafford, Roy, 'Sound on Film – What to Teach?', *in the picture*, no. 25 (Spring 1995).

Stafford, Roy, *Hands On* (London: British Film Institute, 1993)

Stam, Robert, Robert Burgoyne and Sandy Flitterman-Lewis, *New Vocabularies in Film Semiotics* (London: Routledge, 1992).

Stannard, Rob, 'Texts, Language, Literacy and Digital Technologies', *The English and Media Magazine*, no. 34, Summer 1996.

Swanson, Gillian, 'Representation', in *The Media Studies Book*, ed. David Lusted (London: Routledge, 1991).

Tasker, Yvonne, *Spectacular Bodies* (London and New York: Routledge, 1993).

Thwaites, Tony, Lloyd Davis and Warwick Mules, *Tools for Cultural Studies* (South Melbourne: Macmillan, 1994).

Trower, Marcus, 'Dead on Arrival', *Empire*, July 1994.

Truffaut, François, *Hitchcock* (St Albans: Granada, updated edn, 1978)

Vaughan, James C, *Soviet Socialist Realism I* (London and Basingstoke: Macmillan, 1973).

Watson, James and Anne Hill, *Dictionary of Communications and Media Studies* (London: Arnold, 3rd edn, 1993).

Watt, Ian, *The Rise of the Novel* (Harmondsworth: Pelican, 1972).

White, Jim, 'Drama: the last resort', *Independent*, 12 November 1994.

Willett, John, *The Theatre of Bertolt Brecht* (London: Methuen, 3rd edn, 1967).

Williams, Christopher, *Realism and the Cinema* (London: Routledge & Kegan Paul, 1980).

Williams, Raymond, *Keywords* (Glasgow: Fontana, 1976).

Williams, Raymond, *Marxism and Literature* (Oxford University Press, 1977).

Williamson, Judith, 'Images of "Woman" – the Photographs of Cindy Sherman', *Screen*, vol. 4, no. 6 (November–December 1983).

Winston, Brian, 'Was Hitler Really There?', *Sight and Sound*, vol. 50, no. 2, Spring 1981.

Winston, Brian, *Claiming the Real* (London: British Film Institute, 1995).

Wollen, Peter, *Signs and Meaning in the Cinema* (London: Secker and Warburg/British Film Institute, 3rd edn, 1972).

Wollen, Peter, 'Counter-cinema: *Vent d'est*', *Afterimage*, no. 4 (1972).

INDEX